helping
Yourself
With
E.S.P.

helping Yourself With E.S.P.

Al G. Manning, D.D.

parker publishing company, inc.

WEST NYACK,
NEW YORK

LIBRARY OF CONGRESS
CATALOG CARD NUMBER: 66-24968

Sixth Printing.....December, 1971

PRINTED IN THE UNITED STATES OF AMERICA

38674—B & P

TO my wife and divine companion,
Eileen

How This Book Can Benefit You

Everyone dreams of riches, fame, power, and love. Some people's dreams burst into reality as if brought to fruition in another dimension—while other's come to naught! *The fulfillment of your hopes and dreams is not a matter of chance.* Success in any undertaking is a result of the proper use of natural law. And the natural laws work whether our scientists have discovered them or not!

Men traveled over the water in boats for hundreds of years before Archimedes brought forth the concept of displacement of liquids which makes it possible for a boat to stay on the water. And in this "modern" world, some enlightened souls are using laws of the mind to achieve their hearts' desires— even though science is still unable to explain it.

How ESP can enrich your life

YOU can learn to experience another dimension of life through *extra-sensory-perception* (ESP). This unfoldment will bring new meaning and purpose to all areas of your existence. Yes, you can use it to gain health, wealth, power, true love, fame, or anything else you may desire. But its greatest value lies in the change it is certain to bring in your understanding of life. There are depths of meaning and experience far beyond the average man's imagination. The following pages will show you how to develop your extra-sensory powers and use them to attain new understanding and the ability to make your dreams come true.

Wonderfully positive experiences occur in the lives of normal people all over the world—every day. Many are spontaneous, but others happen because some of us are learning the elementary laws of another dimension. Your neighbor may be *working* the same natural laws that brought an ancient prophet to flatly state:

"He will give His angels charge over you, to guard you in all of your ways. They will bear you up in their hands, lest you strike even your foot upon a stone."

This is not an idle dream of some starry-eyed mystic. It is a statement of *UNIVERSAL LAW THAT WILL WORK FOR YOU!*

Why this book is so easy to use

This book is not intended to be "scientific" or "scholarly." It is designed for your use as a tool—to enable you to attain your heart's desires, and more besides! The examples used are from the ordinary lives of normal people. Most of them were obtained from individuals who are eager to share their experiences with others in the hope of bringing upliftment to all mankind. Many came from friends whose integrity is, to me, absolutely beyond question. There may be no incontrovertible "scientific proof" for any of these experiences—but they happened, and lives were enriched as a result!

We start with the assumption that you have never recognized a psychic experience in your own life. This puts you on the same footing with me when I first looked into the confusion of ideas about the next dimension. Then we will *demonstrate to you* that you already have some degree of ESP which you should be using every day. Next we set up a *positive program for your development* of ever increasing ESP. All this is in the first chapter.

The remaining chapters develop the fine points of *application* of your new abilities to each major area of your life. No special talents or aptitudes are required. Nature endowed you at birth with all the necessary tools. Happiness, health, riches, friendship, peace of mind, love, and fulfillment are yours already. This book is designed to show you how to realize your birthright, and attain all these things, now!

Table of Contents

You have already experienced many psychic phenomena. Your five steps to personal success and greatness. How to increase your awareness of yourself and the world around you. Seven simple tests for your special psychic abilities. Your five senses are your link to the psychic. How to develop the art of concentration. How to solve all your problems through concentration and meditation. We learn about ESP from the Orient. The mechanics of psychic sensation —psychic centers. Your seven most important psychic centers. A basic exercise to develop your ESP. How to develop clairvoyance. How to develop clairsentience. How to listen for the voice of clairaudience. How to clear away the blocks to extra-sensory development. Now practice. Points to remember.

chapter 4

A new look at riches. How to interest your spirit helpers in bringing you riches. Your path to riches through ever increasing effectiveness. How to set up a current to draw wealth into your life. Let spirit express riches in your life. How to protect yourself from financial harm. How to enjoy your ever increasing riches. Points to remember.

chapter 5

How to use your psychic centers to extend your personality. How to make other people like you. How to sell an idea. How to attract the right people and opportunities. How to cope with difficult personalities. The give and take of real friendship. Points to remember.

chapter 6

Why some people crack under stress. How to find your source of personal strength. How to understand your stresses. How to ask for help

how to

Develop Your ESP

An old man comes slowly down the street, tapping a white cane to guide his way. Your heart must go out to him in compassion. You have a tremendous advantage over him—you can see, but he can't!

Let's stop and think for a moment! A person with well developed powers of ESP has much the same advantage over the average man that you have over the blind man. Look at this natural occurrence:

"Al, I couldn't tell just anyone about this," the voice on my telephone blurted, "but I know you'll understand. I was coming about sixty-five miles an hour on the Pasadena Freeway this afternoon, lost in thought. About a mile before the big blind curve I saw a vision of a terrible accident with twisted automobiles blocking the two left lanes. The scene was so vivid in my mind that I simply had to slow down. I coasted to about forty and moved over into the right hand lane as I rounded the curve. Sure enough, there was the accident exactly as I had seen it! If it weren't for the vision, I'd have ploughed right into those wrecked cars and I'd be in the hospital or the morgue right now."

This is a simple example of a helpful psychic phenomenon. We will look at many more as we explore practical methods of harnessing this great realm of the unknown. But is the psychic realm really so unknown to you?

You have already experienced many psychic phenomena

Where did your last idea come from? Where did it exist? What is its reality? Its substance? An idea is an intangible substance, a psychic phenomenon! It is an object in that fantastic realm which men call mind, or sometimes even soul. The actual process of thought is not understood by medical men, psychologists, or even philosophers; yet it is the means by which they ply their trades, and the means by which we all comprehend the many experiences of life.

Now you are properly introduced to the world of psychic phenomena. You can't say you have never had a *psychic experience*, because your very act of entertaining the idea is one! There are many uncommon or miraculous psychic experiences, but that is only a matter of degree. The psychic, or intangible, side of life is experienced by every living human, every day of his life, and we will do well to spend some time examining its many mysteries.

Legend tells us that Sir Isaac Newton sat under a tree contemplating a mystery. When an apple fell and hit him on the head, it supplied the missing stimulus. There was a moment of contact with reality, and Newton expounded the law of gravity. Similarly, Archimedes is said to have jumped out of the bathtub shouting, "Eureka!" upon subconsciously solving a problem. His contribution was the principle of displacement of water by immersed objects, which paved the way for the floating hunks of steel we call modern ships.

History records both events as milestones in science's march toward understanding of our universe. The principles seem obvious today, but only after some mind accomplished the original thinking. All progress is a series of steps best described as the unfoldment of an idea, so in a very real sense, *all progress is a result of the psychic*. This means that the psychic is a sure *means to improve your whole life.*

Your five steps to personal success and greatness

A little self contemplation will prepare us for the simple five-step path to personal success and greatness. Let's pause for a brief look at the miracle that is *you*. You are much more than the little pile of chemicals which comprise your physical body. A very real part of you can visit Paris, Sydney, Venus, or the moon while your physical body reclines comfortably in the easy chair in your own living room. You are capable of heights of ecstasy and depths of despondency not experienced by any other species of earth creature, and yet you know less about yourself than about the automobile which transports your body from place to place.

Modern man is a fantastic paradox of wasted potential and pathetic ignorance, boundless love and tender compassion, desolate insecurity and murderous frustrations, mental agility and physical adaptability; all embarked on the journey of life toward he knows not where!

We squander vast amounts of energy seeking *things*. Automobiles, television sets, new furniture, and fancy clothes may bring us creature comforts, but they can never deliver that precious intangible we call inner satisfaction. Your deepest inner hungers can be fed only by *your personal experience of the miracle* which is your inner self. Then you can handle the physical world easily. It is exactly as Jesus taught it, all those years ago: *Seek ye first the kingdom of God, and his righteousness; and all these things shall be added unto you.* (*Matt.* 6:33.)

And where did the Master say to look for it? Within yourself, of course! It's hard to argue with a man who demonstrated so much spirituality along with so many varieties of ESP, so let's consider his advice instead. Let this set the tone for our approach to the five step path to personal success and greatness. Briefly stated, the five steps are:

1. Increase your awareness of yourself and the world around you.
2. Recognize your present psychic strengths and potentials.
3. Use regular exercises to develop your ESP.
4. Learn to contact powers greater than yourself for guidance and help.
5. Apply your ESP to improve and enrich every department of your life.

We will go into the first three steps in detail in the balance of this chapter. Since the 4th step is also an application of what you will learn from the first three, it will be covered in Chapter 2. Then we will devote the rest of our space to the details of application for the enrichment of each area of your life, and explanations of the wonderfully positive results you can obtain.

How to increase your awareness of yourself and the world around you

The owner of a small service company was so wrapped up in his business problems that he could think of nothing else. Any conversation of a cultural or purely social nature made him quite uncomfortable. He developed the habit of interrupting everyone with lengthy discourses on the problems of his daily business operations. Thus, he effectively prevented any possible broadening of his personality or outlook. Because he shut out everything he might have had in common with them, he lost his wife and family. He wound up with not one friend who wasn't some sort of business necessity. His company grew, and the business world might call him a success; but he died a lonely, broken man.

How can you have the business or professional success you desire, but avoid the pitfall this man fell into? Or is it possible at all? Of course it is! But it requires the sincere application of yourself to the development of our first tool. We will call it *relaxed awareness.*

Much study and practice will be necessary to build your relaxed awareness, but the rewards are great. This is one of the most useful of all mental disciplines. Each of us has two aspects of mind: the conscious, reasoning part which is much like a modern computer; and the subconscious part which can be your contact with the accumulated wisdom of the ages. Your relaxed awareness will grow out of the increasing confidence in your ability to cope with life. You gain it by learning to assign each of your problems to the right part of your mind for solution.

Today's computers are being used to solve the most complex problems of deductive reasoning. They can even be programmed to make routine management decisions, but only of a *deductive* nature. Your conscious mind is quite like a computer and should be accepted as such. When a computer receives a problem, all the elements necessary for a solution must be present or it will light up the tilt and reject the query pending the required additional inputs. But how about people? When we encounter a problem but don't have all the necessary data, we become anxious or frustrated! Why? Because we are trying to use the wrong mental machine.

It is only the power of your subconscious which sets you apart as more valuable than a computer. The subconscious is your source of the missing data for the solution of any problem, if you will but learn to *use it*. Next time you are faced with a problem and your reasoning mind can't arrive at a good answer, don't allow anxiety to rob you of your peace of mind. Instead, turn it over to the subconscious and trust your inner self to deliver help at the right time. Meanwhile you can continue to genuinely participate in each moment of life. You will find it no longer necessary to grunt in response to your spouse or child while you are absorbed in anxious thought. You can enjoy your family and friends and get a better solution to the problem as well. A little further along we will present a simple technique for concentration to turn over your knotty problems to the subconscious mind for certain and trustworthy solutions, but first we need to examine some of your areas of psychic potential as outlined below.

Seven simple tests for your special psychic abilities

There are many simple experiences which our materialistic culture has taught us to shrug off as meaningless or sheer coincidence. They are *real psychic experiences,* and they can serve as definite clues to your own areas of special psychic aptitude. All of us are involved in some of these at least once in a while. How often do you experience one of these?

1. *HUNCHES.*

You get a feeling about some present or future occurrence, and it is strong enough that you feel impelled to remark, "I have a hunch that . . . . . ." Sure enough, it turns out that you were right. (Hunches are generally associated with clairsentience or intuition.)

2. *FEEL SOMEONE'S EYES.*

While in a public place, you suddenly feel someone looking at you. When you turn around, you meet the other's gaze and know you were right. (This is also most often a form of clairsentience.)

3. *PROPHETIC DREAMS.*

Last night you dreamed that Aunt Susie came to visit you. Then this morning you received a letter saying that she will arrive on Monday. Or any dream that turns out to be substantially fulfilled shortly afterward. (This is commonly called precognition.)

4. *YOU'VE BEEN THERE BEFORE.*

While visiting some new place, you have a funny feeling you have been there before. You somehow seem to know what type of building will appear as you round the next corner; or perhaps you know exactly the words your companion will use to describe a scene or another person. (This could be clairsentience, or precognition, or possibly a previous astral experience.)

5. MENTAL PICTURES OR INNER VOICES.

While sitting quietly with your eyes open or closed, you see a picture of a scene or a person on the screen of your inner vision. Or you hear someone whisper your name or a short phrase, but you are quite alone. (This would be simple clairvoyance or clairaudience.)

6. TELEPHONE COINCIDENCE.

You want to call up a friend or relative, but while you are still looking for the number, your telephone rings and it is that person calling you. If this has happened to you more than once, either as the one about to make the call or the one actually calling, forget about coincidence. This is a definite manifestation of telepathy.

7. WOMAN'S INTUITION.

The thing called woman's intuition is just as common to men as to women, though men are not as apt to admit it. If you have ever considered using a term like this to explain how you knew something, you admit that you have definite psychic aptitude.

I feel completely safe in saying that everyone who reads this book has had many such experiences. If you feel you have not, it is undoubtedly a matter of awareness. We have been trained since childhood to ignore such things or shrug them off as coincidence. Start looking for it, and within one short week you will notice at least three such experiences.

These simple psychic experiences are important! They can be the beginning of a richer and more meaningful life for *you*. They are your key to the doorway to ever increasing health, wealth, happiness, and spiritual progress. Even if you feel you failed all seven psychic tests, there is no reason to be discouraged. Psychic ability is an inherent part of *every* human being, and like the ability to read, it can be learned at any age. Naturally some people will develop into better psychics than others, just as some learn to read with greater speed and retention than others. But the advantages of a reader over a nonreader are quite similar in quality to those of one who consciously uses the psychic over one who does not.

There is an old truism, "That which you seek is seeking you." In modern language we might put it, the application of your interest tends to attract its subject. Begin *now* to seek manifestations of the psychic in your daily experience. As you progress, we will show you how to build it into a working tool that is *useful in all areas of your life.*

Your five senses are your link to the psychic

Science recognizes five basic senses, or means by which individuals perceive conditions and events in the world around us. They are named sight, hearing, touch, taste, and smell. However they are not as specific and concrete as we might first think. There is a tremendous variation in the degree of each sense as it is demonstrated by different individuals. Glasses and hearing aids bear constant testimony to our many variations of less than normal sight and hearing, but there are also cases of exceptionally keen degrees of these key receptors.

The senses are your mind's basic method of perceiving the objective world. Thus they are a link between the concrete-physical and the subjective-psychic realms. The intensity or effectiveness of this link varies not only from individual to individual, but in the same person it varies as a function of health, inclination, and attention. We all know someone who is quite hard of hearing except when you softly speak something you don't want him to hear.

His teacher reported that young Johnny seemed to be hard

of hearing. She regularly had to call him two or three times to get his attention. Subsequent tests revealed that his hearing was completely normal, but his intelligence level was above the work of the class and he daydreamed out of sheer boredom. A more challenging class and increased parental interest removed the problem in less than three weeks.

Some degree of the same lack of awareness exhibited by the unchallenged child is found in each of us. We often fail to observe events in our immediate vicinity because we "couldn't care less." Conscious development of the power to regularly control and direct your interest will add many degrees to your livingness, and to your ability to recall important facts and events you previously would not have even noticed. This power is most accurately labeled concentration.

How to develop the art of concentration

Concentration is an art, like painting or playing a musical instrument. Your inherent ability must be developed by regular practice, and application of yourself to a program graduated in difficulty to bring you from a point of amorphous potential to a peak of professional skill. The usefulness of a super ability to concentrate obviously extends to every area of your life, and it is certainly worth a little effort to achieve.

Most people actually miss about three quarters of life because they don't observe what they think they see. Listen to three disinterested witnesses of an automobile accident as they give their accounts of the details. Generally you would think they must be talking about events that took place at widely different times and places, because of the conflicting details. The simple ability to accurately observe and recall detail is a manifestation of applied concentration. Let's begin with an exercise to develop yours:

Look around the house and find an old wooden pencil. Examine it carefully and make a list of everything you observed

about it. Finish your own list before you compare it with the
one below.

Details of an old wooden pencil:

A. Colors
   1. Point—dark gray graphite
   2. Wooden part of point—many shades of brown and
      gray.
   3. Shaft—painted yellow-orange, chipped here and
      there with bare wood showing through
   4. Lettering—some black and more by indentations
      in the painted finish
   5. Metal eraser holder—brass with two red stripes
      around it
   6. Eraser—pearly pink with smudges of black and
      gray

B. Shapes
   1. Tip of point rounded
   2. Point conical
   3. Shaft hexagonal, about 5 inches long
   4. Eraser holder—cylindrical, but ribbed and per-
      forated
   5. Eraser—cylindrical, but worn to many shapes of
      flatness and little corners

C. Materials
   1. Graphite
   2. Wood
   3. Paint, orange and black
   4. Brass
   5. Red anodize material on the stripe
   6. Rubber
   7. Flecks of dirt

D. Distinguishing Features
   1. Trademark
   2. Brand name and number
   3. Lead hardness—#3

    4. Made in U.S.A.
    5. Process—"Chemi-sealed"
    6. Quality control number 316325
    7. Many dents and teeth marks
    8. Point very dull

E. Potential Uses
    1. Writing
    2. Erasing
    3. Drawing
    4. Weapon (stab or scratch)
    5. Wedge or shim
    6. Window prop
    7. Lever
    8. Fuel (the wood)
    9. Lubricant (the graphite)
    10. Hair roller
    11. Spool for string or thread
    12. Stirring rod
    13. Dip stick for shallow tank
    14. Measuring instrument (length)
    15. Subject of a painting

This list merely scratches the surface, but it was prepared in less than three minutes and it serves to illustrate our point. Your powers of observation will increase by leaps and bounds as you practice focusing your whole attention on one subject at a time. Practice this exercise on a different object each day for two weeks, and you will be on your way to its mastery. Use simple things at first, like a knife, fork, scissors, mirror, glass, cup, dish, etc. When you think you're good at it, try a flower such as a rose. You should feel that you could fill a whole book with the details of just one rose.

Practice! It is well worth your while. When your concentration is well sharpened by this process, you are ready to apply it to solving real life problems.

How to solve all your problems through concentration and meditation

Somewhere in the psychic realms there exists a creative solution to your every problem. You can tune in on it, and manifest harmonious progress by a combination of concentration and meditation. The preliminary process is applied concentration. By using the powers of concentration you have just developed, clearly analyze and define your problem; that is the purpose of your conscious mind. Then you are ready to use that part of your being which makes you better than a computer.

You will find that your applied concentration reveals the solution to the majority of your problems with no further effort. The remaining ones, being clearly defined, now lack only the creative idea that leads to their mastery. In years gone by, such creative solutions were often chalked up to Yankee ingenuity. *You* are endowed with an endless fountain of this Yankee ingenuity; it is only necessary to open the valve and let it flow into your experience.

The process of turning on your mental tap is best called meditation. Sit quietly alone, and calmly review your analysis of the problem. Next, talk to your own subconscious as if it were another person. Say something like: "O.K., Subconscious, I know you are the source of all creative ideas. Let's see how you handle this one." Then relax and wait. If you get no immediate answer, don't be discouraged. Get busy with your routine chores, and your answer will come in an intuitive flash during a moment of mental relaxation.

A man had just lost $100,000 in a disastrous used car venture. He talked it over with his subconscious like this: "Look here, Subconscious, because of this big loss, I can make $100,-000 tax free in the next few years. What are we going to do about it?" For two days nothing happened, but he didn't worry. There were plenty of tasks involved with winding up his ill-fated venture, and he kept busy with them. On the morning of the third day he awakened with a simple chemical formula running around in his head. By noon it had jelled into a novel process for making a widely used product, so he called up an old acquaintance who arranged the necessary financing. The result? In just 18 months he had his $100,000 back and half of a prosperous business as well.

The real secret of using the meditative art of problem solving lies in the approach of the man in our example. He didn't cry over his loss and wallow in self-pity. Rather, he adopted the most positive outlook. Here was not a personal catastrophe, but a beautiful opportunity to make a lot of money, tax free! Anxiety or despondency will prevent your subconscious from delivering the goods; but a positive, optimistic attitude absolutely guarantees success. Never accept anxiety and frustration as a way of life. Use the meditative process to clear away the pressures by solving all your problems. Begin to enjoy every moment of life, *now!*

We learn about ESP from the Orient

With our materialistic pressures of life relieved, we are ready to look deeper into the realm of ESP. From centuries before the time of Christ, men of the Orient have been teaching the development of the psychic senses. It will help us to examine some of these ancient Eastern teachings. There are practical uses for many of them in our Western world today.

Basically the great Eastern teachers look upon man as a spirit expressing through a soul which uses, among other vehicles, a physical body. This physical body is understood to be a beast of burden, like a horse, which provides transportation for the soul on the earth plane, even as the mind provides a means of expression in the thought realms. The physical senses are tools of the physical body, and the psychic senses are tools of the finer body of light which is most often called the *astral body.*

Under proper conditions the astral body, which contains the

seat of consciousness, can be separated from the physical body and travel independently for great distances. The energy, and the very life, of the physical body comes to it through the astral vehicle which connects with the physical through the sympathetic nervous system. Thus the astral is associated with the emotional part of your being. If you stop to think about it, energy flow through your body is always the result of emotion. There is an energy of love, hate, enthusiasm, pride, joy, jealousy, greed, and the like.

Each one of us has experienced the spark of enthusiasm that drives fatigue out of the body and equips it to enjoy a few lines of bowling or rubbers of bridge after a truly hard day's work. This is only one of many indications that the Eastern masters know a lot more than our modern culture is willing to admit. We will omit much of the detail of their teachings, examining only the bare essentials necessary to a useful understanding. From our standpoint, the main question is: If there really is an *astral body,* can we learn to make conscious, practical use of it in our daily lives? And though many may quarrel with the terminology, we will find the answer to be a definite *yes!*

The mechanics of psychic sensation—
psychic centers

By a process analogous to the transmission of electricity, the physical body is supplied with light-energy through the sympathetic nervous system. A brief review of the household use of electricity will aid our understanding. For purposes of economy, electricity is transmitted from the generating station at relatively high voltages, then it is converted to the safer energy we use in our homes by means of step-down transformers. The energy supplied to most homes comes in at 115 volts, but for many applications, such as your doorbell, other step down transformers are required to reduce the voltage to the 6 or 12 volts used by the more delicate apparatus.

The light-energy is transmitted within your body-house by the nervous system. Each nerve is like an electric wire in your house, and the nerve centers are like the secondary coils of a transformer. Then where are the primary coils? They are in your *astral* counterpart. Consequently, each ganglion or nerve center in your body is also a psychic center, and these are the suppliers of the vital energy which is the life of your body.

Because pain is a form of energy, we see that it is through the astral body that we experience the sensation of pain. When the astral is separated from the physical body, there is no feeling of any kind left in the physical. With this little bit of background, you can readily understand the mechanics of psychic sensation and learn to use it in almost the same way you learned to coordinate your eyes and intellect in the process of reading. There is a special form of yoga used by our Eastern friends to gain conscious control over each individual muscle in their bodies, and another yoga used to attain similar control over the many psychic centers. These disciplines represent truly magnificent attainments, but they are of only academic interest to us. Our purpose is to improve your life in our modern, Western civilization; and we are interested only in that which specifically helps us *here* and in the reasonably near *now*. For our practical approach we need consider only seven major psychic centers.

Your seven most important psychic centers

For those who are interested in more detail, a trip to your public library to look up some topics like *chakra, Ida, pingala, sushumna,* or the *fire of the kundalini* should provide much interesting reading. But we will confine this discussion to the following centers:

1. The *Root Center* is located at the base of the spine. It is associated with the organs of reproduction, and thus with physical creativity of all kinds. It provides much of the energy that

men call get up and go or drive in union with the two other lower centers.

2. The *Spleen Center* is located along the spine in the area of the spleen. It is an energy purifier and a transformer of low vibration energy to higher. As the middle man of the lower three, one of its major functions is coordinating and balancing the activity of its immediate neighbors.

3. The *Solar Plexus Center* is located in the area of the navel or the physical solar plexus. This is the center most sensitive to the animal emotions, and is recognized by modern psychology when it speaks of gut level discussions. All the negative emotions such as fear, hate, anxiety, lust, and despair hit us in the gut; causing butterflies, knots, indigestion, or ulcers. This is an amazingly sensitive receiving station for picking up the lower emotions in other people.

4. The *Heart Center* is located in the area of the physical heart. This is the middle center, representing the balance between the higher mental centers and the lower physical centers. It is the transformer which brings the positive emotions of love, compassion, and enthusiasm into usable energy on the physical plane. Love is the perfect balance between the heat of the lower physical drives and the intellectual cold of the higher centers. Of course all the centers are necessary to the total functioning of a complete spiritual being.

5. The *Throat Center* is located in the region of the thyroid gland. It is the lower center of the upper three, and is associated with creativity like its counterpart, the root center. But this creativity is of a higher abstract nature which includes the arts, literature, music, and science.

6. The *Brow Center* is located behind and slightly above the eyes, in the region of the pituitary gland. Like its spleen center counterpart, it is important particularly in purifying and balancing the energies flowing between its immediate neighbors. The brow center is symbolized by a jewel worn near the center of the forehead, and it is often called the gateway to

illumination because it is our means of activating the highest center.

7. The *Crown Center* is located near the top of the head in the region of the pineal gland. It is no accident that the occult lore of the ages has branded the pineal gland the seat of psychic ability and the instrument of spiritual attainment. The spiritual power flowing through a fully functioning crown center is wonderful beyond finite belief, yet it brings a distinctly personal relationship with God and all his creation. In a very real sense, the purpose of this book is to help you develop this center as your means of certain accomplishment of any goal.

A basic exercise to develop your ESP

As we begin work to increase the activity of your psychic body, it is extremely important that we stress simple *balance*. The Bible insists that you are created in the image and likeness of God. Now this doesn't mean that God has to look like a physical man! But it does mean that, like God, *you are a whole being.* You are a composite whole, made up of physical, emotional-psychic, mental, and spiritual aspects. You attain maximum effectiveness only when all of your parts are working together. On a football team the guard and tackle positions are not the glamor spots. They may be noticed by the average fan only when they miss an important block or tackle, but their devoted performance is the mainstay of the team. Similarly, some spiritual leaders forget the value of the physical body and insist on its subjugation, but without the physical body we are helpless to manifest on this earth. We must bring our *whole being* along on a program of balanced development. True, we must learn to control the wonderful horse that is our physical body, but the stronger the horse the better the ride.

Here then, is our first psychic exercise designed to promote a balanced increase in your overall psychic activity:

Sit or stretch out comfortably where you will not be disturbed. Relax your body and quiet your mind as much as possible. Now concentrate on your *root center*. Try to imagine that all of your consciousness exists at that one spot, that all your thought, feeling, and sensation is centered there. Soon you will feel a warm tingling sensation near the base of your spine. As you begin to feel this psychic response, imagine a whirling circle of flame ever growing and increasing its speed of rotation while stepping up the power of the center.

Now direct this energy to your *spleen center*, causing it to tingle and itself become a vortex of whirling flame. Transfer all your attention to the spleen center, and imagine the flame growing and rotating faster and faster. Feel the increased power flowing through this center! Now direct this energy to your *solar plexus center* and repeat the whole process. Intensify the flame and lift it, repeating all the steps, in turn to the *heart, throat, brow,* and finally the *crown center*. When you feel your crown center tingling with all the energy you can bring to it, make the following statement:

"I seek to promote the growth of my overall being through the stimulation of my psychic senses. This is good for me and I know that my subconscious self is cooperating in every way. I sit in the silence awaiting the voice of my inner self."

Then just sit quietly for a few minutes. You may receive nothing at first, or you may be amazed at the immediate results. But you are definitely progressing! Either way, continue the exercise daily if possible, but at least three times a week.

Understand that you are stimulating the flow of the psychic energies throughout your body as you continue the exercise. If some part of your body is not functioning at peak efficiency, you can help it by directing the psychic energies you are summoning to yourself from the universe. As you consciously bring each center to its maximum vibratory rate, direct its healing force to your afflicted part before transferring your attention to the next higher center. Thus you bathe the limb or organ with healing energy of seven different rates of vibration, and *it must be improved!*

One big word of caution is in order here. There is a potential danger from habitual incomplete use of this exercise! If you regularly fall asleep or quit in the middle, you will be developing your lower centers more rapidly than the balancing upper centers. Such an imbalanced development could lead to an overemphasis of the sex drive or other strictly material urges. Of course sex is beautiful, and material things are delightful; but without the complementary esthetic and spiritual experiences, life is hollow and empty. Health is not of the physical only! It is a natural by-product of mental, psychic, and spiritual growth along a balanced path. All parts of life are equally important, and none should be neglected. As you use this exercise, apply special emphasis to those centers which seem to correspond to your weaker departments. Strive for balanced growth and you will achieve health, prosperity, and happiness beyond your most cherished dreams.

How to develop clairvoyance

As my telephone rang I closed my eyes and got a mental picture of the rabbit which I had previously associated with one particular friend. So I reached for the receiver and answered, "Hello, Eddie, how are you?"

You can easily imagine his reaction. You will find it lots of fun to amaze your friends with simple demonstrations like this. As an interesting little sidelight, you will be fascinated by the resemblance of your symbols to important personality traits of your victims.

Almost everybody does some mental imaging. For instance: When you hear the word apple, what do you see? How about purple? Or horse? Some years ago I still believed I was a non-imager. I took some consolation in the knowledge that words like love, courage, or beauty cannot be seen by mental imaging. In my sour-grapes, I decided that my abstract thinking must be superior to that of an imager because my mind was not cluttered up with a lot of pictures. But that is utter nonsense! *Everyone* sees a mental picture of some sort once in a while and that is all that is necessary.

Clairvoyance is nothing more than the reception of mental images with some recognition of their meaning. Basically, you develop clairvoyance by learning to pay attention to something that has always been with you. Try it now! Close your eyes and stare at the patterns you see. Like a child watching a cloud formation, use your imagination to decide what it is and what it may mean. Form your thoughts into words, preferably spoken aloud, and as you vocalize them, your image will tend to focus itself and confirm the accuracy of your speculation.

Our next exercise concerns telling time. Next time you wonder what time it is, stop before looking at your watch. Close your eyes and picture a large white clock face before you. Now look at the hands and read the time. If it checks with your watch, you have produced an excellent demonstration of clairvoyance. Practice is the major ingredient for successful development of this very useful faculty.

Another good exercise is to use clairvoyance to locate missing articles. Instead of thrashing around the house looking for your scissors or pen, close your eyes and visualize it, carefully noting its surroundings. When you walk to it, there where you saw it, you are demonstrating another practical application of clairvoyance.

Don't become discouraged if you are not highly successful with each exercise in the beginning. The basic exercise to activate your psychic centers will work to improve all of your extrasensory faculties. Persistence and practice will produce startling results in a few short weeks.

Here is another phase of clairvoyance that can be very fruitful. During your quiet, relaxed moments, you will often receive a mental picture with no apparent cause. Learn to pay attention! Recognize these pictures as messages from the great subconscious domain and contemplate their significance. The subconscious speaks to us in symbols, but speak it does and much helpful information and insight can be obtained in this manner. There is literally a whole new world hidden beneath the threshold of our course, normal consciousness, and it has countless practical uses. The key to entering this exciting place is simply to become alert and sensitive to the many little things we have ignored or shrugged off in the past. Let's turn now to another phase of ESP that is even more accessible to rapid development.

How to develop clairsentience

Clairsentience is the extension of your consciousness by the vehicle of *feeling*. A businessman had scheduled the 8 P.M. flight from Los Angeles to San Francisco because it suited his timetable perfectly. On this particular morning he awakened with an uneasy feeling that he should take an earlier flight, even if it meant cancelling his late afternoon appointments. As the day wore on, the feeling became so strong that he "gave in to it" and took the 6 P.M. plane. Next morning at breakfast his paper carried the story of the tragic crash of the 8 P.M. flight. Clairsentience had clearly saved his life.

At some time or other, *everyone* has experienced an unexplainable feeling of uneasiness. This *feeling* is a manifestation of *your* clairsentience. Certainly you have at least one acquaintance whose very presence makes you uncomfortable, and others with whom you instinctively relax. This is an example of elementary clairsentience, but it can also be the basis of a good exercise for further development. Start paying attention to that *feeling!* Next time you get a letter or phone call, observe your feeling about it first. See if you can tell what the subject matter will be and who is trying to reach you before you open the letter or answer the phone.

Your increasing awareness of the little things taking place within and around you will lead to accomplishments and the unfolding of talents beyond anything you can presently imagine. We must hammer away at the concept of *paying attention* to those little feelings and images that were always there, but have regularly been ignored.

The feeling that "I've been here before," as you enter a place for the first time, is generally another manifestation of clairsentience. That feeling is most often produced by our accidentally tuning in to the subconscious vibrational patterns of the new place and finding that they coincide with strong feelings in our memory. We feel that we have been there before because we have experienced feelings like those being picked up before. There may be other instances when you have been there before in your astral body, but we will come to that discussion in a later chapter.

You can learn many things about any place you visit by purposely tuning in on the subconscious feelings that are ever present in its atmosphere. You tune in simply by focusing your attention on the feelings which are impinging upon you from your surroundings. Have those who lived here been generally happy, or sad? Which way do you feel as you mentally ask the question? That is your answer, unless your personal feelings have crowded out the truth. You can *feel* a generally sound answer to almost any question you would expect the place to hold in its memory.

Here is an exercise close to home. How often do you instinctively sense the mood of your spouse or a good friend? That is clearly clairsentience! You can easily improve your ability to sense another's mood by applying more of yourself to it. Let your conscious mind be temporarily pushed aside by the incoming feelings. *Become* the other person for an instant; *feel* his feelings and *think* his thoughts, not as yourself, but as the other person; then bring the impressions back into sharp mental focus. This can be a doubly good exercise. It helps develop your clairsentience and improves your human relations as well.

Common sense will tell you that clinching your teeth, grunting, or anxiously striving will never help you *feel* anything. *Use your relaxed awareness.* It is the key, now and always!

How to listen for the voice of clairaudience

For centuries, poets and clergymen have rambled on about the *still small voice* that speaks to you in the silence. It can become prattling when the writer is talking about a concept rather than a direct experience. But just because an idea isn't always well presented, is not a valid reason to dismiss it as worthless or untrue. There is an allegorical still small voice which is intuitional and directly related to clairsentience, but there is also a *true voice of clairaudience.*

Did you ever think you heard your name whispered softly in your ear, but when you looked around there was nobody there? If you must answer, "no," listen carefully in the future, it will be there. History records an excellent example of guidance and comfort from the voices of clairaudience; and fortunately for us, society is more tolerant today. The voices that led Joan of Arc were real! They stand ready to guide and help you today! You have only to *pay attention.*

We call mental pictures *clairvoyance,* feelings *clairsentience,* and hearing *clairaudience,* but in a larger sense they are all one. They are more likely to manifest in concert with one another than separately. It is the same with the five physical senses, the occasion is rare indeed when one sense is used alone. Taste and smell greatly reinforce one another and a television set minus either picture or sound is much less effective. So it is that all ESP has been poetically called the *sixth sense.* Our goal is to open ourselves to the guidance and inspiration of the great subconscious realm and the name given to the process is of little consequence.

To develop clairaudience you must sit in the silence and listen! But it would be folly to reject mental pictures or clairsentient impressions while doing so. As you practice the exercise for awakening your psychic centers, and direct your relaxed awareness to the whole of the psychic realm, you will get results. You may notice a buzzing or ringing in your ears as you sit and listen. Accept it with thanks as the beginning of your clairaudience.

You have probably spent years rejecting such ideas. Those old thought patterns may impede your progress but *you will improve daily.* Just as it takes time for an athlete to attain a peak of physical condition and develop the skills of his sport, it takes a while to condition yourself to the ways of the psychic and develop your powers of reception. The help to be gained from the psychic is far more valuable than any gold medal won on the field of athletic competition. You can use it to *achieve any goal,* or *open any door!* The price is always growth and self-development. But where else does paying the price so directly enrich the payer?

How to clear away the blocks to extra-sensory development

In the early stages of psychic development we tend to build up blocks to our progress. The three major blocks are:
1. Disbelief.
2. Fear and its consequent tension.
3. Anxiety or just plain overeagerness.

It is important to dissolve these blocks as quickly as you notice their development. To fight them is only to give them strength, but they can be gently dissolved with knowledge and understanding. Let's work on them one by one.

The block of disbelief can rob you of your will to try. It must be dissolved in order to maintain the enthusiasm necessary to success. The great and growing science of Parapsychology gives plenty of intellectual credence to ESP. We will assume your intellectual acceptance for the moment and consider the religious aspect. The greatest value of the *New Testament* lies in the Master's challenge and promise: ... *He that believeth on me, the works that I do shall he do also; and greater works than these shall he do* ... (*John* 14:12.)

And what are these works? Certainly much of Jesus' life story is involved with demonstrations of ESP. There are a good hundred examples of the Master's highly developed ESP in the four gospels. Let's take a brief look at one from each:

Matthew 17:27: *Notwithstanding, lest we should offend them, go thou to the sea, and cast a hook, and take up the first fish that cometh up; and when thou hast opened his mouth, thou shalt find a piece of money: that take, and give unto them for me and thee.* (Clairvoyance and/or materialization of physical substance)

Mark 9:4: *And there appeared unto them Elias with Moses: and they were talking with Jesus.* (Spirit materialization)

Luke 5:22, 23: *But when Jesus perceived their thoughts, he answering said unto them, What reason ye in your hearts? Whether is easier to say, Thy sins be forgiven thee; or to say, Rise up and walk?* (Clairsentience)

John 1:47, 48: *Jesus saw Nathanael coming to him, and saith of him, Behold an Israelite indeed, in whom is no guile. Nathanael saith unto him, Whence knowest thou me? Jesus answered and said unto him, Before that Philip called thee, when thou wast under the fig tree, I saw thee.* (Clairvoyance)

These four illustrative examples were picked for their brevity. There are many longer and more dramatic accounts of Jesus' regular demonstrations of all forms of ESP. Remember that he claimed to be not the great exception, but rather a challenging example to all men! Shall we break the faith and refuse to follow Him? Reread the Gospels while carefully watch-

ing for examples of ESP and let all doubt and disbelief dissolve
in your new enlightened understanding.

The block of *fear* can drive your results away. At the moment
when we experience our first clear demonstration, many of us
feel an almost overwhelming fear of the power of the unknown.
This fear tends to drive away any further demonstrations. There
are only two solvents for this block. They are knowledge and
the familiarity born of broadened experience. It takes real courage to keep on in the face of that formless fear. I freely admit
that the hair stood straight out on the back of my neck the
first time I was aware of the touch of a being without a physical body. There was an almost overwhelming urge to run! But
the conscious mind couldn't answer my next question, "Run
where?" So I sat still and enjoyed a wonderful experience.
There is nothing to fear but your own thoughts!

Now disbelief has been replaced by understanding, and fear
by knowledge and experience; it should all be down hill. It is
here, as we recognize the great value and fantastic potential of
ESP, that most of us get overanxious. We want it all, *now*, with
no further work or waiting. So we tense up and try too hard.
Nothing is more destructive to your ESP! When you get tense,
decide to relax immediately, then help accomplish it with a
simple breathing exercise.

Shut your mouth and inhale through your nose. Fill your
lungs to capacity and hold your breath while you count slowly
to twenty-two. Then exhale slowly through your nose, empty-
ing your lungs as completely as possible. Now immediately inhale through your nose, filling the lungs again. Continue for
from three to seven complete breaths until you feel the anxiety
abated.

Now practice

On May 8, 1965, Randy Matson became the first human to
put the shot over seventy feet, just a few short years after

Roger Bannister broke the four minute mile. How well do you think either of these men did the first time they tried? Success in any worthwhile undertaking is the result of great effort applied in an organized manner. You don't have to become the equivalent of a Matson or a Bannister to bring a good measure of ESP into your life, but you must put forth a reasonable amount of plain old effort. Every moment you spend practicing the exercises will bring its reward of increased proficiency. Then you can turn your attention to the many practical applications of *your ever growing proficiency.*

Points to Remember

    I. The five steps to personal success and greatness
        A. Increase your awareness.
        B. Recognize your psychic ability.
        C. Develop your ESP.
        D. Contact powers greater than yourself.
        E. Apply your ESP.
    II. Work for relaxed awareness.
    III. You already have psychic ability.
    IV. Develop your concentration by use of the exercise.
    V. Apply concentration and meditation to the solution of any problem.
    VI. Man is a spirit expressing through a soul which uses a physical body.
    VII. Practice the basic exercise to develop your psychic centers.
    VIII. Exercise to develop your clairvoyance, clairsentience, and clairaudience.
    IX. Work to dissolve the blocks to your psychic development.

how to

Contact Powers Greater Than Yourself and Get Real Help for Your ESP

If ESP were just a parlor game or something to occupy a few men in ivory towers, we would have no reason to give it our attention. But it has a range of intensely practical applications stretching from the finding of a lost cuff link, acquiring fame and fortune, to achieving an intimate, personal relationship with the Creator of the Universe.

Your place in the universe

Since he first climbed down out of the trees and began to assert his dominion over the earth, man has intuitively sensed a purposeful, creative force underlying the manifestation he calls the Universe. The intricate detail of the atom repeats itself in ever more complex patterns which stretch into the vast galaxies of outer space. Throughout the great scheme of things, the order and intelligence is so obvious that no thinking individual can shrug it all off as a gigantic accident.

History records many changes in man's understanding of the details which make up our world, but the creative intelligence and power behind it all remains forever unchanged. Most men agree to call this intelligent force *God,* and the seeking of a personal relationship with it *religion*. The plain fact is *you can't go it alone*. God is the life and the very substance of your being, whether you like it or not! You will find life a much richer experience when you have surrendered your separateness and replaced it with a *living religion*.

Modern psychology confirms the necessity of religion to our mental health. The brand or denomination is not important: but if an individual is to be a "whole being," it is essential that he establish a satisfying relationship with the power he recognizes as God. Religious diversity is good. It provides a channel of experience and expression for the varied natural inclinations and aptitudes of the hodgepodge we call mankind. But within it all there are many threads of essence, common truths and manifestations which truly bind the entire species of man to the loving worship of *one true God*, though they may call Him (or It) (or even Them) by a thousand different names.

One of these threads is *love*. We find it even in the fiercest oriental-despot type deities conceived by primitive man. The deepest experience of God's love is a common meeting place of all religions. This is the glorious union with everything that is, which is best described as the mystic experience. We will devote a whole chapter to "How to Use Your ESP to Establish a Personal Relationship with God." But meanwhile we want to look at another of the threads which bind the many religions into one.

Most of the religious scripture of our world is believed by its adherents to have come to man directly from God. However, a study of the scriptures themselves reveals that they purport to have come by the intervention of spirit entities on God's behalf. For instance, the great religion, Islam, grew out of a series of mystical conversations between Mohammed and an entity or entities described at different places in the *Koran* as the Spirit, the Holy Spirit, and the Angel Gabriel. Or in the story of the beginnings of Christianity we find, right in the first chapter of *Luke:*

And there appeared unto him an angel of the Lord standing on the right side of the altar of incense. And when Zacharias saw him, he was troubled and fear fell upon him. But the angel said unto him, "Fear not, Zacharias: for thy prayer is heard; and thy wife Elizabeth shall bear thee a son and thou shalt call his name John." And Zacharias said unto the angel, "Whereby shall I know this? For I am an old man, and my wife well stricken in years."

And the angel answering said unto him, "I am Gabriel, that stand in the presence of God; and am sent to speak unto thee, and to show these glad tidings. And behold, thou shalt be dumb, and not able to speak, until the day that these things shall be performed, because thou believest not my words, which shall be fulfilled in their season."

Certainly spirit contact didn't end with the last accepted words of scripture. Down through the ages into the present day, men pray. They pray to the Saints, the Virgin Mary, Jesus of Nazareth, or directly to God; and they *expect to be heard.* By its very definition, any form of prayer is an attempt at spirit contact. Our purpose in this chapter is to unfold your ability to contact those spirit beings who *can* and *will* be of the utmost help to you all the rest of your life. In other words we will learn: *How to be sure of an answer to all our prayers.* We will begin by learning to contact your own higher self.

How to use ESP to contact your higher self

The logical first subject for an attempt at spirit contact is that ever present entity, your higher self. The ancient occult traditions tell us to begin by purifying the temple. Naturally the temple referred to is your mind-body, even as Jesus referred to his body when he said that he could rebuild the temple in three days. It stands to reason that the higher elements of life will not be attracted to a body which is in a run down or degraded condition.

Here common sense is the watchword. It isn't necessary to give up any of life's pleasures, but we should avoid overindulgence of all kinds. The healthier the body, the sharper will be its means of perception, both physical and extrasensory. We won't dwell further on purifying your temple except to say that purity of thought is of even more importance than purity of the strictly physical temple. Your response from the spirit realms will always come in harmony with your dominant mood at the time you seek the contact. Let's take care to seek the higher self only after we have cleansed our mind of its collected negative thoughts.

Now find a quiet place where you will not be disturbed and begin to seek the contact. There is a part of your being which already exists on the higher planes of life. It is the seat of all your morality, and a source of inspiration and positive impulses. It is so much higher than what you normally consider to be yourself that it is easier to comprehend if we think of it as a separate personality and give it a name. For many years I have called my higher self "George," but you should pick the name for yours which seems most appropriate for you. For ease of illustration, I will use the name "George" for your higher self in the following exercise:

Relax in your quiet place and fill your mind with thoughts of peace, prosperity, harmony, health, abundance, love, and joy. Briefly run through our basic exercise for psychic development to sharpen your receptivity. Then call George by name, saying something like: "George, we have been together for a long time. Now I am ready to get better acquainted. What should I be learning from you, now?"

Expect an answer through one or more of your rapidly developing channels of ESP. No one can describe the thrill of that first contact, no matter how slight it may later seem. With a little patience *you will get your response!* You can talk over all your problems with George, and get surprisingly helpful answers. Remember the response doesn't have to come in a loud voice or a thunderclap. Your awareness of the little things and understanding of their meaning is the secret of successful reception. Practice regularly, and *pay attention!* Ask George to set the mental tone for each day before you get out of bed in the morning. This contact is the most basic, and it is certainly worth all the effort necessary to establish it.

How to receive guidance and help from our "older brothers" in the next dimension

Again let's start our approach with a peak at the occult lore of the ages. Throughout the mass of occult literature there runs the thread of the concept of the Divine Hierarchy. This Divine Hierarchy is said to be an organization of members of the spirit world, headed by the *ascended masters* and staffed with many devoted workers whose last earth lives were spent in study and earnest spiritual service to mankind. The express purpose of this organization is the upliftment of mankind and the furthering of its progress or evolution along spiritual lines.

Contact with the Hierarchy can be most beneficial along material as well as spiritual paths. When you have identified your own *teacher* and clearly established your contact, you can expect tangible help of any sort you need. In the next section we will look closely at several specific examples of help in finding a better job, a perfect wife, and a whole new path of spiritual unfoldment; but first we will begin our approach to the source of this help.

Your own higher self is the best means of introduction to your spirit teacher. Go to your quiet place and contact your higher self by the method we just explained. When you are aware of the presence, say something like, "George, I am ready to seek my first conscious contact with my spirit teacher, please help me now." Repeat your request, then relax and await the response. Again it is necessary to be alert and aware of the little things which are slightly out of the ordinary.

Since your spirit teacher is himself (or herself) a complete entity, the method of response may be much more varied than the normally internal response of your "George." It would be quite normal to feel a gentle touch on some part of your body, or a cool breath on your cheek. Or you might see a ball of mist before you, one or more lights of almost any size, or even a full size human shape in a soft misty light. You may hear a voice in your ear, or feel a wave of electricity pass through your body, or you may simply be impressed with a new thought of some kind.

When you recognize that first response, answer immediately. Don't choke up with fear! This is a normal and natural occurrence. Answer with a heartfelt, "Thank you," and, "It's wonderful to know you are here." Then ask for the name of your teacher and the recognition symbol he will send to let you know of his presence. As you progress in this work you will undoubtedly attract many teachers. Each will have his own recognition symbol so you can know who is with you at all times.

To you doubters: *This is not a bunch of hogwash!* The spirit world is just as real as the material, and it is certainly as important to you. Give this a good solid, open-minded try before you dismiss it as nonsense! One good contact is all that is necessary to show you its reality.

How beings from the next dimension can help you

A few words of *why* may make this particular *how* a little easier to understand. Why should beings from the next dimension want to help you? Our answer comes clearly from the concept of one God, one universe, one life, and one consciousness. Dwellers in the spirit world, not blinded by the demands of our kind of physical existence, naturally understand this. They know that we are all *one* in essence, and their individual progress is best furthered by contributing to the overall progress of the species.

Obviously there is only a small portion of our present population which is ready to accept the reality of spirit helpers and try to work with them. So *you* are extremely important as a potential channel for their work *down here*. This is merely a restatement of the ancient truism, "As you turn to God, God turns to you." We are saying, "As you turn to the spirit world, it turns eagerly to you." One of the best avenues of growth for those on the spirit side of life is active help and participation in the evolution of those souls who are currently struggling for growth within the confines of a material body. Thus we can be sure of the wonderful mutuality of spirit relationships—helping you helps them!

Now specifically *how can they help you?* Any way you can imagine another flesh and blood human being helping, and a few ways known only to spirit! Let's look at some real life examples.

A man was completing his divorce, and seriously wondering if there is such a thing as true marital bliss on this earth. He had begun to study and search for spiritual truth, however, and during a period of extreme loneliness he reached a new understanding. He reasoned: I have just conclusively proved that my judgement in the area of marriage is such that I am totally unqualified to choose a mate for myself. But I am not willing to accept a sentence of loneliness for the rest of my life, so I must seek help from a higher intelligence.

In the quiet of his apartment he reached out for contact with his spirit teacher, and asked for help like this: "Professor, I know that Infinite Spirit knows the whereabouts of the perfect companion for me. I know that, of myself, I have not enough vision to pick her, but *Spirit can*. I ask your help in leading me to her now. Thank you for this gift of divine companionship." He repeated this request each evening at bedtime, talking to his professor just as you would talk to a friend or neighbor who you were sure really wanted to help you.

In less than two weeks he felt a powerful urge to visit a strange church. There a medium told him that a wonderful girl was about to enter his life; and followed with a description which included her hair style and color, the color of her eyes, and her first name. He continued his daily prayer, and two weeks later met the girl who matched the medium's description, but at another church not previously known to himself or the medium. The couple's spiritual affinity was obvious from the very beginning, and each found a depth of feeling and companionship more wonderful than either had dared dream possible. They have been happily married for many years now, and the passage of time has added nothing but richness to their relationship. This was not coincidence or accident! It was the certain working of spiritual law. Your birthright is fullness of joy and expression on all planes and in all areas of your life. Now is the time to claim it!

Another man became interested in working with the spirit world, but it seemed that he could find no time for study or meditation. In order to hold his job, he was required to attend meetings in the evening on almost no notice and with such regularity that it made any kind of class work out of the question. He came to me for advice and we reasoned together as follows: In this materially oriented civilization it is absolutely necessary for a man to work and earn the kind of comfortable living he feels his family deserves. However, a balanced life must also include time for recreation, a normal home life, and spiritual study. Naturally the man agreed, but then came the problem: I obviously need to find a different job where I can still make a good living, but I can't afford to quit and go several weeks without income, and I certainly don't have time for job hunting while I'm on my present schedule.

But here was a problem tailor made for spirit help. He was really trying to meet all his obligations and still find time for spiritual work. The only missing factor appeared to be his permission for spirit to help him. He entered his own place of silence and simply presented his problem to his spirit teachers with a heartfelt request for help. He repeated this process each evening just before retiring.

On the afternoon of the fourth day he received a phone call from an old business acquaintance, asking if he knew of anyone who might be available for a position with his company. The old associations were fresh and pleasant enough that it took only two telephone conversations to agree on terms and salary for the new job. He immediately gave notice, and two weeks later he began his new career, but this time with ample opportunity for his spiritual studies. Happily he remembered his obligation to spirit, and he has progressed wonderfully in spiritual things while steadily improving his economic lot.

Let's look at one more quick one before we move along. A woman was waiting for the traffic signal to change at a busy intersection. Just as it turned to "go" she reached for the gear shift to move on, but somehow her hand grabbed the ignition key and turned off the motor instead. While she was restarting her motor, a speeding vehicle came from nowhere through the intersection against the light. That evening in her quiet place she received this answer from her spirit teacher, "The only way I could keep you from being hit in that intersection was to make your hand turn off the motor." Yes, many serious mishaps are avoided by the direct intervention of beneficent spirit forces.

Again a word of caution is in order. Just because a person comes to you without a physical body is not total assurance that he (or she) knows any more about the true nature of life than you do. We are given this admonition in the Bible: *Beloved, believe not every spirit, but try the spirits whether they are of God: because many false prophets are gone out into the world.* (1 John 4:1.)

John continues by prescribing a test: *Hereby know ye the Spirit of God: Every spirit that confesseth that Jesus Christ is come in the flesh is of God: And every spirit that confesseth not that Jesus Christ is come in the flesh is not of God: and this is that spirit of antichrist, whereof ye have heard that it should come; and even now already is it in the world.* (1 John 4:2, 3.)

In modern language, treat any new spirit with the same friendly but cautious reserve you would use on a stranger who knocked on your front door. See that he qualifies himself to you by his words and actions before you place too much trust in him.

Your spirit guides and protectors

It will pay you to spend as much time as possible getting acquainted with your spirit teacher. When you can recognize his presence easily, and your confidence in him is born out of your own happy experience, you are ready to meet other members of your spirit *band.* It is not unusual for one *earth being* to work with a band of from six to twenty-four spirits who devote a great deal of time to the affairs of just this one group. The composition of your group will be unique in character, matching your own special personality. The direction of your natural talents and aptitudes is often obvious from the backgrounds and earthly occupations of the closer members of your band.

If you want to be a musician for instance, you will undoubtedly find several musicians in your group; but you will also probably find a doctor, two or three American Indians, an artist, and business manager. Each one comes to fulfill a specific function in furthering your spiritual progress and such work for spirit as you may be inspired to undertake.

Most of us don't regularly recognize every member of our band, but this isn't mandatory. A friend can accomplish many favors for you while you are unaware of his efforts. Again this is that wonderfully mutual situation where helping you helps them, so always give thanks to your teachers for your "lucky breaks"; but don't worry too much about which individual arranged them for you.

As your spiritual unfoldment progresses, you will experience new urges toward achievement along some line of creative endeavor, and this may attract new members into your band. One woman began her serious study of the spirit world and soon felt a vague urge to paint. At about the same time she noticed two new presences during her meditations, and politely asked them how they would identify themselves. Each showed her a symbol of a painting in a golden frame, one was a landscape, the other a portrait. Thus she learned how these two spirits hoped to improve their knowledge and ability to paint by helping her. She spent several days in the library reading about artists and techniques before she finally bought her first artist's supplies. The beautiful work she now turns out is a delight to her family and friends. It carries a shimmering ethereal quality and somehow seems to bring a personal message to each individual who stops to admire it.

Spirit is interested in the unfoldment of *you!* Your spirit friends are capable of helping in any way you will accept. But they will never act as servants in the sense of doing things for you that you should do for yourself. However, they will be zealous in their assistance of your unfoldment in any way that might add beauty or inspiration to life. The more people who stand to benefit from your success, the greater will be spirit's effort on your behalf. In elementary physics we learn of simple machines by which man has been able to amplify his puny strength. The lever, the pulley, and the inclined plane are examples. By these simple devices man gains what is called a *mechanical advantage.* Similarly, by working with the spirit world, man gains a spiritual advantage which can manifest as tangible help in any worthwhile undertaking.

Enjoy your newly found friends. You will find them loyal and helpful. But remember that working with spirit *is* like using a physical machine. Spirit will happily amplify the force that you supply, but *you must supply some force.*

How to reach out to the infinite

The purpose of all life seems to be continuous unfoldment or evolution. Through the law of natural selection nature tends constantly to improve each species by the survival and reproduction of the fittest. Man often tampers with this law of selection for his own benefit. By scientific breeding, the poultry of today has been made so much better than that of just fifty years ago that you would no longer buy meat from the older strains. Luther Burbank became world famous for his development of superior plants. Everywhere, man is helping nature do things better. The only major exception seems to be in the improvement of the species of mankind itself.

But what is necessary to the improvement of the species, my fellow beings? Logically it is the same basic kind of co-operation with nature that has improved everything else. However in man's case we encounter one big difference. As a self conscious, abstract thinking entity; one man is quite the same in his evolutionary potential as a whole species of plants or lower animals. You can exercise a process of planned evolution upon yourself and produce results every bit as startling and important as Luther Burbank achieved with his plants. In doing so, you will blaze a new path to achievement for all the souls who follow after.

The path of self-improvement or unfoldment logically leads us into a deeper and more meaningful relationship with the source of all life, the Creator of the Universe. The history of man's seeking this at-one-ment with God reveals two quite different paths; the inner path of love, called mysticism; and the outer path of power, called occultism. Let's examine them briefly as follows.

The Mystic's Approach

Traditionally, the mystic spends a life of quiet contemplation, experiencing God's love in the sunshine and rain, the birds and bees, flowers, trees, and even the thorns. The mystic reasons: since God is infinite, he is equally present everywhere; so by contemplation of the essence of my own beingness I must finally experience deity at the center of my being. And through this, I will feel my oneness with all of creation. The keynote of the mystic is *love* of everything as the ultimate form of worship of God.

The Occult Approach

The occult approach is one of action. The occultist reasons: the great unseen forces which created the universe must still be operating or it would collapse back into the nothingness from whence it came. So by learning to direct these forces I can influence the course of creation and thus become more nearly one with God by performing more of his creative functions. The keynote of the occultist is *achievement* as the ultimate demonstration of worship of God.

The Balanced, Combined Approach

The great pitfall of mysticism is the development of a beautifully loving impracticality of existence, while the danger facing the occultist is the tendency to become a coldly calculating egomaniac. Either one is way out of balance! But the solution to this problem is obvious. Why not follow a combined approach, balancing the coldly practical occultism with the warmth of deep mystical experience? This will be the theme of all our study of practical applications of ESP and spirit contact. The truly spiritual approach to the infinite is loving application of the self to improving all areas of the particular. The richer and fuller your life, the more you are fulfilling your destiny as a thinking being.

How to gain complete personal protection

We have looked at several examples of spirit help that amount to protection of your physical being. Now let's discuss ways and means of insuring this help for you, not only for your physical being, but also for all your physical, mental, emotional, and spiritual affairs.

Our example from the science of physics is again in point. Spirit generally works by amplifying your own efforts, so we must look first at what you can do to help yourself.

In discussing what they call accident-prone people, modern psychologists recognize the fact that most accidents are attracted. It is a short step from there to the realization that accidents never just happen, they are caused by people; and the happy occurrences which save others from harm are also caused by people. Your studies are making you more and more aware of the unseen forces whose existence provide your means of extrasensory experience. Even our scientifically oriented society is accustomed to similar unseen things—at least one airliner crash was attributed to interference with the crafts communication system by a tiny transistor radio being operated in the passenger cabin.

We can logically infer that there is some quality of human consciousness which attracts trouble and accidents, and some other quality which tends to repel them. Some people manifest a certain intensity of consciousness that overshadows even their physical senses to a degree, and may make others within their proximity downright uncomfortable. This is the consciousness of the accident-prone, the jinx that attracts disaster of all shapes and sizes. We all produce some degree of this negative consciousness when we become tense or overanxious, and simply learning to eliminate these conditions will be a major step forward. The greater your success in achieving the *relaxed awareness* we discussed in Chapter 1, the more you will be eliminating the sources of trouble. The achievement of a reasonable degree of relaxed awareness is a prerequisite for obtaining effective protection through the aid of our friends in the spirit world.

Let's contemplate the nature of the next dimension as a means of understanding the mechanics of spirit protection.

Without the impediment of the sluggish reactions of dense matter, dwellers in the spirit realms must find the mind to be a somewhat different tool than it is on our lower earth plane. Here *below*, thought is certainly creative, but it is impeded by the inertia of material objects. But mental creation and even travel in the spirit realms is essentially instantaneous. This also gives a completely different meaning to the concept of time. Thus to a tremendous extent, each spirit lives in a world of his own mental creation; and this is formed at first from the beliefs and quality of consciousness he brought with him from his earth life. Then it is modified by his newly acquired knowledge and experience as his spirit life progresses.

Thus a criminal or ne'er-do-well passing into spirit will probably enter a world of misery and hate such as we might expect his mind to create. Now if such an entity should wander into your quiet place and try to communicate with you, you would be in danger of being deceived or even driven toward some negative act. Our Bible often speaks of *spirit possession* as an affliction like any other disease. Modern science pooh-poohs this as ancient superstition, but there are those in mental hospitals today who might return to normal lives with a little old-fashioned "casting out of 'evil' spirits." Since such entities will only enter a thought atmosphere which is compatible with their own, you can best avoid them by maintaining an attitude of happy spiritual aspiration. Fill your quiet place with your own bright spiritual light, then you can expect the most help from your spirit band.

Let's return to our Bible for help in this understanding. Creation is associated with light—*And God said, Let there be light: and there was light. And God saw the light, that it was good: and God divided the light from the darkness. (Genesis 1:3, 4.)* In the world of spirit, those who have gained understanding live in the light, while the confused souls dwell in a darkness of their own creation. Now if you have been in a dark room for some time, and someone suddenly turns on a bright light, you experience a very real discomfort. In much the same way, those spirits who dwell in the darkness cannot stand a bright spiritual light. Thus your effective prayer for protection is: I dwell in the bright Christ Light, all goodness is attracted to me, and nothing of the darkness can come near me; I give thanks for the wonderful light.

Use this prayer each time you enter your quiet place for meditation, and *any time* you feel uncomfortable. Spirit protection is yours for the asking. It can be the most positive influence in your life. Use the little prayer just on general principles at least five times every day—I dwell in the bright Christ Light, all goodness is attracted to me, and nothing of the darkness can come near me; I give thanks for the wonderful light.

Your special place in the divine scheme of things

Wherever we look in this tremendous universe, we see order and organization. From the tiny particles which make up one atom, to the vast galaxies of space, man has observed a consistent manifestation of law and intelligence which keeps the electrons in their orbits around the atomic nuclei and the planets in their paths around the suns. If this were not so, the universe would disintegrate into a giant chaotic mess. Back of all manifestation is an Intelligence minute enough to control individual electrons, yet vast enough to direct the course of whole galaxies. There can be no doubt that this Infinite Intelligence has some sort of a master plan for the development of its manifestations.

From our vantage point astride this speck of dust we call the earth, we are in position to understand only a tiny fraction of the Creator's over-all plan. But how much is a fraction of infinity? The part *we can experience now* is close enough to infinite that we won't know the difference for many incarnations to come. Now how shall we perceive mankind's part in the Divine Plan? How shall you discover your special part of it?

Life, as we are able to observe it, is embarked on an apparently endless spiral of evolution or improvement. So far, man is the only earthly manifestation of self-consciousness with the power of choice best described as initiative and selection. Therefore we are the first earth beings with the power to choose whether or not we will cooperate with the laws of evolution. To continue to ignore the laws leaves us no worse off than we have ever been, but what is the potential reward of complete cooperation? Isn't it the achievement of a new level of consciousness where man understands the true meaning of being created in the image and likeness of God?

In truth, we are intended to grow into the realization that man is God in potential, here and now! And we should begin to demonstrate this truth by manifesting beauty, peace, abundance, love, and joy as a beacon of hope for all those who have not yet grown to this beautiful realization. Now why are you so important to this Divine Plan? Precisely because this great realization must be experienced by *individuals!* Since the realization and the *power* both exist only deep within the recesses of individual beingness, *you* as an individual are the only avenue through which mankind can achieve this great evolutionary advance. Thus, as you help yourself the most, you simultaneously make your most important contribution to the advancement of mankind.

You are entitled to tangible help from spirit in every phase of your existence. But isn't it logical that spirit will tend to shower the greatest help on those who are consciously striving for the advancement of the common cause by the sincere improvement of their own beings? The Master left us this same thought when he said: *And seek ye not what ye shall eat, or what ye shall drink, neither be ye of doubtful mind. For all these things do the nations of the world seek after: and your*

Father knoweth that ye have need of these things. But rather seek ye the kingdom of God; and all these things shall be added unto you.

Spiritual growth is the key to all progress, happiness, fulfillment and joy. Join your spirit teachers in mutual seeking and you will unfold a life of joy beyond the limits of imagination.

Points to Remember

I. All major religions have a heritage of spirit contact.

II. Purify your "temple" before seeking contact.

III. Start by contacting your higher self.

IV. Ask your higher self to introduce you to your spirit teachers.

V. Ask for help whenever you need it.

VI. Live always in the bright light of spirit protection.

VII. Find your place in the Divine Plan and grow in joy, usefullness and fulfillment.

how to

Attain Perfect Health
for Yourself and Others

Let's begin our quest for perfect health by agreeing that any healing is good, regardless of the method by which it is attained. Some religious and occult sects preach against doctors and medicines, but this is obviously foolishness. Divine protection is a fact for many of the faithful, but if you have a physical problem, it simply shows that you haven't yet attained the perfect consciousness of protection. So why suffer needlessly when medicine can help?

The value of modern medicine

The science of medicine has unquestionably grown up into sophisticated adulthood. Through applied research, it has nearly doubled our average life expectancy in the last fifty years, and made the process of daily living more comfortable along the way. As the frontiers of medicine push ever forward, dread killer diseases of years ago are one by one becoming only bad memories. To deny the good works of medicine would be ridiculous, but to consider it the only hope or the omnipotent fighter of disease would be equally silly. Let's quickly agree that there is a time when any prudent individual would consult a competent medical doctor.

Certainly you would expect to let a good doctor set your broken leg or stitch up a nasty cut. And for any persistent ache or pain, it is a good idea to let your physician decide whether there is an organic problem. Then pay attention to his diagnosis and submit to expert treatment. But we should carefully understand that doctors treat the symptoms, or at best the secondary causes of our symptoms. The physician's field is basically restricted to treatment of your physical body; but we will clearly see that all disease originates in the mental or astral bodies. Your doctor does his best with the knowledge and tools at his command, but without your help in removing the mental and emotional causes underlying the symptoms, his results are bound to be limited both in scope and duration.

Don't be misled by this line of reasoning. Some people refuse to take aspirin for a headache because it "doesn't cure the cause." But others take aspirin and find that they are much more comfortable while waiting for nature to remove the cause. And it seems to take the same length of time with or without the medication. There is no reason for you to be foolish about it. *Use anything that will help!*

Then if you should happen to be one of the many people who enjoy a physical problem that medicine has not yet cured (or perhaps even found a name for), you can join that growing group of sincere spiritual workers for the comfort and upliftment of man. We call them spiritual healers. Most of us who become interested in spiritual healing do so because of personal experience in an area of modern medicine which has not progressed far enough to cure our problem. Then when spiritual healing works for us, we somehow feel bound to repay our spirit friends by helping others. As is so often true in this work, you will find that the best way to help yourself is to set out to learn how to help others. So let's start helping ourselves now by learning the rudiments of spiritual healing.

How you can become a spiritual healer

The big advantage of the spiritual healer is his approach to the individual as a spiritual entity—a whole being, consisting of a soul which is manifesting through mental, emotional, and physical bodies. A simple recognition of the vital energy flow from the emotional body to the physical, as directed by the mental body (or mind), gives the healer more ammunition than all the scalpels and antibiotics in the country. You will learn that every physical symptom is the result of a maladjustment in the energy flow coming into the solid body. Careful cooperation between the patient, the healer, and the spirit forces can always correct the adjustment and bring about the return to the original health state of the divine archetype.

With only a little practice, you can learn to see the energy field around yourself or your patient, so you will know that we are not carrying on a modern witch hunt. The field of energy which holds your physical body in shape and vitalizes it is known as the *aura*. It is most easily noticed around the head or the fingers; but it actually permeates your physical body, and extends beyond it in all directions for several inches in the easily visible spectra and for much greater distances in the finer, less visible vibrations. Your first glimpse of your own aura is important because it proves that your body is much more than a mere pile of clay. It is a new look at the *livingness* which is you!

The aura is light. Now if you want to get a careful look at any subtle light source, how do you go about it? Naturally you try to set up conditions that provide a minimum of interference from other light sources or variegated backgrounds. For your first attempt to see your aura, try this simple experiment:

Sit in a room that is dark except for one or two candles burning on the table. Spread a few pieces of clean white paper on the table and against the wall to provide as unbroken a white background as possible. Now hold your hands at a comfortable reading distance in front of you with the palms facing each other and the fingers comfortably curved. Bring your hands near each other until the fingers almost touch, then slowly pull them apart for a distance of three to five inches. Stare carefully at the space between the tips of your fingers as you move your hands slowly together and then apart. Soon you will notice the shafts of light running between your fingers. You may sense the vibrations more like the *waves of heat* that we often see rising from a dark surface on a hot day. But whether you see light or vibration, watch it stretch thin as you move your fingers apart, then grow fatter as the fingers come closer together again.

Continue the exercise and notice how you are using your eyes when the aura of your fingers seems most visible. Then try to see the aura around your head in a mirror, using your eyes the same way. Next, observe the effect on the aura around your head when you bring your open hand near it. Then try a mental exercise: see if you can expand the visible aura around your head by *willing* it. Can you vary its shape? How about changing its color?

Since the aura is a special kind of light, we can learn to turn it into a *healing light*. This, too, is a matter of *will*. You have mentally affected the aura around your head, and the same principles apply to any part we choose to work with. Start controlling the energy around your hands and directing it to become a most beneficial healing agency for anyone you touch with this light-energy. A good exercise for developing your healing faculty is to sit before a mirror and hold up your hands like a saint giving the benediction; then ask your spirit teachers to join you in sending forth the healing energy to bless all mankind. Feel your hands tingle as the healing energy flows out of them. Regular practice of this universal healing exercise will improve your effectiveness and prepare you for the time when you need to help someone close to you (or even yourself) by using your wonderful new healing hands.

You will have an unquestionably positive effect on *all who cooperate*. An excellent example of the need for your patient's cooperation came in my relationship with a lady in the business world. Because we worked fairly close together, I learned that she often suffered from headaches. One day I offered to help her get rid of a bad one she obviously suffered from at the moment. Without telling her what I was doing, I worked with the spirit forces to manipulate the healing energies and easily removed the psychic block which was causing the trouble. In less than five minutes her headache was completely gone and she was very thankful for the assistance. However, she was a rather high-strung individual and managed to produce a new block for herself every few days. For several weeks I was able to cure each headache with dispatch. But finally her curiosity got the better of her and she pointedly asked me how I did this. She had a strong anti-religious prejudice, and my explanation unfortunately angered her. From that day forward, I was completely unable to relieve her pain. Her elimination of the element of receptivity blocked the flow of beneficial energy from my hands and even from my spirit helpers, so she resumed her use of aspirin and tranquillizers.

The example serves to illustrate two important points. First receptivity, or at least the absence of conscious resistance, is definitely required. But second, and perhaps more important, the energy flow itself works primarily on the symptoms. So without the removal of the mental cause, it is no more able to effect a permanent cure than the aspirin. The only way to produce a permanent cure is to move from the mind through the emotions to the physical. Let's begin to examine the following basic steps in spiritual healing.

The five steps to spiritual healing

We will examine the five steps to spiritual healing in detail, but first here they are in brief:

1. Determine the broad mental cause and explain it to the patient.
2. Invoke spirit world help in breaking the basic thought-reaction patterns of the cause, and healing of the mental, emotional, and physical bodies.
3. With the cooperation of spirit, apply the healing light to the afflicted area. (laying on of the hands)
4. Assist the patient in establishing healthy new mental and emotional patterns to prevent further outbreaks. (He must change his way of reacting.)
5. Keep up the prayer and healing work until the patient has completely recovered.

How to determine the mental cause of illness or disease

Obviously no one can make a simple table that says exactly what thought pattern causes each physical disorder. Life isn't nearly that simple. Apparently identical thought patterns in two different individuals may cause a heart attack in one and nothing worse than a simple headache in the other. However there is some general correlation between the major negative thought patterns and broad groups of physical troubles. In *The Miraculous Laws of Universal Dynamics,* I presented a table of mental poisons and their general symptoms. It seems useful to reproduce it here with only minor variations from the original.

The table should be studied like a mystical poem, for the *feeling* it produces within you, not for specific case information.

Obviously everyone living here on this earth still has a few negative thought patterns. It will pay you well to look within

Table of Mental Poisons and Their Symptoms

Mental Poison	Resulting Symptoms
1. Resentment, bitterness, hatred.	Skin rash, boils, blood disorders, allergies, heart trouble, stiff joints.
2. Confusion, frustration, anger.	Common colds, pneumonia, tuberculosis, disorders of the respiratory tract, eyes, nose and throat, asthma.
3. Anxiety, impatience, greed.	High blood pressure, migraine headaches, ulcers, nearsightedness, hard of hearing, heart attacks.
4. Cynicism, pessimism, defeatism.	Low blood pressure, anemia, polio, diabetes, leprosy, low income, kidney disorders.
5. Revulsion, fear, guilt.	Accidents, cancer, personal failure, poverty, poor sex, "bad blood."
6. Antagonism, inferiority, introversion.	Allergies, headaches, lack of friends, heart murmur, accidents.

yourself and root out as many as possible before they have a chance to cause more trouble. For every negative pattern of your own that you notice, you will find that you have a neat bit of mental gymnastics by which you justify harboring such a dangerous felon. It will be an excellent exercise for you to write down each justification, then study it carefully to detect the basic flaw in your reasoning. Now *throw out the negative pattern,* but keep your understanding of the flaw in your rationalization to use in helping someone else get rid of the same sort of mental poison.

Whether the patient is yourself, a loved one, or a complete stranger, his (or her) cooperation and straight-forward honesty are the keys to success in this part of the treatment. With enthusiastic spirit cooperation you may accomplish a perfect physical healing, but unless you also break up the mental cause, you will discover that the healing is short lived. This is what Jesus meant when he so often cautioned someone he had just healed, *Go, and sin no more.* The only sins in the universe are negative thought patterns and their manifestations.

So how do you discover your patient's mental cause? If it is yourself, by detached introspection; if someone else, by psychic communication and the art of conversation. Caution your patient of the need for directness and honesty, then ask a few simple questions like: "What do you resent the most?" or, "Tell me briefly, what are you most ashamed of?" or, "If a good fairy gave you a choice of one person or condition to be removed from your life, what would you pick?" As you learn to relax during such sessions, you will find that you receive psychic impressions which will also help in your understanding of the problem.

Now let's become fully aware of a most important point. You *are not to be a judge!* The Master cautioned us, *Judge not, lest ye be judged.* Then He demonstrated his practice of what he preached. For instance, there was His conversation with the woman taken in adultery. After they had been left alone, He asked her, *Woman, where are those thine accusers? Hath no man condemned thee?*

She said, "No man, Lord."

And Jesus said unto her, *Neither do I condemn thee: go and sin no more.* (*John* 8:10, 11.)

No matter how terrible a confession may seem, if you show the slightest revulsion or condemnation, you will lose any ability to help your patient. Discuss all problems with warmth and understanding, and be ever alert to hear the voice within which prompts us to say just the right thing to help your patient reach a new insight. This new understanding is a major factor in the success, since the spirit world is bound to respect an individual's wishes. In other words, it is only when your patient *wants to change* his thought patterns and *asks* for help, that a permanent cure becomes possible.

How the spirit world helps break old reaction patterns

O.K.—now your patient wants to change, and wants spirit help to accomplish it. Logically it's time to assist him in asking for it. First call on your own spirit teachers and ask them to invite your patient's teachers to join in prayer. Then pray aloud somewhat as follows: "Infinite Spirit, in its own way and through the agency of our wonderful helpers from the spirit world, is helping Joseph (your patient) to break up all his negative mental and emotional patterns now. His mind is becoming highly sensitized to notice his negative tendencies before they get a chance to manifest as emotions, thus he can choose to react with divine light and love to all situations. He is inspired to find the hidden good in all his experiences and seek always to let spirit express through him as harmony, health, wealth, peace, unfoldment and fulfillment. Thus he turns to God, and God answers with showers of blessings. We sit in the silence now, giving thanks for these wonderful changes."

After a reasonable pause, repeat your prayer, then pause again. Continue until you or your patient feel some form of definite response from spirit. Spirit will always respond by sending positive thought vibrations to the mental body and soothing energy to the emotional body. Your patient may feel a wave of warmth pass through his physical body, or he may describe it as a tingling feeling like a mild electric shock. Others will simply feel a sensation of peace stealing through their being. If you have done your work properly, *there will be a response from spirit!*

You must expect your patient to feel this response. Your faith will help open the path for the downpouring of the beneficent energies. Now you are ready to add your own light to the helpful spirit energies.

How to apply the healing light to the afflicted area

We opened this discussion with exercises to develop your aura vision and your ability to control and direct this visible part of the vital life force. With the help of your spirit teachers, you can direct this powerful force to cleanse and heal the patient's physical body by application through his aura. Understand that the aura is *light* which is in the nature of pure emotional energy, and it can be directed by the mind to produce important tangible effects on the physical body.

The process is simple. Ask your teachers to participate, then mentally direct the powerful light to flow from your aura into the afflicted area of the patient and exert a cleansing, healing influence on both the emotional and physical bodies. As you work in this way, you will make an interesting discovery: that you don't lose any vitality in your part of the process. If anything, you will feel invigorated by "giving a healing." This is because you are only acting as a pumping station for the vital energy that is present throughout the atmosphere, and many of your own needs will be met by the rush of vital energy through your system to that of your patient. How shall we go about this?

If your patient is present, the best method of applying the healing energies is by the laying on of the hands. Prepare your patient by sitting him in a straight chair with the back turned around to one side, leaving you clear access to his spine and the seven major psychic centers. Prepare yourself by holding out your hands, palms up, and taking a deep breath. While holding the breath, mentally send a short prayer to your spirit teachers to help in directing the healing energies through you to the patient. Then hold your palms about four inches apart and feel the energy flowing between them. You can tell by the tingling sensations that one hand seems to be sending, while the other receives the energy your body is pumping between them, much like an electric circuit.

Begin your treatment by placing your *sending hand* on or near the base of the patient's spine. Now hold your *receiving hand* about an inch above your patient's head, and move it around until you feel the maximum current flowing up into your outstretched palm. At different times this flow of energy may feel hot or cold or just tingly, but you should always feel something, no matter how slight. Hold this position and let the current flow for something over sixty seconds. Then keep your receiving hand in place, but move your sending hand up to the area of the spleen center. Again hold this position and let the current flow for about a minute. Next, go on with your sending hand to the point on the spine directly behind the solar plexus and let the energy flow some more. Repeat the process for each of the first six psychic centers. When you are ready to treat the seventh or crown center, move your receiving hand to the forehead directly above the eyes, and this time feel the flow from the crown center out through the brow center. As you get used to working with the energies, you will develop your own techniques and variations because some things will feel more natural and effective for you than others. This is good, since no two really effective healers ever seem to use identical techniques. Even the same individual healer will find his techniques evolving with time, and also adjusting themselves to meet the needs of particular patients.

Now that you have cleared the seven major centers with your healing light, you are ready to concentrate on the specific area of your patient's symptoms. As best you can in the particular circumstances, get the afflicted area between the palms of your hands and *will* the energy to flow again. It helps to mentally picture a rushing stream of light flowing from your sending hand through the afflicted area and back into the receiving hand. Picture this light as the spiritual equivalent of a swirling torrent of water which sweeps everything of a diseased or negative nature before it, back into the nothingness from whence it came.

End the treatment with a prayer of thanks to your spirit teachers and the Heavenly Father for the perfect healing of your patient. Visualize him as absolutely whole, complete, pure, and perfect, expressing more and more of the God-life as he continually grows in spiritual understanding. Then release him to God and *go wash your hands,* while mentally affirming that you are washing away any remaining trace of negativity. If you forget this ceremonial cleansing process of the hand washing, you may pick up a few of your patient's symptoms and wind up needing a healing for yourself.

Don't get the idea that this is just for professional healers!

You can use it to help your spouse or child, or even your pet. And it will benefit your own spiritual growth for the trying. By willingly giving of yourself to help someone else, you make it easier for your teachers to send help to you. Don't scoff at this or shrug it off! Develop your healing ability now, so you will be ready to help someone who really needs it tomorrow or the day after.

If you know of someone who needs healing help, but you can't be present, you can still participate. Go to your quiet place and call on your teachers to help. Then mentally picture the whole process being administered to the patient by your spirit healing teachers. Again end the *treatment* with a prayer of thanks and a visualization of your patient as absolutely whole and perfect. And again wash your hands for your own protection and to give a feeling of release for the treatment. This is called absent treatment. You will be amazed at the excellent results you get with just a little practice.

How to establish healthy mental and emotional reaction patterns

Now the healing is well under way, and our main concern is to prevent recurrence of the mental causes. A simple explanation of the interrelatedness of the whole of the human entity will be most beneficial. Logically show your patient that he is a soul expressing through mental, emotional, and physical vehicles; and he must look upon himself as a whole being rather than a group of isolated parts. Use the example of psychosomatic medicine to demonstrate that the mind and emotions have a definite effect on the physical body. Then follow with the next step—a healthy mental and emotional pattern must have a positive, healing effect on the physical body.

Convince your patient that he can't afford to harbor negativity. Then review the trouble areas you turned up while seeking the mental cause of his problems. Help him find new and positive attitudes to replace the newly uprooted negative ones. Review and repeat the teaching until you are convinced you are really getting through to him. The ultimate success of the entire treatment depends on the effectiveness of the joint effort to change the underlying thought patterns. Your own completely positive approach to life is the best possible argument. It will show through your words and win for you if you have taken the trouble to develop it. Similarly, any negativity that you demonstrate will work to the detriment of the healing process, and could even make the patient worse. Work constantly to improve your personal attitudes and reactions to help yourself and your ability to inspire others.

Keep working until the healing is complete

Some healings are dramatic and instantaneous, but these are relatively rare, and they often degenerate into a later relapse. By far the most common and the surest healings are the result of a form of growth. Now the most obvious quality of physical growth is its lack of noticeable speed. A seed sprouts and sends the first little shoot up through the ground, then the tiny plant slowly unfolds, and even more slowly grows into a bush or tree. The naked eye is not capable of registering the moment to moment progress of the growth of a plant or a human baby, but we know that it is growing all the same. Careful observation from week to week or month to month reveals definite progress.

Such is the normal progress of spiritual healing. New life and muscle is added to a shriveled limb or a useless eye, one cell at a time; and this only by faith and constant vigilance to prevent the negativity of the cause from returning. Certainly there are instantaneous healings like those recorded in the Bible as accomplishments of the Master, but if your initial attempts are not so spectacular, there is still no reason to give up. In the world of track, the distance runner will tell you it's not so much the start, but the finish of the race that counts. Many a mile run has been won by a man who was fifty yards behind the leader at the half mile point. Success comes to the man who doesn't quit! A man who keeps trying in the face of failure is called dumb and stubborn until he succeeds, then he is lauded for his insight and perseverance. You can't win a fight unless you get up one more time than you are knocked down!

Keep your faith! Work until the healing is complete and can be verified by medical doctors or anyone else who may care to pay attention.

Some seeds take longer than others to put a sprout above the ground. One sure way to prevent results is to keep digging up your seeds to see if they have started to sprout. The Master had an excellent bit of advice for this situation: *If ye have faith as a grain of mustard seed, ye shall say unto this mountain, Remove hence to yonder place; and it shall remove; and nothing shall be impossible to you.* (*Matt.* 17:20.)

How to heal yourself

Basically the same five steps apply to a healing, whether it is given to yourself or to someone else; but it will be worthwhile to review the process as it is applied to your own body and affairs.

1. Determine the mental cause and explain it to the patient. This step always seems easier for someone else, just as it is easy to look over someone's shoulder and tell him what he is doing wrong. If your most objective searching fails to turn up the mental cause, ask your spirit teachers for help. Then pay careful attention; you will be tempted to shrug off the answer as not applying to you, but no matter how absurd it may seem at first, face up to it. In some stubborn cases you may consider seeking help from another student of the healing art. In any case, root out the trouble no matter how much effort it takes!

2. Seek spirit world help in breaking the old negative reaction patterns. Your spirit teachers are anxious to answer your calls for help. Now that you have determined the mental cause, it is well to renew your request for help in breaking the negative thought patterns each morning just as you get out of bed. Again, pay attention! The more you cooperate and listen for the promptings of spirit, the quicker will you get rid of the mental poisons.

3. With the help of spirit, apply the healing light to the afflicted area. For yourself it is just like giving someone else an *absent healing*. Sit quietly and visualize your spirit healer applying the light by laying on his own hands. Then feel the light as it surges through each of your major centers and moves on to cleanse and renew the problem area.

4. Establish healthy mental and emotional patterns to prevent new outbreaks. This step is much more important for you than for any of your other patients because you are working to activate your psychic faculties and thus are more sensitive

to all your thoughts and reactions. The best possible advice on this subject was given by the Apostle Paul: *Finally, brethren, whatsoever things are true, whatsoever things are honest, whatsoever things are just, whatsoever things are pure, whatsoever things are lovely, whatsoever things are of good report; if there be any virtue, and if there be any praise, think on these things.* (*Phil.* 4:8.)

5. Keep working until the healing is perfect. Since we are so very susceptible to our own thoughts, it is of greater importance than ever that we do not become discouraged. *According to your faith is it done unto you.*

Learn to live constantly in the healing light. To the extent that you are successful in mentally living in the pure white light, you will be healed of all your present problems, and you will remain radiantly healthy and happy until you are ready to lay down this physical shell and graduate to the next classroom in the spirit world.

Expect excellent results

The level of confidence that you project to your patient is a key factor in the success of the treatment. However it is not your outward expressions so much as your inner feelings that control your projected faith. The healer must remain completely optimistic throughout the course of the treatment, giving thanks to spirit for each tiny physical manifestation of improvement. And when no outward manifestation is yet visible, you should continue giving thanks for the fact that the healing forces are acting so effectively on the unseen side of life that the healing is about to show through into the physical like a bud suddenly opening into a beautiful blossom.

A man suffered terribly from a spine infection called Pott's Disease, for which the medical profession had not yet found a cure. His seeking of some form of help led him to a small Spiritualist Church where the twice-a-week services began with individual spiritual healing treatments for all who would accept them. He instinctively felt a great power there, and began attending each service with a prayer for help in his heart. The philosophy imparted by the sermons slowly helped change many previously negative thought patterns, while the healing light administered through the laying on of the healer's hands continually cleansed his physical body. It is difficult to imagine such a slow, and yet so steady an improvement in a condition. After the third week his regular answer to the question, "How are you feeling?" was, "Better." And he did get better, mentally, financially, emotionally, and physically. At the end of the first year his doctors were amazed that his spine had completely ceased draining, and the deformity was noticeably reduced. No one would care to say exactly when the healing was complete. He still takes his twice-a-week *treatments* for the benefits of well being in other areas of his life as well as the peace of mind that comes from knowing that the old problems can never come back through that wonderful light.

Not all good healings take that long. A business executive developed a huge hemorrhoid. He decided to postpone the recommended surgery for two weeks because of the press of business. During this period he sought spiritual help. A simple pattern of anxiety coupled with lack of physical exercise was noted by the healer. An intensive program of twice daily absent treatments by the healer, coupled with a simple yoga exercise relieved all the pain in two days. Within a week there was no evidence of a hemorrhoid at all. Thus he avoided both the time loss from work and a very painful operation.

A migraine sufferer was accustomed to being knocked out by her attacks to the point of simply going to bed until they passed. Generally she had an attack about every ten days which lasted twelve to thirty-six hours. One evening she arrived at a spiritual gathering to take part in a ways and means discussion, but an attack had begun to hit her while driving to the meeting. She sank into a chair and commented that she would have to head for home and bed, and she "sure hoped she could make it that far." The work was new to this sufferer so she was amazed when two women suggested she stretch out on the couch and let them try to help her. They formed a human-spirit chain with one woman sending the powerful light into the patient's head while the other pulled it out through her feet and the spirit helpers purified it and completed the circuit back to the first healer. Within ten minutes all the pain was removed, and the patient was able to enjoy the meeting and go home afterwards with a living hope for a new pain-free life. No, this was not her last migraine headache, but the attacks were quickly reduced in frequency to about three a year of a much milder variety. After three years of study and practice, she was able to report no headaches that couldn't be relieved by simply taking a couple of aspirin tablets.

It is not necessary to accept any physical condition as incurable. The same forces which built your body are available to repair it. The price of the repair job is complete cooperation with the great healing forces of the spirit world.

How to handle special healing problems

Sometimes a physical problem is aggravated by seemingly impossible surroundings such as extreme poverty, a totally sadistic spouse or head of the family, unrequited love, or a career that is obviously slipping due to the force of circumstances. An individual may have been born into a difficult situation in order to learn some special lesson, and no healing efforts can be expected to be successful until the lesson is digested. At times like these you should give extra thanks that it is not you who performs the healing. The power of God manifesting through your spirit helpers performs the healings, and it is as infinite as you are willing to believe.

Any time you feel that external conditions are a major stumbling block to the healing efforts, talk it over with your spirit teachers and ask for their physical help. Often a joint meditation with your patient will quickly reveal the basic lesson required, or some simple change of approach to the patient's thinking habits which will be the key to a perfect healing. Of course you are working with a whole being which you cannot isolate from its surroundings, but regardless of any astrological or karmic influences, each individual is entitled to grow constantly into better and better conditions of health, finances, happiness, peace, and joy. Teach your patient that this is his birthright, and encourage him to claim it every moment of his life.

Mental cases present a different problem of approach. Obviously it will accomplish little to reason with a catatonic or a paranoid who is playing Napoleon. In these cases the laying on of hands can often work wonders, but we must take care not to frighten or unduly excite the patient. The soundest and surest approach is directly from the spirit side of life. If the trouble is being caused by obsessing entities, spirit world intervention may be the only way to reach your patient. Group healing prayer and requests for help from the assembled spirit teachers of the group can produce enough force to bring any patient back to some greater degree of rationality. Seek whatever help you feel is appropriate. Certainly this is a most wholesome time to prove the promise of the Master: *Ask, and it shall be given you; seek, and ye shall find; knock, and it shall be opened unto you.*

Use your healing ability as often as possible

Whether you use it to help yourself, your family, or all mankind; you must agree that proficiency in the healing art is a gift of great value. But like a mind or a muscle, it requires the right exercise to develop its maximum utility. A muscle will atrophy with disuse, or a mind will become dim; and so it is with your ability to assist the spirit world with the healing process. Never hesitate to help! If your assistance would be misinterpreted or resented, give it silently at the altar of your own heart, and tell no one. When you can help by injecting yourself directly into the situation with prayer and laying on of hands, all the better.

In truth we are all one, and anything you do to help someone else *must help you* as well. The Master expressed this thought: *And the King shall answer and say unto them, Verily I say unto you, Inasmuch as ye have done it unto one of the least of these my brethren, ye have done it unto me.* (Matt. 25:40.)

You don't have to get yourself a reputation as "that nut who is always butting in trying to heal somebody," but with discretion, tact, and prayer you can perform many healing miracles for the good of your *brethren*. As you give of yourself in loving service, you are blessed in many more ways than you can imagine. Add this as a new dimension to your life, now!

Points to Remember

I. Modern medicine is good. Never hesitate to call on it.

II. The spiritual healer treats his patient's whole being by redirecting the energy flow from the astral or emotional to the physical body.

III. Learn to see your aura, and mentally vary its size and shape.

IV. Practice directing the flow of healing energy from your hands.

V. The five steps of spiritual healing are:
   A. Determine the mental cause.
   B. Seek spirit help both in breaking the negative thought-reaction patterns and in the physical healing.
   C. Apply the healing light to the afflicted area.

      D. Help establish new healthy mental and emotional patterns.

      E. Keep working until the healing is complete.

   VI. In working with negative mental patterns, judge not! Merely heal.

  VII. Expect excellent healing results.

 VIII. Practice often

how to

Use ESP to Gain Riches in Ever Increasing Abundance

Ever since society became complex enough to outgrow the barter system, people have suffered from real and fancied troubles with money. The average American feels that he is restricted in his ability to express himself and accomplish worthwhile things by his lack of unlimited funds. A special few inherit great material wealth, then have to strive all the harder to keep it from destroying their ambition and drive. Since money is some kind of problem to almost everybody, a closer look at what it really is will help us get better control of our relationship to it.

A new look at riches

What is money, anyway? For most of us it has long since ceased to be pieces of silver or green ink on pieces of paper. Now, money is simply a few assorted numbers appearing as an abstract thing we call our bank balance. We all tend to become greatly excited over nothing where our bank accounts are concerned. You will say, "Not me!" But let's think about it. The mathematical symbol for nothing is zero, which we express as 0. If your next bank statement arrived with one or two symbols of nothing placed between the numbers and the decimal point, *you would get excited!* But if it showed a check charged against you with the same extra nothings inserted, *you would panic.*

Money is simply a symbol, an *idea,* a convenient way of measuring your claim to future goods and services. We entered this classroom called earth to learn to be masters of life. Our purpose is to control and direct our ideas, *not to be enslaved by them.* We are intended to express more and more of life, not limitation. The Master taught us simply on this matter: *And ye shall know the truth, and the truth shall make you free.* (*John* 8:32.)

I am come that they might have life, and that they might have it more abundantly. (*John* 10:10.)

The *Gospels* are full of examples of Jesus using the higher laws for what we might call economic purposes. He turned water into wine, found his tax money in a fish's mouth, and more than once fed the multitudes by dramatically multiplying a food supply. Clearly the great Christian example taught us not to accept material limitations. We must learn to recognize apparent shortages of money as glorious opportunities to develop our mastery over earth life.

Begin to become a magnet now; attune your being to riches. A young man had an idea for a product which he was sure would make life more enjoyable for many people. He had only $100 to spend toward promoting it. Most of us would despair and submit to the limitation, thinking "this is just too big for me to attempt." This man managed to produce a few samples from materials he wheedled from his potential suppliers. So he spent his $100 for the biggest advertisement it would buy. He sold enough from the first go-round that he had $300 to spend on advertising the next week. Instead of just spending the $300 on advertising, he borrowed another $300 from a friend and spent the whole works on advertising. His confidence prompted him to continue pyramiding his business spending, and in less than three years he sold his company for several million dollars.

The reason this doesn't happen every day is lack of that confidence in an idea which makes a man give the *extra bit of himself* which is the ingredient of all success. You are standing on the threshold of greater financial success than you have dared to dream. Let's step across!

How to interest your spirit helpers in bringing you riches

Many religionists have a terrible habit of degrading money, both in their thinking and from the pulpit. It is a crime against the well being of humanity to preach that money is filthy lucre or that love of money is the root of all evil. As long as you make the awful mistake of believing these things, your spirit helpers will naturally strive to help you avoid any unpleasant contact with nice sized sums of money.

It is time to understand the truth. *Love of money is a good emotion!* To love money is to use it wisely, and spend it happily in the comfortable knowledge that there is an abundant supply. The negative emotion concerning money is *greed*. But this is exactly the opposite of love, because greed is *fear* of lack. To clutch and hoard money in fear of not having enough, is a powerful prayer for poverty. But financial comfort is simply a proper understanding of the laws of earthly living.

You agreed to be born into this particular earth life to further your personal evolution and thus advance the whole species we call man. Part of coming back into material existence is a set of physical requirements for the proper maintenance of the vehicle of manifestation, and these needs must be met so long as you remain here. You are given your own unique equipment for supplying these needs as you grow toward the age of responsibility. You have a set of aptitudes which fit you for some particular kind of loving service which will allow you to *earn* your keep. And you have a mind which equips you to discover your potentials and develop them. Let's be sure we understand that you don't have to be the economic bread-winner to earn your keep.

A child earns his way in a very real sense by entering whole-heartedly into the growth process. No amount of money can express the feeling of joy in a parent's heart that comes from seeing his (or her) child realize his potential by achievement of some small goal (like an *A* in second grade math or a home run for his little league team) that will seem inconsequential in just a few short weeks or months. And a wife certainly earns her share of the income by her care of the children and by providing loving encouragement for her husband.

But there is a deeper lesson hidden in this analysis. Spirit is primarily interested in the progress of the spiritual side of your life. Like a parent who may reward a child's accomplish-ments with candy or a new bicycle as well as love and joy, spirit can and *will* shower you with material blessings as you ear-nestly strive for spiritual growth. The requirement is roughly the same as the parent-child relationship. No parent will give a child something he knows will detract from its growth and development, but he will be quick to give any gift which will obviously be beneficial. So if you can demonstrate to your spirit helpers that money will definitely *aid* your spiritual progress, they will help you attract it in ever growing waves of prosperity.

A young married man felt he should provide more material and financial blessings for his wife and children. He had started at the bottom in his factory job just three months before, and the economic pressure of four people to support on his modest wage left no margin for error, much less any luxuries. His interest in spiritual progress heightened at about this time and he reasoned that he could unfold spiritually with much greater effectiveness if his mind weren't so full of the pressures that stem from lack of money. So he began to talk it over with his spirit teachers twice a day. His part of the conversation went something like: "Beloved teachers, you know I am striving to grow on the spiritual plane, but I need your help. My deep desire to provide a better material life for my family keeps trying to crowd out the spiritual, but I realize that both are necessary. Please help me progress in the business world as an aid to my spiritual development. Thank you for your loving help."

Soon he started to get simple ideas of how to do things better on his job. The quality of his work improved as he seemed to apply more creative attention to it, and his sound suggestions to the foreman shortly earned him a substantial raise in pay. He continued to look upon his work as an exercise for spiritual as well as material improvement, and in three short years he progressed all the way to assistant plant superintendent. That is far from the end of his story, but it is enough to illustrate the truth of material progress under the guidance and direction of spirit teachers by a human who is willing to cooperate

Your path to riches through ever-increasing effectiveness

"Seek ye first the kingdom of heaven," is the injunction in point. But there is a rule of reason that comes with it. We live in a materially oriented, economic society, so your path to riches must lead through ever increasing effectiveness in the material world. Improved health is the logical first step. Any day you are not feeling your best, your effectiveness is bound to be lessened. Apply the lessons of our chapter on physical healing and gain ever more radiant health.

Next comes your attitude toward life in general and your work in particular. In all of life, but especially in the business world, there is room for only one emotion. It is that manifestation of positive love which men call *enthusiasm*. Life is an endless series of games by which we strive to attain real spiritual advancement. One of the very important games is the complicated riddle called business. The game attitude gives us the best clue to the most healthy approach toward getting ahead. On the football field it is well known that the enthusiasm generated by desire can make up for much lack of natural ability. Certainly, given two equally matched teams, the one with the greatest *will to win* will put the most points on the scoreboard. We must constantly strive to generate willing enthusiasm for the accomplishment of each assigned task, but it should be tampered by a good gamesman's sense of sportsmanship. Of course we will gamble and take calculated risks to achieve spectacular gains, but we must abide by the established rules and sound ethical judgement. A spectacular gain that costs us the support of our spirit teachers would be a tragedy! This prompted the Master to remind us, *What profiteth a man to gain the world, but lose his soul?*

Enthusiasm and good sportsmanship will get you maximum mileage from the application of ESP to your work problems. Often there are several possible answers to a business problem, but there is always one *most creative* solution. Since it will benefit the most people, your ability to regularly come up with creative solutions guarantees your continued advancement. Truly creative solutions most often come from your higher self or your spirit teachers. Talk over your business problems alone in your quiet place with your spirit helpers. Explain each problem exactly as you understand it, and ask for creative advice. Then relax and *pay attention!* Sometimes an apparently wild idea will come drifting into your consciousness. Before you dismiss it as ridiculous, talk it out with your spirit helpers, it may have an intensely practical application.

An expediter had a chronic problem getting good quality parts out of several plating shops his company was using. In his quiet place an idea kept pushing its way into his consciousness. At first it seemed to say, "Why don't you set up your own shop?" He knew that his company didn't have nearly enough work to keep a plating shop of its own in operation, and he would have dismissed the idea as worthless, but he paused first to talk it over with his teachers. As he verbalized the question, how could I sell an idea like this when we obviously don't have the volume for it, he was met with this response: "Why not buy one of your suppliers? You can streamline its operations to do a better job for your company and for its other customers as well." He approached his boss with the idea, and together they went to see the president. A supplier was interested in selling, and our expediter was offered the position of manager of his company's new division. This was only the first of a long series of promotions, each based on one or more creative solutions to chronic problems.

No one can use these ideas for you. But if you pay attention and *apply what you receive,* there is no limit to your progress.

How to set up a current to draw wealth into your life

Seen from the spirit side of life, wealth is as abundant as air or ocean water. Both air and water move in currents, and so does material wealth. You can set up a mental current to draw riches into your life in tidal waves of abundance. The first step is to eliminate those thought patterns which have been blocking the flow of abundance to you. In our last chapter we set out a table of mental poisons and their symptoms. You may have noted references to lack of money as part of the symptoms. Actually, any negative thought pattern will tend to restrict the flow of riches into your experience. Deliberately set out to clear your mental channels of all obstructions to the smooth entry of wealth, now! You should spend at least ten minutes each morning and evening in your quiet place seeking contact with your spirit teachers. During each contact period, ask for guidance and help in ridding yourself of the habit of negative thinking. Then pay attention to the little reminders of the areas where you are falling short, and resolve to improve a little more every day.

A woman of some means had been experiencing an undue amount of financial difficulty. She came to me with the complaint, "I have eliminated all my negative thinking, but my affairs are still in a mess and I seem unable to straighten them out."

As we talked, she explained how she had carefully weeded out her resentment of the people whose efforts had caused her problems; and I agreed she had done this job well. But further discussion clearly revealed a deep seated fear of financial ruin. Such a strong fear is a very effective prayer for the manifestation of the thing feared, and this was completely negating her positive prayer work. Her efforts to gain new perspective by looking on the whole problem as if it were a checker game slowly dissolved her mental block and brought about her return to financial peace.

A special area that demands our careful attention is your acceptance of financial responsibility. Some people hate to pay their bills, and shirk carrying their share of the financial load in social as well as business situations. This is tantamount to praying for poverty and lack! Learn to *enjoy* paying your bills promptly and fulfilling your obligations graciously. Give thanks to the Infinite Source of all for the abundance you have now, and spend it intelligently. Maintain a never ending vigilance to keep obstructions to the flow of wealth from creeping into your mental environment.

Now that your channels are prepared, let's look to starting the flow of wealth into your personal experience. In the physical world, when you want to get water out of a well, it is necessary to prime the pump. A similar pump priming is necessary in the mental-spiritual world we seek to master. How shall you prime your spiritual pump? Again we can find our answer by looking at the material world. When you want to get water out of a physical well, you prime your pump with the same substance, water. So when you want riches, money is the best substance to use in priming your pump. The Christian concept of tithing is an excellent method, but only if it is done with the right attitude. In a very real sense, a farmer tithes when he gives his seed into the loving care of the soil. There is no sense of loss or holding back at planting time because the farmer visualizes the joy of harvest. If you release your tithe to spirit with the same happy expectancy, your harvest will be similarly bountiful.

But some of us may say, I haven't the resources to tithe, I can barely make ends meet now. That feeling is undoubtedly the cause of your problem, but any attempt to use the law of abundance while harboring such an attitude would be disastrous. If you feel too short to give money, then find a way to give of yourself in loving service. But look forward all the time to the happy day when you can also do your share with plain old-fashioned money.

Spirit has infinite ways of multiplying your good. Scientific giving is as certain a way to improve your financial lot as modern farming is a way to produce food. As you release each gift in love, you set up an irresistible spiritual current to draw wealth into your experience. It is only necessary to accept without anxiety or greed as the increased flow of riches begins.

A young typist encountered these ideas and decided to give it a try. Instead of the quarter she had been dropping into the collection plate on Sundays, she decided she could spare a dollar for openers. Each Sunday for four weeks she made her dollar donation to the church and sure enough, nothing happened, except that she began to feel better somewhere inside her being. In fact she felt so good that she decided to increase her weekly donation again, this time to two dollars. As she continued to feel better inside, it reflected in the quality of her work. On the tenth week of her program an opening developed for a junior executive secretary, and her new radiance and effectiveness led the personnel manager to offer her the position. The thirty dollar a month raise that came with it made our new secretary so happy that she decided to increase her donation again, this time to three dollars a week. We will sum-marize the rest of the story, just in case you haven't guessed the outcome. She married the junior executive and taught him the simple secret of her own advancement. Today she is the happy wife of a successful senior executive.

Let spirit express riches in your life

Now you have deliberately set up the current of wealth and it is only necessary to *let* spirit express riches in your life. Build an attitude of gracious acceptance as the happy changes begin to enter your experience. Spirit regularly operates through ap parently natural and normal channels. Don't expect the heavens to open up and dump a million gold doubloons on your front porch. Your wealth will seek you through new ideas and op-portunities, and again it is your responsibility to *pay attention.* Yours could come from a new train of thought triggered by the chance remark of a friend or even a child.

Act when the spirit impels it! The best idea in the world is no good to anybody until it is put to some practical use. As your idea unfolds, keep asking your teachers what is the best way to implement it. Never brush off an idea because it seems too simple or commonplace. Imagine the value in today's market of a patent on the principle of the safety pin! Or the zipper! There are just as many concepts waiting to be realized today. But your good doesn't have to come in the form of a new product. It could just as easily be a series of individually insignificant ideas about doing your present job better, or a promotion, or the unfoldment of a completely new career. Know that the tendency of the universal laws is to increase the happiness, health, peace, abundance and wealth in the lives of all who will cooperate. Use your relaxed awareness to notice and capitalize on your opportunities. Then remember to give thanks, spiritually, mentally, *and financially.*

How to protect yourself from
financial harm

In our economically oriented society, it is a truism that any form of harm to you or a member of your family will have some negative effect financially. So it is necessary that we seek protection in its broadest sense. By this time you should be aware of the deeper truth of that wonderful passage from the 91st *Psalm*, *"For He shall give his angels charge over thee, to keep thee in all thy ways. They shall bear thee up in their hands, lest thou dash thy foot against a stone.*

You are certain, now, that the *angels* referred to in the *Psalm* are your own spirit teachers. As you earnestly work to co-operate with the great evolutionary plan of the universe, they will provide you with just such protection. You will live the truth of the promise, *A thousand shall fall at thy side, and ten thousand at thy right hand; but it shall not come nigh thee.*

As always, your own efforts provide the small force that is amplified by spirit into an irresistible protective influence which you can place around yourself, your loved ones, and your belongings. In the old occult terminology, you can fashion a "ring-pass-not" which will absolutely prevent the approach of negative occurrences. How shall you build your own ring-pass-not?

Our modern world has many examples of effective protection from unwanted conditions and influences. One in particular will help us understand the principle of the ring-pass-not. Many supermarkets, department stores, and other public buildings are air-conditioned; yet their doors stand wide open all day. The cool inner air is protected from invasion by the undesirable outside air by a simple *curtain* of air in motion. This invisible curtain allows normal in and out passage to the desirable elements like customers and employees, but it effectively seals out the external heat, smoke, dust, fumes, and smog.

Your Heavenly Father provided just such a *curtain* of protection for you. Are you using it? It works quite like the protective air curtain of the supermarket, but it uses currents of thought and living light for its protective shield. *It will work successfully for you*, but only if *you* choose to use it. You must build your own personal consciousness of divine psychic protection.

Start in a quiet moment and visualize a space suit of dazzling white light surrounding your body and extending its protective force a foot or more in all directions. Then say to yourself: "The white light of divine protection surrounds me now, sealing out all negative thoughts and experience. Only goodness and purity can penetrate this wonderful light, and I will send nothing but goodness out through it. Thank you, Heavenly Father, for your perfect protection." Now bask in the lovely white light and consciously feel its loving protection. Repeat this simple exercise as often as possible while building your certainty of personal divine protection.

You should renew your protection by using the exercise at least mornings and evenings for the rest of your life. Then any time you feel you are in a tight spot either physically, mentally, financially, or psychologically; simply call on your teachers and the Heavenly Father to intensify your protective white light. This will not only help you, but it will exert a positive influence on all others involved with you. It will take much mental work before your light can give you 100% perfect protection, but it will give you some degree of tangible, positive help from the very beginning. Start to practice now! The life you improve is not just your own!

You can extend this protective ring-pass-not to include your home, your automobile, and to some extent the members of your family. The limit to family protection is cooperation in thought from the individuals you wish to protect. Although you can exert some positive influence, every human being is entitled to exercise his own freedom of choice in the matter of accepting such protection.

Let's look at an example of protection of your automobile. Many years ago, after a series of three very minor accidents, I began nurturing the idea of an inch of psychic armor plate around my vehicle. Since that time, I have driven in the extremely heavy Los Angeles area traffic for over twenty years in perfect safety within my inch of *armor plate*. In a couple of emergencies I could swear that another car has been stopped at just that one inch point, and an accident averted. There is one exception to the perfect twenty-year record. During one short period of great emotional stress, I decided that this whole spiritual business was a bunch of hogwash, so I dropped my daily renewals of the protective white light. In less than two weeks, I got clobbered in my brand new sports car! I regularly give thanks for this experience. It was the best lesson anyone could ask for. Take it from someone who's been there, this thing really works! And *you* can't afford to be without it.

You can lead a charmed life from now on. The great strength of the whole Judeo-Christian tradition is its generous, loving God who wants only to shower blessings and protection upon his human images. The Master brought us the instruction, *Hitherto have ye asked for nothing: ask, and ye shall receive, that your joy may be full.*

This is one thing that no one can do for you. *You* must do the asking. Ask your Heavenly Father for the protective white light. Then accept the loving gift, and lead a spiritually charmed life forevermore. Do it now! "The white light of divine protection surrounds me now, sealing out all negative thoughts and experience. Only goodness and purity can penetrate this wonderful light, and I will send nothing but goodness out through it. Thank you, Heavenly Father, for your perfect protection."

How to enjoy your ever increasing riches

You have paved the way for spirit to manifest ever growing abundance in your life, so now it is only necessary to learn to enjoy it. This may sound easy, but it is spotted with pitfalls left over from your past attitudes. A man who entered adult life shortly before the great depression of 1929 makes an excellent example of the problem. This man lost his savings when the bank failed, then went for some time without a job when his employer failed. Over the years he learned some of the laws of prosperity, but they were tempered by the vivid memories of the early thirties. He established a goal of success as $10,000 a year, and attained it reasonably easily; but he could never let himself progress any farther. At every meal he kidded about carving very thin slices of meat to be sure there was some left for tomorrow, and his general attitude was one of looking over his shoulder for the coming disaster. By his own standards he was a success, but there was something drastically wrong with his yardstick. He might have progressed so much farther into the good life if only he could accept the infinite supply of the Almighty.

As you grow spiritually, it is natural to grow financially also. Don't restrict the wonderful flow of riches by doubting the infinite nature of its source. Accept the flow and use it! Your natural desires are good, and it is good for you and the economy to gratify them. Of course there is a point of balance between gratification and overindulgence, but your own intelligence will guide you if you pay just a little attention.

Then enjoy paying your bills! Look upon each invoice as a wonderful reminder of God's loving opulence. It is your happy pleasure to keep the flow of riches ever growing and circulating in your life by paying each bill as it becomes due. Mail your checks with a word of thanks to your bountiful Heavenly Father for your many blessings, and watch your goods grow and grow. Let your riches buy you time for things that are uplifting. There can be time for travel and mingling with people of other cultures and religions, for academic or spiritual study, and for those periods of relaxation that precede great spurts of spiritual growth. Relax and enjoy your ever increasing riches. You will bless many others as well as yourself!

Points to Remember

I. Money is merely an idea.

II. Love of money is a good emotion.

III. Demonstrate to your spiritual teachers that money will aid your spiritual growth.

IV. Attract your riches through increased personal effectiveness.

V. Practice creative problem solution.

VI. Improve your flow of riches by clearing your mental channels of the old negative blocks.

VII. Set up a current to attract riches by priming the pump.

VIII. Accept the flow of riches into your life.

IX. Build your ring-pass-not to protect you from all harm.

X. Enjoy your ever increasing riches.

how to

Use ESP to Build a Dynamic Personality That Attracts the Right People

Have you ever noticed how little groups tend to center around certain individuals at a party? If the center of attention is a woman, you may try to shrug it off as a low cut evening gown, but in your heart you know there is much more to it. There is an intangible something which attracts people in much the same way that moths are attracted to a bright light. You have some of this power now, but you can develop much more. *You can become a center of attention wherever you go!* It is only necessary to learn the simple laws involved.

How to use your psychic centers to extend your personality

The real secret of personal popularity and effectiveness in social and business relationships lies in an ancient saying often blamed on Emerson. It goes something like this: *What you are speaks so loud, I can't hear what you say.* All people are psychic to some extent, although many don't call it that and tend to ignore it. But this is no reason for us to skip over it. Let's restate our proposition for emphasis: *All humans receive psychic impressions from their surroundings,* though this reception is

101

largely unconscious to many people. Many times in your own experience, you have been touched by the obvious sincerity of one new acquaintance or the complete lack of scruples in another. You can be certain now that the feeling was psychically received. Similarly, you are instinctively drawn to some people and quickly form deep and lasting friendships, while it may take months or even years to learn to tolerate others.

Let's examine the psychic reasons for this instinctive behavior as our best approach to gaining control over it. In spite of his reverence for intellect, psychologists insist that modern man is governed by his emotions to a much greater degree than he realizes. We play great games with ourselves trying to believe that our major decisions are based on sound intellectual judgment, but we rush into marriage or purchasing homes, cars or minks without so much as a shred of reason to support our actions. This is not necessarily bad, it is simply a fact worthy of careful contemplation. How long has it been since you got good and mad at somebody? Now that you have had time to cool off, you can see the tremendous power of emotion to cloud or completely obscure intellectual reasoning. Now what is that power? Does it have other effects on us?

This brings us right back to the psychic centers. Your own psychic centers are active twenty-four hours of every day. They constantly send and receive the vibratory energy which is the power of emotion. Your aura is a field of the blended energies from each of your centers, and it is regularly changed by your changing thought and emotional patterns. It is also affected by similar patterns in people with whom you come in close contact. Physical proximity to another person naturally brings your auras closer together, and your emotional reactions to each other are the result of the harmonic blending of these vibrations in the case of pleasant relationships or dissonance when the relationships are negative. Certainly you have at least one friend whose very presence is a comfort to you. You may have thought it silly to feel that way, but there is a sound basis in fact for it. Some auras react upon each other to produce emotional and psychological peace of much greater quality than either person seems able to attain alone. It falls in with that interesting promise of the Master, *Where two or three are gathered together in my name, there will I be also.* Don't hesitate to enjoy such relationships without reservation, it will advance the spiritual progress of all concerned.

What of the few persons whose presence seems to make you tense and uncomfortable? Some auras don't naturally blend with each other without the conscious effort of at least one of the parties. It is reasonable to avoid contact with people whose presence makes you uncomfortable. But you should look forward to the day when you learn to adjust your own aura to compensate for the difference in vibration. Still it may require substantial effort to adjust your aura enough to remain comfortable in the presence of one who is intensely self-centered and materially grasping. This may help us to understand why we seldom receive physical visits from our own spirit teachers. They certainly want to give us all the encouragement and help we need, but to bring their highly refined auras too close to our relatively coarse ones must make them just as uncomfortable as some lesser developed humans make us. Give extra thanks next time you are aware of a spirit teacher's presence, and strive to purify your thoughts and aura as much as possible to help make your friend's stay more pleasant. The same basic techniques apply to making a visiting spirit or a visiting normal person comfortable by adjusting your aura. It is the secret of making other people like you.

How to make other people like you

Regardless of your opinion of them or their station in life, it is to your advantage to be liked by as many people as possible. Others' feelings about you do have an effect on your aura.

The positive feelings are helpful of course, but any negative vibrations must be continually cleansed out of your being if you are to remain at maximum effectiveness. Now the less negativity that impinges upon you, the less energy must be wasted in purifying your aura, and the more you will have left for constructive accomplishments.

The universe tends to return your basic projections as the pattern of your own daily experience, so let's start by examining the sort of vibrations you project into your surroundings. It should be obvious that the more positive the emanations from your aura, the more pleasant will be the response from your environment. The sincere, confident approach to life is the most effective way to tune your psychic centers for this purpose. You may hide your true feelings from the conscious minds of others, but you can't keep from projecting them into the great psychic stream from which everyone receives impressions. *There is no escaping it!* If you expect people to be comfortable around you, you must project sincere goodwill at all times. There are no shortcuts, no gimmicks, and no pills that will do it for you. But a habit of genuine goodwill toward all your fellow beings will bring you many side blessings while it truly makes everyone like you.

Projecting genuine goodwill is the first half of the battle, and it will give excellent results just by itself. But let's also consider a more positive use of your ESP in this area. If you could tune in to the other's moods by sensing the projections of his centers, wouldn't you know just what to say and do to achieve the maximum positive response? You already have a tool to do just that! Use your rapidly developing clairsentience to tune in on the other's psychic wave length. Everyone has some experience in sensing another's moods, but you will increase in accuracy and sensitiveness as you apply your conscious attention to this very practical psychic application.

As you sense your friend's mood, a combination of intuition and good judgement will lead you to adjust your own projections to blend and harmonize. You will make a substantial contribution to the goodwill of the world by spreading peace, happiness, encouragement, and joy by entering into the spirit of applied psychic goodwill. Give of yourself to promote the good of those around you. Provide the light touch that gently kids a comrade out of a bad mood, or helps him adjust to a personal disappointment.

Build the habit of psychically seeking the best method to bring out the good in your associates. There is no better way to add to your own good than by seeking good for others. Pay attention to your clairsentient impulses, and act on them for the upliftment of everyone you contact. Often you will find that helping someone else involves selling an idea.

How to sell an idea

The first principle of idea selling is communication. Most often an idea has to be sold because your friend has a psychic or emotional block to clear thinking in his problem area. The direct approach is seldom effective, as typified by the old adage, "A woman convinced against her will is a woman unconvinced." And that is equally true of men. If you would effectively reach your friend, it must be from a position of psychic rapport. Similarily in the commercial world, a salesman will attempt the psychologically symbolic act of sitting on the same side of the desk as his prospect in order to create the impression that both men are on the same team, rather than being adversaries. You will rarely sell anything as an adversary, but the job is easy from a position of psychic rapport. Take the time to build it with friendly topical conversation. Then begin a friendly game of verbal fencing while your conversation skirts the fringes of your main point.

A typewriter salesman's approach to one particular office manager is a good illustration of the technique. During most of the period in question the office had no machines of the salesman's make, but they operated about thirty competitive machines standardized as to model and typestyle. The salesman's first visit was strictly a get-acquainted contact where he probed for future conversational material. Then on each subsequent visit he opened with friendly questions about the office manager's family and the progress of his son in the Little League. On his second visit he inquired about maintenance problems and down time on the existing typewriters. On his third visit he sold them a dozen ribbons which proved to be slightly better than the ones in regular use. It was almost five months before he got around to leaving a demonstrator of his latest model, and all this time he kept the personal relationship uppermost in the conversation. Eventually he replaced every competitive machine with his own by clearly demonstrating the savings in repair cost and lost typist time to be gained from his product. The toughest part of his job was in overcoming the office manager's emotional resistance to change and to admitting that he might have made a mistake in standardizing on the other line in the first place. This could only be accomplished by indirectly approaching the subject, so the office manager never had to admit even a hint of an error.

Note the details of the technique. Send your message psychically while your conversation skirts the main issue. Carefully avoid statements or implications that your prospect is completely wrong about anything. Instead, lead him slowly to see that there is a potential benefit to him from opening his mind to a new idea. When he is finally interested in exploring the new idea, ask a leading question like: why don't you try it? Or in the case of our typewriter salesman: how about my bringing a demonstrator for you to play around with for a couple of weeks?

You are a master of the art when you can get your prospect to verbalize the idea as an outgrowth of your carefully directed discussion. Then praise him as if the idea were really his own. You don't have to have credit for a good idea as long as it is actually hatched. People like to believe they are doing their own thinking whether it is true or not. Let them, as long as it helps. But remember that this technique should be used only if you are genuinely interested in the other's welfare. Otherwise your lack of sincerity will reach your friend's psychic centers and eventually give you away. Always be sincere, and work to help your associates tactfully but effectively.

How to attract the right people and opportunities

Your sincere desire to be a positive influence in the lives of all who come into your sphere of activity is the secret of attracting the right people and opportunities. As you seek to bring light and happiness to others, your spirit band will seek the same for you. They are particularly interested in your happiness as an aid to your further spiritual evolution.

Thus you can see that when you are experiencing great happiness, the best way to insure its continuation is to give thanks and pray for continued spiritual growth. The bumps and hard places in life come to jog us back onto the spiritual pathway by reminding us of the extremely precarious nature of our physical existence. When we stray from the path of growth, life will keep bumping us harder and harder; and only as we seek spirit do we begin to find respite.

But you have a personal contact with His *angels* now. Go into your quiet place and talk over your needs with these spirit helpers. They are real friends, and you can kid with them just like any other people. If anything, their sense of humor is better developed than ours, and a good joke often works to improve your contact. I have felt closer to a particular teacher for a long time because of the running bit of banter we carried on for the two years it took to complete our first book. Relax and enjoy good fellowship with your spirit friends, and ask them for help. Then observe the little indications of its forthcoming. Since our channels of communication are not yet as effective as those between occupants of physical bodies, you won't necessarily understand exactly how spirit intends to help you. But if you remain alert, expecting help and guidance, it will always be there at the right time.

A widow sat down to talk over her problems with her spirit teachers. She expressed her feelings like this: Look here, friends, the children have grown up and left the nest, and things are pretty lonely for me. There must be a good man who needs warmth and companionship as much as I do, please help us find each other. She lost count of the number of weeks she daily repeated her request for help, but she never lost hope. Then one Sunday in church her meditation was interrupted by what felt like a sharp electric shock. She looked in the direction of the energy *source* and found herself staring into the eyes of a man in the row in front of her and two seats to the left. She smiled and returned to her meditation. Instantly she received an impression that she should arrive early for the next few services and be sure to get the same seat. She carefully made it to her seat next Sunday, and again felt an electric shock just as the same man found the seat next to her. Again she smiled, and they exchanged a few pleasantries before the service. By the fourth Sunday he asked her to join him for coffee before going home. It wasn't what we would call a whirlwind courtship, but it did develop into a warm and happy marriage that has added much pleasantness to the later years of both these wonderful people.

Notice that, as always, the spirit forces guide and help, but you must follow up with your own best efforts to manifest the desired results. One young man had been out of work for three weeks before he realized he could ask for spirit help. Finally he went to his quiet place and talked to his teachers: "Somewhere there must be a job that needs me as much as I need it. Please, my teachers, help us find each other." As he started on his daily round of job seeking, he barely missed a bus, so he decided to walk along to the next stop to help pass the time. Along the way a local newspaper that he seldom read caught his eye and he was impelled to pick it up. He was still looking at the new batch of help wanted ads as he boarded the bus. He noticed a particular ad just as his bus reached the corner mentioned in the paper. He hopped off, rushed into the building, and was hired; almost before he realized what was happening.

Your spirit friends are always ready to help you. And you understand the truth that you help each other by cooperating in positive undertakings. Nothing is too big or small to deserve help from spirit, but only if you are doing your best to help yourself. Give it a try!

How to cope with difficult personalities

Now you are doing beautifully, attracting new and interesting people and opportunities into your experience. But every once in a while you seem to attract someone who proves very difficult to get along with. How shall you handle yourself?

First adjust your attitude toward the situation. Be thankful for this wonderful new opportunity to demonstrate your mastery over problems which have previously plagued you. Next understand that the reason you rub each other the wrong way is an inharmonious blending of your auras. Obviously you can't expect to change your adversary's aura, but you have now learned to adjust your own. The secret is in your preparations *before* you deliberately enter the proximity of such a person. When you know a meeting is imminent, arrange to be alone for a minute, if only in the bathroom. Consciously call on your spirit teachers for help in controlling your reactions and adjusting your psychic centers to produce the changes in your aura that will help blend with the other's and protect you from any negative influence. Then mentally will your psychic centers adjust under your teachers' direction. Now set your own attitude. Remember that no matter how offensive a person may seem to you, he or she is an expression of the same God and the same life that you are. Mentally salute the God-self in the other, put on your warmest smile, and walk out to your meeting.

If you are caught off guard by a chance meeting, mentally go through the whole process while you are exchanging greetings. Use your smile liberally, and constantly keep in mind the simple fact that it takes two people to disagree or argue. Here is a perfect opportunity to practice selling your ideas. You will never be sure of your effectiveness in this area until you can consistently sell your sound ideas to the acquaintances you consider the most difficult. You can enjoy a happy relationship with *anyone* you meet if you will take the trouble to make it that way.

A company had contracts with several unions but seemed to be having particular difficulty with a small local which covered only a dozen of its employees. There was a running battle for almost two years which consumed enormous amounts of time for both sides. Every meeting seemed to break up with threats and bitterness, and strike preparations were underway almost constantly. When a new beef developed over the company's refusal to take a man sent over by the union hiring hall, the young vice-president decided to attend this meeting along with his usual set of negotiators. Just before leaving the office, he sat for a few minutes in the rest room making his mental preparations. He asked his spirit teachers for help, and resolved to see only the God-self in the business agents throughout the meeting. His friendly smile and warm handshake started things off on the right foot, and he seemed led to say exactly the right thing at every tense moment in the discussions. At the end of a two-hour meeting, the union representatives were convinced that the company had acted in good faith, and a friendly ending to a meeting took place for the first time. This marked the beginning of a long period of peaceful relations between the two sides, all because some·

body took the trouble to be spiritually prepared for a difficult meeting.

You can win understanding and sympathetic consideration from *anybody,* if you will conscientiously use what you know Never hesitate to call on your spirit friends for help. Helping you helps them also! Let spirit participate in making your daily round of experiences more pleasant for you and everyone you contact. It's fun and profitable, too!

The give and take of real friendship

Now that we can get over the rough spots, let's take a look at what we should expect from a real friendship. When auras naturally blend and produce the happy sensation of effortless comfort in another's presence, you have discovered the basis for a deep and lasting friendship. True friendship is characterized by the absence of dependence or need. It is a special relationship for the simple sharing of experiences which enrich both lives in the process, or it is something else. It is the same with earthly or spirit friendships, the sharing of experiences and mutual striving for growth and the good of mankind helps all parties.

Either an earthly or a spirit friendship can of itself be an expression of the mystic experience. When auras blend in the deeper relationships, the light of each is strengthened and a new plateau of spiritual consciousness may be attained. Sitting in near darkness with your friend, you may actually light up the room, or produce such a spiritual vibration that one of the higher spirits can bring a special manifestation. Your totally unselfish admiration for each other may lead to a momentary flash of consciousness where you literally think and feel, not as yourself, but *as your friend.* Welcome any such sensation, because the surest way to the experience of complete oneness with God is directly through the ability to think and feel as someone else. The ability can then be expanded so you think and feel as the whole planet, and finally the universe; and thus you find the ultimate in spiritual companionship with the God-essence itself. We will discuss the mystic experience in detail in Chapter 9, but let's close this section with one quick brush at how to find a true friend.

The secret of finding true friendship lies in your answer to the question: What do you expect to get out of a friendship? If you are looking for material gain, prestige or the like; you must realize you aren't seeking true friendship at all. But if you can say you want just the happy sharing of warmth and unselfish affection for the sheer joy of the experience, you undoubtedly have many friends already. So you'd like to have more? O.K. If you don't hide in a box under the stairs all day, you must regularly find yourself around people. They are your new friends. Treat them that way! Greet everyone you encounter with a warm smile and a friendly hello.

For you ladies (and sometimes even gentlemen) who say, I don't dare smile at strangers because it will probably be misinterpreted; there is an obvious answer. *Nobody will misinterpret your smile unless you want him to!* We all respond pleasantly to someone else's warmth, but we are still ready to give it *all the respect it requires.* The way to find a friend is to give friendship. All strangers are made of the same God-essence as you are, so they must be friends already. It's just that you haven't found out yet. Treat everybody that way and you will never be lonely. You will never want for true friendship either.

Points to Remember

I. You can become a center of attention wherever you go.

II. You constantly send and receive psychic impressions through your aura and psychic centers.

III. Psychological comfort or discomfort in another's presence depends on the degree of blending of your auras.

IV. Project genuine goodwill to everyone you meet.

V. Let your clairsentience guide you in sensing other's moods and blending harmoniously with them.

VI. Ask for spirit help in attracting the people and opportunities you need.

VII. You can learn to adjust your aura to blend with difficult people.

VIII. To find a friend, give friendship.

how to

Find the Strength to
Face Any Crisis

Our workaday world gets much pleasure and respite by poking good natured fun at itself. One of my favorite expressions of office humor is the little sign that says: "If you can remain calm while all around you people are screaming and tearing their hair, you just don't understand the situation!"

There may be much truth to that little slogan, but there is another kind of calm which results from knowing *more* than those who panic. This *more* gives us all the strength we need to face any crisis. Let's start building our strength with a look at the sources of stress, and the havoc they often cause.

Why some people crack under stress

Whether you like it or not, God is the substance and very life of your being. Some people refuse to accept this simple fact, and so build up an illusion of separation from God. They think of their being as bearing the same sort of relationship to God that a fountain pen bears to the engineer who designed it. Thus they feel isolated and on their own, and they have nothing to fall back on when the going gets rough. They expect about as much help from God as if they were a fountain pen praying to its designer for help after being stepped on. So that's what they get.

Our study of the psychic energy centers shows that we are much more intimately connected to the universe and our fellow creatures than any materially oriented individual could realize. We understand that the rest of the world tends to treat us exactly as we expect it to in the depths of our own being. Thus we recognize that we attract all our own bad breaks as well as the good that so regularly come to us. We easily understand that guilt and fear are deadly negative prayers which summon bad breaks with irresistible power. So we strive daily to rid our mental and emotional lives of all negativity. And we are making real progress! But nobody is immune to the sin of backsliding. We get all wrapped up in the apparent importance of our own little sphere of activity, and literally forget to keep our perspective. So we lapse back into some of the old negative patterns, and cry out in anguish when we begin to reap the disastrous results.

If you have allowed the illusion of separateness from God to creep back into your being, you are in a very miserable state. When things look hopeless and the world seems to be closing in on you, where shall you turn? Some people reach the breaking point and crack under the stress. Our mental hospitals and psychiatrist's couches are full of them. But there is no need to let this happen to you. Turn back to God as the only real source of personal strength, and you will make it safely through the most difficult situations.

How to find your source of personal strength

Down through the ages, men have found their greatest strength in the same place. It comes from an unshakable faith in God, such as that which prompted the psalmist of old to exclaim: *I will lift up mine eyes unto the hills from whence cometh my help. My help cometh from the Lord, which made heaven and earth. He will not suffer thy foot to be moved: he that keepeth thee will not slumber.* (*Psalm* 121:1-3.)

Even before you embarked upon this earthly life, He gave his angels charge over you. In the work of our second chapter you met your own guardian angels. We most often call them our spirit teachers, but regardless of the label, they are an ever present source of tangible help in any emergency. They have helped you many times in the past, whether you are aware of it or not, and the variety of their methods is infinite. A devoted student of this work told me the following story in complete sincerity:

> Last year while I was still driving cross-country trucks, I had an excellent demonstration of spirit protection. Late at night I got very sleepy, so I pulled my rig off the road to take a short nap. It happened that I stopped at the top of a long grade, and I must not have set the brake properly. I woke up with a start to see that my truck was careening down the hill at terrific speed. But my fear quickly vanished as I noticed the shadowy form of a powerful Indian handling the steering with a skill that was obviously out of this world. He kept the truck on the road around a couple of wild curves and finally brought it to a stop in a safe place on the shoulder. I had seen Tomahawk in my meditations before, but this was my first obvious demonstration of his physical protection. I am sure I owe him my life from that instance, and I feel his presence now every time I get at the wheel of a motor vehicle. He is a constant source of physical protection.

This is not such an unusual story. Normal people are helped by the spirit world in countless ways every day. A middle-aged woman was walking home from an evening church meeting. As she passed a tall hedge, she found herself looking right into the muzzle of a revolver. The voice said, "let's have that purse," but it was interrupted by a flash of blue light like a tiny lightning bolt which knocked the gun to the pavement. The bandit fled in terror, and the woman hurried home to give thanks to her spirit helpers in the safety of her own sanctum. A young boy was swimming alone in a secluded bay. As often seems the case for young boys, he overestimated his prowess and soon found himself over his head and sinking from panic and exhaustion. Suddenly a hand grabbed his trunks and lifted him just out of the water. He was transported in this fashion back to where the water came up only to his waist, and deposited back on his feet by the invisible hand.

These are not *pipe dreams,* they are natural examples of the help you can expect when you are working in tune with your spirit teachers. You earn special protection by spiritual striving, and by consciously working with your spirit band. You are privileged to stop at any time and return to the capricious rule of the law of averages, but very few who have tasted this protection do. If you haven't yet started to seek contact with your teachers, *now* is the best time!

How to understand your stresses

Most of us would agree that life on this earth is very much like a chess game. Your various activities correspond to your chess pieces, and you move them about trying to gain an advantage. But the rest of the world seemingly acts as your opponent, and tries to counter your moves. All the stresses in life result from frustration and disappointment arising out of our own poor moves or the excellent moves of our opponent. This is the simple reality of life until you *decide to change your relationship to it.*

There are two ways to work from this analogy to alleviate our stresses. First we called it a chess *game.* Now if you can really understand life that way, you will realize that it isn't a tremendous tragedy to lose a game once in a while. This can be a mighty help in regaining your perspective, no matter how bad a pickle you manage to get yourself into. But most of us also like to win our share so let's get back to the board and play. We started out by looking at the whole world as the opponent, but an old saying is in point here. It goes: "If you can't lick 'em, join 'em." The world will remain your opponent *until you choose to join it.* What are you trying to accomplish anyway?

Instead of trying to scratch a living out of a hostile world, a small change of perspective can do wonders for your peace of mind. Why not adopt a basic purpose to work for the good of mankind? Of course you still have to work! Man needs the honest sense of accomplishment that comes from a day's job well done. But what of your attitude? A man who has scratched hard for a living comes home weary and discouraged at the end of his day. But another man who worked on the same job all day for the benefit of his fellow men, comes home with a smile on his face, a song in his heart, and the same wage in his pocket. The *reason* you do a job, and your *attitude* toward it, have a lot more to do with the fatigue factor than the actual amount of physical energy you expend. Check your feelings on the way to work each morning. Be sure you have the right attitude and perspective!

Often we think we need help when we really need only to correct our approach to the problem. Then we get disgusted with our God and our spirit teachers because we are not rescued by some spectacular super-normal intervention. It is important that you learn to recognize the times when you actually need help. In times of genuine need you can take comfort in the unbreakable promise of the Lord, *Before they call, I will answer; and while they are yet speaking, I will hear. (Isaiah 65:24.)*

You will never be forsaken by His angels! They may let you stay in the uncomfortable situation you have built for yourself just long enough to be sure you learn your lesson, but they will *never* let you come to lasting harm. When the world seems to be closing in on you, go to your quiet place and call on your spirit teachers for help. Then sit in the silence until you get the response. But don't be surprised if the answer is, "You are perfectly capable of working this out for yourself." A significant part of your mission on earth is to learn your own mastery over physical and material conditions. Tangible help when you don't need it would be weakening, so this you will not receive. But when the chips are down, and your best is not good enough, you are in the same position as Jesus when he said: *Thinkest thou that I cannot now pray to my Father, and he shall presently give me more than twelve legions of angels?* (*Matt.* 26:53.) Let that be your faith also.

A teen-age girl was exploring a small cave alone. She tripped on a timber and caused a collapse of part of the roof, apparently trapping herself inside. In the utter darkness she knelt to pray. Soon tender hands lifted her to her feet and guided her faltering steps around two small bends to a brush covered hole just big enough to climb out. If you have *faith*, the Father will send *more* than twelve legions of angels when you need them.

How to ask for help for others

The farther you progress in this work, the less apt you are to need help for yourself, and the more you will want to seek help for others. This sharing of our spiritual blessings is an essential requisite to further growth. As always, sincerity and faith are the two greatest keys. Let's look at the methods of the Master.

Jesus often brought healing help by the laying on of hands or some other form of definite physical contact. Follow his example and practice the healing work you started in Chapter 3. But the true catalyst in all his ministry was the Master's great faith which is perhaps most clearly demonstrated before the tomb of Lazarus.

Then they took away the stone from the place where the dead was laid. And Jesus lifted up his eyes, and said, Father, I thank thee that thou hast heard me. And I knew that thou hearest me always: but because of the people which stand by

I said it, that they may believe that thou hast sent me. And when he thus had spoken, he cried with a loud voice, Lazarus, come forth. And he that was dead came forth. . . .

In more modern times, the great Hindu leader most often called Mahatma Gandhi used a somewhat different approach to helping others. He entered the silence to pray for help, then demonstrated his faith by announcing a personal fast until his prayer was answered. His spiritual leadership was the inspiration behind the birth of the great nation which is modern India. You will gain much by entering your quiet place to ask your teachers for help in understanding the deep faith of such a spiritual man. Then strive to build an equal faith in *you.*

The simple trust in the power of God demonstrated by a grandmother brought many blessings to the people around her. She talked to God in her room, in the garden, and even on the streetcar; regularly asking help for her neighbors. All the neighborhood animals were her friends, including two little mice who occupied a hole in the wall of her room. She fed them and prayed for their welfare also. Her faithful prayers healed a dying rosebush, and produced the most beautiful camellias in the city. She was so close to God that her very presence had a healing effect on anyone in need. When she passed on, she was missed by people and animals alike. Do whatever is necessary to satisfy your intellect and build a faith like that—it is worth more than all the material possessions you might accumulate!

How shall *you* ask for help for others? Go into your quiet place and greet your spirit teachers. Talk over your friend's needs as you would with someone on earth; and *ask* for spirit help. Then *according to your faith* it is done! *Believe* that God is helping your friend through the agency of the spirit world, and *it is so.* Then give thanks. Know that spirit is working to bring the highest good into the lives of all concerned. With this technique you can obviously do no harm, and the potential good is beyond the limits of human imagination. Never refuse to ask for help for anyone in need. The asking will truly benefit you both.

The secret of getting help for yourself

It's relatively easy to ask for help for someone else, because the question of whether *you* deserve it doesn't get in the way. But the first thought that hits most of us when we feel we need personal assistance is, "Am I worthy of it?" It seems that we can remember our every shortcoming just when we need help the most.

Modern psychologists call this guilt, and it is the most destructive commodity in the universe. The first thing a mentally healthy person learns is not to carry a grudge against any fellow man, but we somehow forget to apply that to ourselves. There is a beautiful passage in the *Lord's Prayer* which bears directly on this: *And forgive us our trespasses, as we forgive those who trespass against us.* You are entitled to forgiveness from the universe in the same measure that you forgive others for real or fancied wrongs against you. Meditate upon this carefully. Then proceed to honestly and fervently forgive anyone and everyone who may have wronged you. Now claim your own forgiveness! Remember, the Master came to show the way, not to chastise or condemn. Even on the cross he said, *Father, forgive them....* Go before your spirit teachers in your quiet place and claim your forgiveness for everything that seems to stand in the way of your worthiness.

Once you have dissolved the blocks of guilt, the only limit to progress is your own faith. A living faith must be built on a sound base of understanding, and it should be renewed by twice daily contacts with your spirit teachers. Each time you sit in your quiet place and receive a positive response to your call, the reality of the spirit side of life becomes more certain to you. Strengthen and renew your ties with your spirit teachers throughout the good periods of life, so you can count on their help when you really need it.

How shall you go about asking for help? How can you be sure you are heard? Any time or place you are accustomed to talking to your teachers, you can be sure they are there, and *they will hear you!* Tell them your problems and the extent of your efforts to solve them. Demonstrate that you are doing everything within your power to achieve the solution with your own efforts. Then ask for that little extra push from spirit which is certain to tip the scales in your favor. Feel your teachers' response, and *believe* they are helping you. Then according to your faith, you will receive whatever you need the most. Let's look at a detailed approach to some typical situations.

How to get a new job

At some time or other, each of us has the feeling that the secret of all our future personal happiness lies in landing a new job. This is a time of special crisis, and we should begin with a careful assessment of the factors which have put us in this uncomfortable situation. Whether you are out of work or just plain miserable on your present job, there is a deep lesson to be learned *before* you blindly strike out on a job hunt. All of life's bumps come to teach us some special lesson, and we will be stuck with our problem until we wake up enough to digest its inner meaning.

The place to start is in your quiet place, meditating on the lesson to be drawn from your difficulty. The question to ask is: "What are the qualities or attitudes in me that have brought me to this uncomfortable situation?—or, How did I go about attracting this?" When I am in difficulty, I have to find the key and *change something within me* in order to accomplish the cure. Ask the question of your higher self and your teachers, then *pay attention* to the answer. This is no time to rationalize and make up all sorts of excellent excuses. The only way you can claim the power to extricate yourself is to admit it was your misuse of your power that got you into this fix in the first place.

A man was on the verge of quitting his vice-presidency of a small but rapidly growing corporation. For several months it had seemed that his efforts were not appreciated and somehow it was all for naught anyway. Before taking any action, he retired to his quiet place and asked the key question: "What is there in me that makes my job seem such a waste of energy?" In the peace of his silence the following train of thought unfolded: Because of your intense interest in spiritual things, you will never achieve the depths of satisfaction from your job that most executives do; *but you do have an obligation* to your family, and it will be to your spiritual advantage to continue fulfilling it. Your satisfaction is to be attained from helping other people, and your executive position gives you the wherewithal and opportunity to bring inspiration and tangible help to many. You need a change of attitude, not a change of job! If you switch jobs in your present frame of mind, the next one may turn out to be even more miserable.

He took his lesson to heart, buckled down on the job, and eventually amassed a fortune sufficient to retire to a happy life of philanthropy.

Another man who was out of work got quite a different answer. The voice within him said, "Your cynical attitude toward your employer and your immediate supervisor lowered the quality of your work so much you had to be fired. It's time for you to adopt a completely positive approach, clean yourself up mentally and psychologically, get off your fanny and go looking for your new job, now!"

Only when you understand the lesson of your situation are you ready for spirit help in correcting the physical and material aspect of it. When you feel you understand, send your call for help loud and clear. Say, "Beloved teachers, I'm doing my best to assimilate my lesson and change for the better, now please help me find just the right spot to unfold more of my talents in loving service to mankind."

Then keep the faith! Do everything you know how to help yourself, and you can be certain that spirit will come through with all the extra help you need, now and forevermore!

How to find your perfect mate

Marriage is one of the least understood of our major institutions. Regardless of our age, education, or emotional maturity we tend to rush into it blindly; then spend years in suffering or trying to patch it up. Our psychologists and marriage counselors preach constantly that the key to a successful union is *compromise,* but there is a higher truth that is worthy of careful examination. Compromise will certainly make a bad situation more comfortable, but a marriage without compromise is infinitely more desirable. Your ideal mate is so completely in tune with you spiritually, mentally, and psychologically that compromise is rarely necessary.

The idea of compromise assumes initial disagreement and infers some pushing and pulling at each other. If you are already married in a less than ideal relationship, I certainly don't advise a bunch of hasty actions. Each individual situation carries its own set of special obligations, and differences should be resolved along carefully directed spiritual lines. But if you are single, and looking forward to marriage sometime in the future, *take heed.*

There is a great deal of truth to the old idea that marriages are made in heaven. The good ones really are! But many times the most completely unlikely people find some attraction for each other and confuse it with love. They get a silly idea that the simple act of a marriage ceremony will somehow dissolve all their differences and they will "live happily ever after."

This is one of the areas where we need the most help from our spirit teachers. If you already have your eye on a potential partner, bear with us for just a little way while we discuss that important preliminary.

Your own quiet place is the best base of operations for the seeking of a soul mate. Call on your teachers and talk it over with them. Tell them of your desire for true spiritual love and marriage, and tell them what you expect to bring to your mate. Listen to the little impressions that warn you of too much selfishness in your dreams of the ideal marriage, and work to polish and beautify your concept. Then ask for guidance and help in locating your ideal mate. Know that somewhere there is another person whose being will blend perfectly with yours in the creation of an ideal marriage, and this person is seeking you even as you are seeking.

Then go to places where people of like nature to your own are likely to be attracted. If you are religiously inclined, the church of your choice is an excellent place to meet new friends. Or try a course in night school, the neighborhood little theater, civic activities, or charitable work. Wear your friendly smile and be easy to meet. Any new friend may be the instrument of your introduction to your soul mate. Sooner than you dare expect, you will meet someone you think (or hope) is the wonderful mate you are seeking. As the acquaintance begins to warm into friendship or infatuation, you are nearing the critical point where spirit help is most important.

With your teachers' help, you must decide if this is your soul mate, or if you should just keep right on looking. Understand that *unless you are a saint,* it would be a grave mistake to contemplate marrying one. The real question is, do your faults and weaknesses blend along with your strengths? Do you want to change the other person? Or does he want to change you? If you are interested in the other for anything except exactly what he (or she) is right now, forget it! Go into your quiet place and ask your teachers if you are glossing over anything in the other's character or personality that will be unbearable in the long run. Are you relaxed and comfortable at just being your-self in your potential mate's company? Does he pay attention to you when you are out with other people? And vice-versa? Could you just sit back to back for an hour without talking and feel uplifted by the warm glow of the blending of your auras?

Listen to your higher self and your spirit teachers; they are not blinded by the strange workings of body chemistry we so often mistake for love. A natural blending of spirit and aura, completely without the necessity for compromise, is the ideal state. And *it is attainable on our earth.* You settle for less at the risk of years of tugging and compromise. Marriage is a classic example of the value of *quality* as opposed to quantity.

I don't necessarily subscribe to the theory that there is only one soul mate for each of us, but I'm certain that for every one individual who would make you a good soul mate, there are at least a million who would make you a lousy marriage partner. Without spirit guidance, *you are not equipped to make a wise decision* in the heat of a courtship. Go into your quiet place and commune with your spirit teachers as often and as long as necessary to be sure you are not heading into a disaster. *Spirit guidance is real and it will never fail you!* This may be the time it is hardest to do so, but it is to your best advantage to pay attention to the voices of those whose vision is clear.

How to get instant help in an emergency

There was a terrible screeching of brakes, and two auto-mobiles that had been apparently bound to wind up as a tangled mass of metal stopped fractions of an inch apart. So instead of becoming a stretcher case, the young salesman met a corporation president who offered him an excellent chance as his new sales manager. Not disaster, but new opportunity! This man seemed to lead a charmed life, and so can you.

All life as we know it on earth is maintained by an extremely delicate balance of seemingly hostile forces. Without the insulating effect of the atmosphere, we would burn to death in the sun during the day, then freeze in the darkness at two hundred degrees or more below zero. Every day we read of individual lives snuffed out by literally thousands of different methods, yet many of them were in the very prime of their usefulness to society. If the world's great poets, doctors, authors, and scientists don't naturally receive special protection from the spirit agencies why should we expect that *you* can?

The answer is contained in the question itself. Because you dare to *expect it,* spirit help is available to you. Of course there is the inevitable price. We never get something for nothing, even from spirit. The price for complete spirit protection is your sincere and steady effort to work with the spirit world in uncovering your "mission" in life and unfolding your greatest potentials for good to the whole of mankind. Don't wait until it's too late to put on the brakes! Start earning your spirit protection, now. In a very real sense we each have a spiritual bank account, much like a checking account in a commercial bank anywhere in the United States. The primary rule for using such an account is *you can't take out more than you put in.*

If you haven't already, *now* is just the right time to start making twice daily deposits to your spiritual account in the peaceful atmosphere of your own quiet place. In a broader sense, the spiritual communion in your quiet place will begin to color your whole life with a richer understanding of people, and you will be impelled to shine your light to help them over the dark spots. As you devote more attention to the world of spirit, you will notice more and more evidence of tangible spirit help in your routine affairs. Give thanks for it and resolve to earn more of the same. We will begin the search for your mission in the next Chapter.

Points to Remember

I. The illusion of separateness from God robs men of the emotional strength to handle stress.

II. Faith in God is the source of all personal strength.

III. Stress is caused by our wrong attitudes toward the world.

IV. Spirit protection is tangible and sometimes dramatic in its handling of emergencies.

V. Spirit will never forsake you.

VI. You are richly blessed by sharing your spirit help with others.

VII. Your honest striving and faith in your spirit teachers guarantees all the help you need.

VIII. Work with your spirit teachers and build a charmed life.

how

ESP Can Reveal Your True Reason for Living

Step outside on any clear night and look up at the myriads of stars shining in the great nothingness we call the sky. Science tells us that each star you see is really another sun, probably much bigger than ours and quite possibly surrounded by orbiting planets like this one. The magnitude of the universe remains beyond the ability of our intellect to encompass, yet in all its vastness, it seems to be made of the infinite repetition of a few simple patterns. No matter how complex the organism or galaxy, it is made up of nature's basic building blocks, all assembled according to logical patterns.

From the submicroscopic world of atoms and molecules to the marvelous milky way, man looks at nature's patterns and ponders his own meaning.

The age-old question, "Why am I here?"

One of the major characteristics which distinguishes man from the lower animals is his ability to objectively contemplate his own nature and seek a meaning and purpose for his existence. Man has asked this burning question since he first began to think, "Why am I here?" Brilliant philosophers have devised a fantastic multiplicity of answers based on sound logic and monumental soarings of reason. No matter what your in-

131

clination, you can find someone's philosophical system that will help you for a time. But philosophy somehow seems to get bound up in an intricate series of mental gymnastics until the poor struggling student gets ready to accept the old jibe that goes something like, "An expert is a person who knows more and more about less and less, until finally he knows everything about nothing, and becomes a philosopher." Things aren't really that bad, but it is certainly true that no purely mental system can lead you to the *personal experience* of meaning in your own life.

Jesus had a stimulating answer to our basic why. He said, *I am come that they might have life, and that more abundantly.*

With this simple concept as our clue, we can gain much insight by looking at nature herself. Throughout all of nature we see life striving for expression, seeking constantly for improvement of form and being through the process of evolution. If we can sense a purpose in nature, it must be simply the expression of life. But this brings us smack up against the next logical question, what is the purpose of life? If we can understand the purpose of life in its general sense, perhaps there will be the answer to the meaning of our individual existence.

What distinguishes a living organism from a blob of dead matter like a rock or a clod of dirt? We might say the ability to reproduce its own kind, or the method by which it derives nourishment from its environment. But the truly significant feature of life is *consciousness.* Some degree of consciousness is exhibited by every living organism from the single-celled amoeba through the plants and lower animals to its highest earthly form in man. When viewed from this standpoint, the whole process of evolution is obviously aimed at producing ever higher forms of consciousness.

It is as if the Infinite Consciousness which created the universe is seeking to duplicate its infinity of consciousness on the plane of the particular. Therefore we can reasonably equate consciousness to livingness. But this brings us to the simple conclusion that the purpose of life is to express more and more of itself in ever upward spiraling approximation of the infinitude of the Creator. You may ask if there is any practical application to this bit of speculation. Yes! It can lead us to a useful understanding of our individual reason for living.

Your place in the scheme of things

In order to find our individual place in the scheme of the universe, it is necessary to dig a little deeper into the details of the great pattern. We have agreed that the expressed purpose of life is continual development of higher and higher forms of consciousness through the evolutionary process. But just how does that work?

Within each species, the law of natural selection works for the constant improvement of the type. This is also called the survival of the fittest, and it means exactly that. Only the stronger and more intelligent members of a species survive and thus have the opportunity to reproduce the kind. Thus the basic weaknesses are gradually weeded out of a species by the simple expedient of the death of those who have them. Throughout the world of nature we see how careful the great mother is of each species, but how unconcerned about the individuals within it. All the so-called laws of chance serve to perpetuate and improve the species at the expense of the inferior individuals.

The lower animals, lacking the precious gift of self-consciousness, don't understand this hard fact of nature, and so go on being chewed up by the laws of chance. This is also the case with most individual humans. They live from day-to-day subject to the unmerciful caprice of accidents, microbes, disease, pestilence and the like; living, suffering, and dying with little thought to the reasons back of it all. It's a terrible waste for man to believe himself subject to these ancient laws! The first key to freedom lies in our objective consciousness, the ability to understand our relationship to our environment and to the Creator.

Now if the purpose of life is evolution, and the pattern for the lower species is chance, we are bound by the same laws until we figure a way out. But there is a way out! It lies in using our objective consciousness to establish a new relationship with the principles of evolution, based on our exercise of the *power to choose and cooperate.* The consciousness of *one* individual human being is sufficiently developed that it may realize and claim the same care from the forces of nature that is lavished on a whole species of lower creatures. *You can decide* that the old laws of chance shall be replaced as they apply to your personal existence with a new set of laws which we might call the *laws of conscious cooperation with the evolutionary force.*

This understanding led the psalmist of old to exclaim, *What is man, that thou art mindful of him? And the son of man, that thou visitest him? For thou hast made him a little lower than the angels, and hast crowned him with glory and honour. Thou madest him to have dominion over the works of thy hands; thou hast put all things under his feet.*

Make your own decision to cooperate with the great forces of evolution! Then go to your quiet place and announce it to your spirit teachers. Send out your call to your spirit band; then in the silence say aloud something like this, "Beloved teachers, I am happy to tell you that I earnestly want to cooperate with the great evolutionary plan of the universe. I realize that I have much to learn, but even that is part of working for my own evolution. I pledge my best efforts henceforth to the accomplishment of my personal evolution and the maximum contribution to the upliftment and progress of all mankind. I will seek your special guidance in a quiet moment at least twice a day, and be alert at all times to your impressions of inspiration and help. I accept the tender, loving protection of all emissaries of God in whatever form they come, and proffer my wholehearted cooperation."

Then set out to discover your personal mission or reason for this particular incarnation, and fulfill it to the best of your ability.

How to discover your individual mission in this life

All of life is like a great symphony; and we, as individual expressions, are like the notes that combine to make the whole composition; complete with melody, harmony, counterpoint, and all the glorious details. When the orchestra is assembled to play, if just one note is omitted or comes out of sequence, the whole performance is something less than it might be. *Your individual contribution* is important to the great symphony we call life. And it is a fact that you agreed to achieve certain definite goals before you entered the tiny body that has grown up to be what the world considers *you*.

You are necessary for a special contribution to the progress of mankind during your lifetime. Isn't it about time you set out to discover what it is? There is a *wonderfully reciprocal relationship here;* your own spiritual progress is advanced most by your special contribution to mankind's upward march. So how shall you look for your mission?

Your first step is a careful review of the subconscious pattern of your past to get a look at the direction in which you have been led. Your subconscious is aware of the needs of your mission and has been working throughout your life to prepare you. Even your most glaring weaknesses were designed to assist in your grooming for the culmination of a lifetime of devotion to the progress of mankind. Some missions may seem bigger or more important than others, but that is only the appearance to our egocentric lower selves. In any symphony, some notes may stand out more than others, but all are necessary to the perfect whole.

We may gain an important insight by contemplating a story from the life of the Buddha. It is said that after six years of seeking enlightenment through the ascetic path, Gautama sat near a garden on the verge of death from his long starvation. A woman appeared bearing an offering of thanksgiving for the birth of her son and, mistaking Gautama for the wood-god, fed him with the precious offering prepared from the milk of one hundred newly calved cows fed to fifty white cows and their milk fed to twenty-five and with theirs twelve more and again with theirs to the six best of the herd, and that yield boiled with fine spices and finely ground rice planted and individually picked with a pure heart. The purity of the nourishment so rejuvenated the young prince that he arose and proceeded to the Bodhi tree where his meditations brought on the enlightenment which made him the Buddha. Without those simple ministrations of the grateful mother, the world might well have been deprived of one of its greatest teachers.

Some of us have tasks to accomplish that may stand out like those of the Buddha, but most of us will find our lot to be more like that of the grateful mother. But each person's mission is well suited to his talents and experience, *and it is important to the over-all progress of mankind.* The process of evolution, like its tool, the process of physical growth, is a steady heaping up of many, many small achievements.

As you carefully review the subconscious pattern of your past life, pay attention to your chronic problems as well as your special aptitudes and experience. Quiet meditation on the patterns you have discovered and prayerful consultation with your spiritual teachers will begin to reveal the general outlines of your mission. It is not necessary that you know the exact details until the time draws near for its fulfillment, and no amount of impatience will get the knowledge for you. Consider it enough to realize the broad outlines of your daily preparations, and strive to improve your effectiveness and your channels of communication with your spirit teachers whose guidance will be invaluable when it becomes your turn to take positive action. Work with them towards the time when you are meant to achieve.

How to direct your efforts toward accomplishing your spiritual mission

What is the best way to set about accomplishing your mission? *First* and most important, maintain your balance and continue to lead a normal life. The Oriental religions teach that life is divided into three major epochs which we might call childhood, the householder stage, and the later life when the family has been raised and there is more time and energy left for cultural and religious pursuits. It is important that we don't shirk our material responsibilities. How could you expect to stand in the presence of the Master and ask to join in service to mankind if you have not even fulfilled your regular obligations as a householder? That would be obviously absurd! We can take a lesson from the approach to the material world expounded by our Hindu and Buddhist friends. They tell us to *kill out all ambition for material advancement,* then *work as one who has it.*

Sounds shocking at first, doesn't it? But a little reflection will show you that here is the best way to succeed in the material world; without ambitious emotional involvement in your progress to cloud your thinking, you will naturally do a better job and so get ahead faster. The by-product is an absence of guilt arising out of petty little plots to get ahead or yielding to temptations for unethical practices. Thus you can enter your twice daily meditation periods with a clear and untroubled mind, and progress unimpeded along the path of spiritual growth.

It is during your meditation periods that you should properly turn your attention to receiving guidance as to your spiritual mission and the means of accomplishing it. Your ever-improving relaxed awareness will reveal each opportunity for spiritual sèrvice as the time is right. Pay attention, but *keep your balance.* Nothing is as destructive of good spirit contact as anxiety. Be willing to take one simple step at a time, without always knowing what the next will be. Keep your faith, and enjoy being a spectator as much as a participant in the unfoldment of your earthly sojourn.

Dr. George Washington Carver regularly talked with his *dear Creator* in the silence. His loving attention to the peanut, the flowers, and the clays of the soil in his *dear Creator's* presence brought forth such a multitude of new and useful products that he revolutionized the entire economy of the South. The depth of his personal faith shone so brightly that it profoundly influenced the spiritual lives of countless thousands. If he were standing before you now, his words would tell you that any man can accomplish truly wonderful works if he has enough love in his heart for his fellow man and his *dear Creator.* Let your love shine out through all your actions as you strive toward the accomplishment of your mission.

How to start your spiritual chain reaction of gcod

There is a great deal of truth to the old adage, *The Lord helps him who helps himself.* Spirit works most effectively by amplifying the efforts of a human agency. Ask for guidance, then *act on it* to the best of your ability, always keeping a strong faith that your help will be there whenever you need it. As you learn to work more effectively, spirit will increase the level of its help. It is rather like canasta or a paratroop invasion—the most successful people get the most help. Start your own spiritual chain reaction of good, now! Go into your quiet place and ask your teachers for instruction. Then act on the impressions you receive. It can be the turning point of your whole life.

A middle-aged woman was impressed by her teachers to seek a class in psychic unfoldment. Her children were grown now, so there was no question of lack of available time. She made a few phone calls and the same class was recommended by several friends. Her progress seemed painfully slow at first, but after six months she suddenly unfolded a wonderfully accurate ability to bring through messages from those now living on the spirit side of life. She has since served thousands of people, bringing many little personal proofs of survival of the individuality after the change men call death. The passing of her husband left a physical void, but her ability to communicate with him in her own quiet place considerably lessened her loneliness. She was able to live an economically productive later life by providing private readings for the assistance of many seekers of truth.

A young man was finishing his second year of college, still with no idea of what he wanted for a career. Late one evening in his quiet place he saw a very clear symbol of himself in hospital garb performing an operation. A review of his first two years' classes showed he had been taking an excellent pre-medical course. He gave thanks for the previous subconscious guidance and threw himself into the study of medicine with a zeal born of the wonderful feeling of spirit cooperation. He is an excellent and highly successful surgeon today.

Your life can be enriched by *unfailing help* from on high! Seek your guidance, then start to help yourself. His angels will go before you, making your way happier and more productive than you dare even dream. Now is the best time to start!

Your path to peace of mind

Many people subscribe to the fallacy that contentment is the measure of peace of mind, but this tends to deflect their striving into less spiritually productive avenues. Peace of mind is a dynamic product of *achievement* that knows it can *and will* continually do better. Discontent can be an excellent tool of the spirit world in guiding us along our individual pathways of growth. We should always give thanks for our healthy discontent as a precious spiritual gift. It is the expression of our subconscious desires to work toward the fulfillment of our spiritual mission. You are assured of ever increasing peace of mind if you train yourself to regularly view your discontent in these terms. Ask each little feeling of restlessness to reveal its spiritual message. Then pay attention to the answer—it will tell you more about your mission in life.

Progress in any field of endeavor is a direct result of somebody being dissatisfied with the status quo. In modern religious parlance, the driving force behind the advance of mankind is divine discontent. It is spirit urging us onward! By cooperating with the directing forces of spirit, you can turn each apparently negative emotion into a stepping stone to glorious growth for yourself and others. Ask each uncomfortable feeling for its spiritual message, then respond to your teacher's direction. As you regularly respond to the promptings of spirit, your life becomes a panorama of joyous progression. This is the true source of all personal peace.

Henry Ford's discontent with the transportation of the day led to the first mass production of the automobile, and changed our economy forever. Whitney's cotton gin, Douglas's airplane and Land's Polaroid camera are similar examples of applied discontent. Each brought new comfort and happiness to many people.

Don't be afraid to think big, but don't refuse to take the small steps either. A mother was uneasy about the lack of crosswalks for children on the way to a nearby school. Her perseverance gathered enough signatures on the petition to get a city survey which resulted in boulevard stop signs, and a crossing guard during school hours. Who can tell how many young bodies were saved from harm by her efforts? Every step that helps others must help you. Start now!

Points to Remember

    I. Nature's purpose is the expression and improvement of life through the process of evolution.

    II. Life's purpose is to express ever more of itself, and thus the infinitude of the Creator.

    III. The laws of chance serve to improve the species at the expense of its inferior individuals.

    IV. You can lift yourself above the laws of chance by conscious cooperation with the forces of evolution.

    V. Seek to discover your personal mission in this life— your planned contribution to the progress of mankind.

    VI. To gain control of your progress: kill out all ambition, then work as one who has it.

    VII. Spirit speaks to you of your mission through the avenue of divine discontent.

    VIII. Peace of mind is a dynamic product of achievement.

how

ESP Can Insure the Success of Your Every Undertaking

It is the spirit that quickeneth; the flesh profiteth nothing: the words that I speak unto you, they are spirit and they are life. (John 7:63.) As you learn to use your ESP to stay in contact with spirit, your own life will be quickened. You will find that the success of any undertaking is directly affected by its relationship to your spiritual mission. It is so certain that we can express it as a natural law.

The law of personal success

We can safely state that none of us is a Master, or we wouldn't need to be spending our time in this earthly classroom. Therefore our own efforts are never enough to insure the success of our undertaking. *Spirit help is our key to success!* But your spirit teachers are not particularly interested in your worldly or material success. They hover near to assist in your personal growth and to see that you accomplish the tasks you accepted before you voluntarily entered the present earth life.

In this respect, worldly life is like a swiftly flowing stream. Any fool can float downstream with little or no effort simply by clinging to a passing log or piece of debris. But if it should be desirable to go upstream, you need a boat with a powerful motor. The power for any upstream accomplishment must

143

come from spirit, and this leads us to infer our law of personal success: *Any undertaking which prepares you for, or contributes to your spiritual mission will succeed; and any undertaking which is incompatible with your spiritual mission will fail.*

You can avoid costly mistakes and failures by checking out each potential endeavor with your spirit teachers *before* you decide to try it. A successful corporation executive found an excellent opportunity to help a friend go into business for himself. Their special aptitudes were complementary, and the executive's contributions of time could be in his hobby hours, so he rushed into the deal without bothering to check with his spirit teachers. The enterprise was well planned and got off to a rousing good start. It made a profit the very first month, and after four months success seemed assured. But suddenly the executive discovered that his friend had been systematically diverting collections on account into his own pocket instead of into the business. In the legal battle that ensued, the business was ruined. Net result: the executive lost ten thousand dollars, five months of hard work in the moonlight, and what he had thought was a good friend.

A somewhat belated meditation in his quiet place revealed the reason for his setback. The time he spent working in the sideline business was needed for him to begin writing a short self-help course in practical metaphysics. So six months late and ten thousand dollars short, he began a successful metaphysical writing career in his hobby time. Spirit could care less that he lost the money—it was a good spiritual lesson for him, and as soon as he got back on the spiritual track, prosperity again flowed to him in waves of abundance.

Another executive regularly paid more attention to his spirit teachers. One evening as he reached out to spirit in his quiet place, a strange light appeared on the wall. It formed itself into letters which said, "In three months the parent company will close your division with very little warning. Start discreetly sending out résumés as soon as possible, and we will help you relocate painlessly."

It came as quite a shock because he was happy with his position and knew that he was doing a good job in every way the situation allowed. But you don't argue with spirit when you receive such positive advice, so he followed directions. On the same day he was informed that the division would be closed, he received an offer of a new position with a local company at a slight increase in salary. By following directions, he was not jobless for even one day, and he avoided the anguish that naturally accompanies the unexpected closing of a material door.

The advantages of working with the spirit world are tremendously greater than anyone who hasn't experienced it can imagine. Let's look further into your part of working with spirit on new ideas.

How to examine a contemplated new undertaking in the light of your spiritual mission

You were given a mind as one of the tools to be used during this earth life experience, and this is a good place to exercise it. Why bother spirit with questions about undertakings that common sense will tell you not to start? It should be obvious that anything you do must be honest and should not be harmful to others. Certainly it should be compatible with the spiritual view of life. If it fails to pass these simple ground rule tests, drop it at once!

If your idea passes the general ground rule tests you are not yet ready to take it to spirit. You also need a set of specific rules for you. Let's put them in the form of simple questions.

1. Does it provide new uses for many of your already developed aptitudes and strengths?

2. Will it provide opportunities to develop new strengths?
3. How would you feel about it in the awesome presence of your Maker?

If you can give positive answers to all three questions, you are at last ready to take it into meditation in your quiet place. Call for the presence of your spirit teachers and carefully explain your idea to them. Then *ask if it is compatible with your spiritual mission*. Be careful that your anxiety and/or enthusiasm doesn't close your mind to spirit advice, and *wait for the answer*. It will always come. Feel it before you leave your quiet place!

As a simple example let's say you are thinking about taking a course in evening school. This is certainly honest and harmless, and advancement of personal knowledge is always compatible with the spiritual view of life. How about the personal tests? You would not be allowed to take the course if you had not fulfilled the prerequisites, so we can assume it will provide new uses for your present strengths; and its whole purpose is to provide opportunity to develop new strengths, skills or knowledge. I can think of no course offered by a socially responsible educational institution that might cause you to feel uncomfortable in the presence of the Creator. It has now passed all the mental tests, and as far as you can logically tell, it should be a good move for you. Now you are ready to take it before your spirit teachers for their special council. Go to your quiet place, relax, and call for your teachers. Tell them, "I am considering taking this particular course in night school, and it seems like a good thing for me to do. Please give me the benefit of your wider vision. Will it fit into my spiritual mission?" In the ensuing silence one may be impressed, "It is good for you, little sister, do not hesitate!" Another may hear, "Not this year, my brother, it would be too great a strain on your health." And yet another might suddenly feel, "It would be good for you, but there is something much better just over the horizon. You would be wiser to wait for it."

When you ask in this manner, your teachers will consistently give you sound advice, but it is important to realize that the *decision is always your own*. It is your personal responsibility to decide and act in your own life! This can never be delegated or abdicated. It is analogous to consulting an expert on earth. You may go to your attorney with a legal problem and receive sound advice as to your alternatives and their probable outcomes; but the decision and the responsibility remain forever your own. The more you think and act responsibly, the greater help you will naturally draw from the spirit world. It is another working of the law of natural selection—*them as has, gets*.

Coming out of the armed service just after World War II, a man was pondering his choice of two proffered positions. One appeared to offer better opportunity for advancement, while the other offered a better starting salary. Certainly he needed to work for a living, so the ground rule questions were satisfied. He decided to take both offers into his quiet place and consult his spirit teachers. In the silence he received an unexpected answer: "You are leaning toward the position that seems to offer the best chance of future progress, and that is laudable. But there is a setback coming to that company within the year, and it will keep the occupant of your potential position tied down for several years. Take the job that pays more money, and apply yourself. You will be pleased with your progress."

By listening to the voice of spirit, the man avoided a material setback and launched a highly successful career. The same good guidance is yours if you will but ask, *and listen!*

How to summon your spirit teachers to assist you

When you reach the point in your meditation where you know spirit agrees your undertaking is in keeping with your basic mission, rejoice! You can be sure, now, that your teachers are ready and eager to help you. But they can do little without your specific permission for them to help.

Don't be the "Please, mother, I'd rather do it myself" type. Ask for spirit help. Your teachers are real people, and you will get the best results if you treat them that way. Talk to them just as you would talk to a good friend who still inhabits an earthly body. You have attracted your special set of spirit teachers because you all share in the same basic mission. They are literally partners in your progress, so your success is theirs also. They will help you in countless ways, but they won't do the things you can and should do for yourself. Again remember that spirit works best by *amplifying your efforts*. So put out some effort for your friends to amplify.

A young man working at the very bottom in a furniture factory began to get an urge for a career in electronics. He took this feeling to his teachers in his quiet place and asked for guidance. In the peaceful atmosphere of the meditation, everything seemed to make sense, so he enrolled in an electronic assembly class at night. After twelve weeks of hard work he received a certificate and began his search for a suitable job. He was chosen over fourteen other applicants with similar backgrounds for his first job in electronic assembly. Next came the urge for an engineering degree, and again he sought guidance in his quiet place. This time help came in the form of his company's financing the cost of books and tuition in the evening section of a local college. It took eight years of hard work, but he regularly advanced on the job as the new educational work improved his qualifications, and his years in the shop contributed to his being one of the top electronic production engineers in the state.

A middle-aged man was told that his wife needed a very serious operation. They were both working, and it seemed to take all they could earn to keep the children in high school and make ends meet. In his quiet place he talked over his intense desire to find a way to finance the operation. After he covered all the details, he sat in the silence and waited. After about ten minutes a voice seemed to say, "Worry not, good brother, you will have help within three days."

On the third day there was a check for $2,000 in the mailbox together with a letter from an attorney in a distant state explaining that this was a bequest from the estate of a distant uncle.

Regularly call on your spirit teachers for help, then cooperate! *Help will be there whenever you need it.*

Your law of growth

We have regularly alluded to the price of all this spirit help as your striving to align yourself with the goals of your personal spiritual mission. Regardless of what direction that might lead, your personal growth is the best possible catalyst for its accomplishment. Look around you at the lower animals and the plant kingdoms; the lower a species in the evolutionary scheme of things, the more certainly its individuals lack the choice of their activities. For instance dogs and monkeys move about freely, but trees and shrubs are restricted to one location for a whole lifetime. But the *one major requirement* of *all* individuals of *all* species is *personal growth.*

The law of life is growth, and its opposite is stagnation or decay. Everywhere you turn, you see evidence of vigorous growth or signs of decay. *Nothing ever stands still!* The law of nature is *grow* or *die* and make room for the new growth of something else. It matters not if your chronological age is 20, 60, or 99; your choice is still the same: grow or die! Because we humans are blessed with the most comprehensive mental faculties, it falls upon us to take a greater initiative in directing and perpetuating our personal growth processes.

Yes, I believe you can grow a new hand or foot if you need it! But if you are blessed with a complete and well functioning physical "horse" to ride through life, it is all the more important not to relax your striving. We began the first chapter with simple exercises for psychic and spiritual growth, and everything that has come since is pointed in the same direction. What are your personal weaknesses? You can grow by consciously working to improve each weak area, be it physical, mental, financial, psychic, or spiritual. Most intelligent people would want to do that anyway. But by itself this is not enough! Your true fulfillment will come as you strive to exploit your strengths in the direction of accomplishing that part of your mission which is most obvious to you now.

A young man in a junior supervisory position began to feel the stirring of an urge deep within his being. It kept saying, perhaps you were meant to be a minister. For a long time he contented this urge by reading books on comparative religion and metaphysics. Then he subscribed to several *New Thought* publications and started to take courses in metaphysics. His embryonic attempts at application of the principles he studied brought advancement on his job and added new meaning to his daily existence. More and more he felt he must definitely contribute to mankind's progress in these broad fields. As time passed he became increasingly successful in his material work with personal earnings near the top ten percent of individuals in the nation, but he was still stirred by the urge to serve in a religious capacity. In his late fifties, he began courses in the "development of mediumship" and gradually unfolded an excellent ability in that field. It was not until he reached what most men called the retirement age that he found himself in a position to serve with his new ability. But all the later years of his very productive life were brightened by the joy of serving as a medium for messages from the spirit world. He would be the first to agree that his material success was tremendously aided by his lifelong preparation for that vague spiritual goal.

Your spiritual mission may not be scheduled for accomplishment tomorrow or next week, but your earnest seeking and preparation will certainly benefit every area of your present life. Follow that urge to learn something new! Every talent you develop will contribute to your progress and to that of mankind as a whole.

How to succeed every time

Some men seem to succeed in everything they try, while others crawl along over the carcasses of their many failures. *Success is never an accident!* It may look easy for some, but it is always a result of carefully laid spiritual groundwork. We might describe the secret of success by a simple three-step formula:
1. Unify with your spiritual mission.
2. Summon your subconscious and spirit help.
3. Let it grow and *work* to make it even better.

Whatever you undertake must be compatible with your spiritual mission to insure success. Screen each desire carefully, and take the worthy ones into your quiet place for spirit help in determining their compatibility. When you get the spiritual green light, ask for help from your subconscious realms and from your personal spirit helpers. Renew your spirit contact twice daily in your quiet place, and ask for help each time, never forgetting to give thanks for the help you have already received. Then make your physical start and give spirit plenty of your own effort to amplify on behalf of your success. Keep faith with your spirit teachers and they will never forsake you. Success in any endeavor is yours for the spiritual trying.

Walter Russell combined his concentrated desire with a deep abiding faith in God to become successful in music, literature, architecture, painting, sculpture, and philosophy. He attributed his success to his unity with the *Universal One* and to his belief that he *must* do each thing as it presented itself, and he *should* do it as a demonstration of his belief in man's unlimited power. He left us the challenge that communion between the self and the *Universal Self* is the only way to achieve the impossible.

With God, all things are possible. Tune in on the spiritual success wave length, now!

Points to Remember

I. The law of personal success: any undertaking which prepares you for, or contributes to, your spiritual mission will succeed; and any undertaking which is incompatible with your spiritual mission will fail.

II. Use your common sense in evaluating potential new ventures.

III. Specific rules for spirit help:
   A. Does it provide new uses for many of your already developed aptitudes and strengths?
   B. Will it provide opportunities to develop new strengths?
   C. How would you feel about it in the presence of your Maker?

IV. Then ask your teachers if it is compatible with your spiritual mission.

V. The law of growth: grow or die!

VI. The three steps to success:
   A. Unify with your spiritual mission.
   B. Summon your subconscious and spirit help.
   C. Let it grow, and *work* to make it better.

how to

Use ESP to Establish a Personal Relationship with God

As you improve your contact, and learn to work with your spirit teachers, you will quite naturally feel a closer relationship to the great life force of the universe which men call God. Certainly no one in communication with the other side of life would deny Its existence. But there is a much deeper personal experience of God that longs to manifest for you. Down through the ages, spiritual men of all faiths have experienced momentary periods of communion with God in a personal way, beyond time and space. Religionists generally call this the *mystic* experience, Freud called it the *oceanic feeling*, and Jesus called it the *pearl of great price*. Regardless of the name you choose to hang on it, we can agree that this is the most important single experience of any person's life. Let's begin a systematic search for your personal experience, now.

How your active intuition expands your concept of God

Primitive men of all ages recognize a whole host of gods. There will be a god of the river, of the wind, the hunt, the sunshine, the rain, the tree, the rock, and on and on. By looking at the personalities projected upon their gods by these backward believers, we can get a better understanding of our own concepts. And what are the principal characteristics? First the gods are all more powerful than man, but they demonstrate very human emotions and weaknesses. The regular practice of the primitive is the attempt to flatter or bribe the gods with praise and sacrifices in order to seek favor or ward off wrath.

An interesting remnant of this old process is the rain dance of the American Indian by which the spirit of rain is propitiated and drought is brought to an end. Similarly, it is normal in some primitive cultures to bring a gift to the river god to bribe his favor for a safe crossing. We snicker at such practices in the smugness of our modern society, but in a larger sense we haven't come so very far from those things ourselves.

We claim to worship one living God, but what is our concept of him? The old testament is full of descriptions of the anger and vindictiveness of the Hebrew idea of God. For instance, in (2 *Judges* 2:13, 14.) we find: *And they forsook the Lord, and served Baal and Ashtaroth. And the anger of the Lord was hot against Israel, and he delivered them into the hands of their enemies round about, so that they could not any longer stand before their enemies.*

Have you really come so far from that concept? Isn't this the basis of what our psychologist friends call subconscious guilt? Fortunately for the collective psyche of the whole Western world, there entered upon the scene a man of great stature whose mission was to emphasize that our God is a God of love. For those who can simply accept the concept of vicarious atonement, Jesus of Nazareth brought the perfect gift of freedom from guilt. After all, if the Master gave his earthly life on the cross for the forgiveness of your sins, what have you to be guilty about?

This was a simple teaching for the primitive mass mind of its day, and it is harder to swallow by today's intellectual standards. The modern thinking man finds it just as hard to accept the dogma of original sin as vicarious atonement, and that is good for him. Thus he is in a position to make his own peace with the Universal Life Force, but only if he can free himself from the haunting subconscious doubts and guilts of yesteryear. It is good for our wavering subconscious to be treated with some of Jesus' teachings of love and law to offset the collective race sense of guilt that impinges upon us in unguarded moments.

These things have I spoken unto you, that my joy might remain in you, and that your joy might be full. This is my commandment, That ye love one another, as I have loved you. Greater love hath no man than this, that a man lay down his life for his friends. (*John* 15:11-13.) Some meditation on this in your own quiet place will help prepare your subconscious for its part in your coming experience. The basic idea is to get more and more love attached to your concept of God. We have chosen these words of Jesus because they are the prelude to our understanding of that often misconstrued statement:

... he that hath seen me hath seen the Father ... (*John* 14:9.)

Obviously Jesus wasn't referring to his physical body as the *me* which to see is to see the Father. We must make a distinction in our thinking between the man, Jesus, and the Christ Spirit which manifested through him. Our best translation of the quotation would probably be, "He who has seen the pure love of the Christ Spirit manifesting through me has seen the Father."

You can never reach God through your intellect. In a larger sense you can never reach God at all—that is, without a gift from on high which the orthodox Christians most often call *grace*. The mystic experience is indeed a gift from God himself, but you must first be prepared to receive it. The beginning of preparation is to expand your concept of God. This is a job for your intuition. Spend a little time in your quiet place, daily for as long as is necessary, meditating on your highest concept of God. Let your intuition explore the depths of the infinite love which created the beauty of life and the vastness of the universe, and yet has a tremendous individualized love for something as tiny as you. Grow yourself a wonderful new, living concept of the infinite, loving God.

The reciprocal relationship between you, your spirit teachers, and God

A closer look at your spirit teachers will help your expanding concept of God. Truly, He has given his angels charge over you, and they do keep you in all of your ways. But just who and what are they? *All* of them have had bodies of earthly flesh and have experienced the strange mixture of suffering and joy that we call living on earth. Many of them will have new earthly bodies one of these days, and the accomplishments they help you attain here and now will certainly help them then. Where are they? What are they? In the *Bhagavad-Gita* the Lord, Krishna, explains to Arjuna that: When a man *dies* he first goes to the exact heaven of his own belief. Then after a stay of an appropriate time, the soul enters again into the scheme of things on the other side of life while preparing for a new birth into a brand new earthly body.

Whether or not you agree with the two-thirds of the world's population that believe in reincarnation, you can accept the simple fact that your spirit teachers once had bodies of flesh, but now have been relieved of the confines and demands of their mortal bodies. Therefore they have no requirement to earn a living in the same sense as we who remain on earth; and the absence of the demands of the flesh gives them the opportunity for much clearer spiritual vision, and in some cases even the ability to predict selected future events on earth. Yet, one who has passed over prematurely will feel a tremendous handicap in trying to complete the projects he left undone.

Plainly, the better communications you establish with your spirit teachers, the better you will be able to learn from them and profit by their guidance. Always remember that you attract the kind of spirits which more completely blend with your personality and approach to life. If you should receive a suggestion that you do someone physical or psychological harm or commit a criminal act, break off communications at once and begin praying for the blessing of light to come to the offending spirit. Such occurrences should be extremely rare in the experience of any spiritually oriented person, but we all have negative periods during which we might attract one of lesser evolvement. This is simply a word of caution. No spirit of the light would advise you to hurt another person or commit anything resembling a crime! *You are always responsible for your own actions,* regardless of whose advice you are taking.

Now back to the good part. Use your ever growing rapport with your teachers to help expand your concept of God. You can talk to them about God and receive many uplifting impressions and ideas. When you enter your quiet place to meditate on your growing relationship with God, invite your teachers to be present and participate. The beautiful part about spiritual work is that there is no competition. There will be no jealousy on the part of your teachers, and absolutely no feeling that you are trying to go over their heads. Everything that helps your personal progress also helps them, and from their spiritual vantage point they are totally aware of it. Best of all, they are able to feed you new ideas on the fringes of your current understanding, thus helping you grow into a richer, fuller relationship with God. There is a deeply personal experience and relationship to be gained! Seek it either through the intercession of your teachers, or directly by your own efforts. But *seek* it!

How to reach God through your spirit teachers

In the modern Catholic Church it is considered normal and even necessary to pray for help to the Saints of the Church. But who are the Saints? They are people who led such exemplary lives while in the flesh that some time after their passing they were, in effect, voted into sainthood by the Church Fathers. Thus we can postulate that one of the great foundations of the Catholic Church is *spiritual contact* in the form of prayer to the Saints and answers received by those who pray. This is not too different from Oriental ancestor worship which also involves spirit contact. In the *Bhagavad-Gita,* Krishna himself gives the mystic experience to Arjuna; and in most forms of yoga the master works with the student to assist in his achievement of the same result.

Thus it is not only reasonable, but also nearly universal, to ask for individual spirit help as one truly aspires to the depth of mystic experience. When your meditations have unfolded much of the vast subliminal-intuitive area of relationship to the Living God, you are ready to ask for help. Ask always, call on your teachers and talk it over with them. They are your best friends as well as your most effective helpers. As for their guidance in your preparations to receive the mystic experience, and for their specific help in attaining it. Your own relaxed awareness is your best contribution to the cooperative accomplishment. Pay careful attention to the guidance and direction, and *follow it.*

How Gladys G. found enrichment

For years Gladys G. had been pushed by a vague but persistent inner spiritual longing. She investigated several *mystery schools,* belonged to several *new age* churches, and had finally unfolded a goodly measure of ESP. It seemed that each new bit of progress only whetted her appetite for much more. Her husband was patient with her seeking because she had always been a loving and good wife. One day he was inspired to ask her a startling question: "Why don't you use this ESP of yours to ask some spiritual being what it is that seems to be gnawing at you?"

Recognizing this as a wonderful piece of spiritual advice, she took the question into her quiet place for meditation. The first time she asked there was no answer because she had become so anxious and excited that she couldn't receive anything but spiritual static. She worked at relaxing, and by the third morning she reached a degree of serenity that could not be denied. In an intuitive flash came the answer: *You seek a deeply personal relationship with God.* Naturally her immediate question was, How shall I go about attaining such a wonderful gift? And again came that flash: "Your own spirit teachers will help you tomorrow morning. Arrange an uninterrupted hour and begin it in meditation. You will be directed and assisted by the highest help we can summon."

This time Gladys knew better than to go in excitement or tension. She spent the evening in attentive care of her husband and managed to stay relaxed enough to get a good night's sleep Next morning she approached her quiet place with relaxed but happy anticipation. She called on her teachers and waited in silence. Shortly she was impressed to lie down on the bed. Following directions without question, she complied and soon was comfortably relaxing in the horizontal position. In a few minutes she fell into a light trance and was treated to an out of the body experience she can find no words to describe. Suffice it to say that her life was enriched and given new meaning and purpose from an inner certainty that is unshakable.

This gift can be yours also. Seek it!

How to reach God directly

For those who were raised in the Protestant faith, it is encouraging to know that the mystic experience can be yours directly and without your conscious knowledge of help from the spirit world. Ever since Martin Luther introduced the *do it yourself* movement into Christianity, hardy souls have been seeking the *light* on their own. And seeking always pays off to those who are sincere.

Generally the first experience is spontaneous when it comes directly, and it comes as quite a surprise to its recipient. As an excellent example of this, I quote from a letter sent to me by a lady in the midwestern United States:

> One morning I had already risen for the day but something prompted me to flop across the foot of my bed and sort of wake up more fully. And a strange sight came in view like two diamond shaped frames in which were enclosed sparkling jewels (not lights) like the glitter of precious stones. Some blinked off, others on—off and on they went, all colors for a few seconds, beautiful beyond description. Then they dimmed out and I saw sky and stars like the whole universe moving to the right and gradually fading out. Something within me made me reason, I'm seeing the whole Universe, but it neither excited me nor scared me.

I had an experience in the spring of 1953 that was the beginning of my earnest seeking in this field, and it may help your understanding to share it. It was my first out of the body experience, and I found myself standing in utter darkness in the center of a huge dome-shaped structure. Suddenly a great shaft of light shone down from somewhere above, engulfing me. I felt that I was completely alone in this light when a voice spoke with great authority, "Let him whose eye is single lift himself up and reveal God."

Then a tremendous power surged through my being and I

was able to levitate my body and float through the air with ease. This seemed to be the normal method of travel between various groups of people whom I addressed from a floating position about six feet above the ground. You can imagine my disappointment upon returning to my physical body and finding that these wonderful powers had not returned with me. This was the initial challenge to do something spiritually worthwhile with this life.

But we don't want to wait for some chance bit of *luck* to bring our mystic experience. Let's get on with a program to bring it about for *you*. By now it should be deeply meaningful to you to contemplate the fact that *you are spirit. God is spirit and you are created in his image and likeness.* We have agreed that the self contemplation of spirit is the original creative force. Since you are spirit, your contemplation of God is truly the self contemplation of spirit, and as such must be itself creative. So the secret is to enter your quiet place and contemplate God. Imagine the richest personal relationship with God that your expanded concepts can encompass, and claim it as yours now. Thus, as spirit, you can truly create your own mystic experience.

Of course it is necessary to surmount the same old stumbling blocks of doubt and fear. They will try to haunt you with questions like: Do you dare? Are you worthy? Isn't this all really just nonsense? If you are bothered by these doubts, read some Whitman, or Meister Eckhart, or Thomas Aquinas. The mystical writings of great men such as these will convince you that there is nothing more worthwhile than the mystic experience.

Then go into your quiet place and reach inside yourself to the infinity which is God. I want to share one more experience with you. It was a quiet Saturday afternoon, and I was stretched out on the couch contemplating these great truths. Suddenly I seemed to enter another realm of consciousness and I felt those great words of the 91st *Psalm* spoken not as words, but as *the law of the universe. Because he hath set his love upon me, therefore will I deliver him: I will set him on high, because he hath known my name. He shall call upon me, and I will answer him: I will be with him in trouble; I will deliver him, and honor him. With long life will I satisfy him, and shew him my salvation.* Seek it! There is nothing beside it.

How your mystic experience will change your life forever

No amount of words spoken or written will ever take the place of your personal mystic experience. Whatever you may imagine of the splendor and wonder of it will prove incomplete by a whole dimension when you have the real thing to compare with it. It may last for a few moments or an hour, or it may come and go regularly. But your first glimpse will show you that *the light is real.* Something happens deep within your being, though it may seem to be happening outside somewhere. For the truth is that at that moment, you and the universe *are one* in a totality of feeling and realness that defies the limitations of the language. Suddenly you *know,* and you need no further proof. But what do you know? Even that defies description, but it includes your *ownership of eternal life,* your brotherhood with all living creatures, and your personal relationship with God. It is suddenly yours forever, and nobody can take it away from you!

Now it's time to get this experience into the proper perspective. Spirit used an interesting analogy to help me, and it seems worth passing along here. Think of yourself as a very young flying fish. You have lived all of your short life beneath the surface of the ocean in the relative darkness of the deep. This compares to the normal physical life we all lead on earth. Now the wonderful day comes when you are attracted by the shimmering surface above. Instinctively you gather the necessary speed and make your first fantastic flight up into the sunshine and air above the water. For a few seconds you soar on your young wings, completely exhilarated by the new experience; but just as surely as you soared up there, you must shortly fall back into the great ocean. Your consciousness is forever changed, and you will seek to soar in the wonderful world above many times during your lifetime. But you cannot escape the fact that you are a fish. It will avail you nothing to bemoan the fate that has made you dependent for the life of your body upon the sustenance to be derived only from living under the water.

There is much to be learned from this little analogy. We have come to the classroom called earth life to learn and to grow. Some of us realize our potential as *flying fish* and manage to soar momentarily in the great mystical union with God and His Universe. But just as surely as we enter this wonderful experience, we are deposited once more into the same life, with its same mundane problems and the same seeming drudgery of routine living. Shall we be stupid and bemoan our fate? That could only hurt your progress. The wise man will give thanks on his knees for the momentary respite from the classroom of life. He may look upon this wonderful experience as recess and look forward to another with the same happy anticipation as a young schoolboy awaiting the recess of his class. But *this is not an excuse to abdicate our earthly responsibilities!*

Yes, your life is changed permanently. You can't help but be happier and more at ease for the rest of your life. But you created a set of earth problems that you must still work out, and you contracted to accomplish a mission before you entered the body of this incarnation. Your mystic experience shows that you are making wonderful spiritual progress. This is certainly not the time to fall by the wayside and waste your golden opportunity for service and growth. Give thanks for the infinite joy of the mystic experience, and seek it often, even as the flying fish often soars. But come back to earth refreshed and willing to be an *effective part of society!* Live the practical mystic life.

How to live the practical mystic life

One of the great gifts of your mystic experience is a new frame of reference for all of life. You have a new feeling of oneness with all of God's creatures, so you will be much less inclined to hurt anything or anybody. Such sports as hunting and fishing lose much of their luster, and some mystics go to the point of becoming vegetarians so as not to take their sustenance from the killing of sentient beings. There is a danger of going out of balance with such practices, and you should be careful of the effect on others if you carry your new inclinations to extreme. Having spent an interesting three years as a vegetarian myself, I can tell you for sure that you can be a double barreled nuisance to your friends without half trying. A vegetarian is almost an impossible guest to normal people, and a bit of perspective will help you understand that it is all a matter of degree anyway.

Yes, it's good to live such a life that you bring a minimum of suffering to your fellow creatures. But science has shown that even a tomato registers anxiety or pain when cut with a knife, so why should we kick up a big fuss? The Creator in his infinite wisdom gave us bodies which require much of the protein and amino acids found in meat, and who are we to question Him? There are many carnivorous animals besides man, and we don't condemn them for living as their bodies were designed. So don't condemn yourself either! Live as normal a life as possible, and let your new light shine through in the many acts of kindness and friendship you find the opportunity to bestow upon your fellow creatures.

You should be a joy to all who meet you! Follow your happy impulses to kindness and generosity, but again a note of balance is in order. You may feel impelled to save the whole world, but your resources may temporarily limit you to simple and inexpensive acts of kindness. The tendency is to forget yourself completely, but this is as utterly ridiculous as complete selfishness. You are very like the goose that laid the golden eggs. The goose must be fed and cared for if it is to continue to produce. Don't let some greedy imbecile kill it and cut off the supply for everyone.

Because of your mystic experience, you are now God's personal ambassador to mankind. Strive to follow the injunction of your *older brother* who came to show us the way, *Let your light so shine before men, that they may see your good works, and glorify your Father which is in heaven.* (*Matt.* 5:16.) But it isn't prudent to run off looking for some personal cross to get tacked up on! The Master's sacrifice was intended to be enough to last mankind for all time. You are of more use to the world healthy and alive. Live to experience the true joy of helping others, and of fulfilling your own spiritual mission. Your achievements will bless you into all of eternity.

Then let's be sure we understand that the mystic experience is not the ultimate achievement, either. It is indeed the most wonderful individual experience presently imaginable, but it should be considered more as a new beginning than as an end in itself. In one sense it is like the proverbial carrot held in front of the rabbit to induce him to pull the cart faster. Here is your taste of what true spiritual oneness with God can mean, now come on back to earth and *earn* the right to dwell there always. As you labor in His vineyards and strive to feed His sheep, you will unfold ever more of your inner spirituality until you learn to dwell in His secret place of the most high. "He that dwelleth in the secret place of the most high shall abide under the shadow of the Almighty. I will say of the Lord, He is my refuge and my fortress: my God; in him will I trust. . . . He shall cover thee with his feathers (of love) and under his wings shalt thou trust. . . ." These words are no longer just the poetic mouthings of an ancient shepherd boy, *they have shown themselves to be the law of your being.*

Enjoy your sojourn with the Creator and let it be the inspiration for your life of meaningful service to mankind.

Points to Remember

I. Our doubts and guilts stand between us and our personal mystic experience.

II. In meditation, let your intuition grow you a wonderfully new, living concept of the Infinite, loving God.

III. Ask your spirit teachers for help in achieving your mystic experience.

IV. Seek it directly; claim your personal relationship with God.

V. Your life will be changed forever but keep your balance!

how to

Use Advanced
Psychic Phenomena
for ESP

You may have wondered why we stuck with just the very elementary and basic forms of ESP throughout the first nine chapters. Even though there might be more glamor in some other approach, all educators agree that a sound groundwork of fundamentals is necessary before building the superstructure. My personal feeling is that the work of Chapter 9 is an absolute prerequisite to any intelligent excursion into advanced psychic phenomena. But we have worked for lo these nine chapters, now let's play! Let's have a go at the glamor part of ESP.

Now you are ready for advanced phenomena

The humility that comes from a deep mystical experience, or at least from a thorough understanding of the idea, gives you a sound appreciation of the next dimension. You can easily understand the simple confession of the Master, *When ye have lifted up the son of man, then shall ye know that I am he, and that I do nothing of myself; but as the Father taught me, I speak these things.* (*John* 8:28.)

It is for lack of this humility that many areas of ESP have accumulated what we might call a bit of a bad name. A few psychics and mediums seem to forget that it is not their little self which is doing the work, and the unfortunate result is jealousy, back-biting, and even fraudulent demonstrations. Happily these people are few in number, but the sincere workers have a great task in living down the negativity. However we have long since ceased to condemn the whole medical profession for an occasional quack, and we must now do the same for the workers in ESP. If you feel impelled to do so, enter the work; but take care to bring your humility with you.

We are about to survey a vast panorama of fascinating psychic phenomena, but it is important that we pause for one more word of caution. The Master cautioned us, *"Give not that which is holy unto the dogs, neither cast ye your pearls before swine, lest they trample them under their feet, and turn again and rend you.*

Psychic phenomena is for the use and instruction of seekers and believers, not for parlor games. Use sound spiritual judgement in when and where to use it. Its misuse will set you back much farther than you might think. From this somewhat sober mental platform, we will begin our happy exploration of the deeper psychic realms.

Types of experience you may expect

In a work of this size we can hardly scratch the surface of the wonderful world of the psychic, but we will begin with a brief description of some of the more common occurrences.

1. *Knocks and Raps.*

Spirits often indicate their presence, or even enter into the conversation, with distinct knocks or raps on the wall, a window, or some piece of furniture. This simple manifestation is present in many places where it is ignored or shrugged off as *the house settling, the wind blowing,* or the like. Just the other day I attended a gathering of people at a very nice lady's house. During an interesting bit of conversation about spiritual things, there came a loud rap on the wall indicating a visiting spirit's agreement with what was said. A little dog heard, and I believe saw the spirit and barked a friendly greeting. I looked up and said, "Hi, there." But our hostess immediately said, "Oh, it's just the wind."

It is highly unfriendly to snub our spirit friends in such a manner. Yes, some creaks may be from strains on the structural members of a house, but there are unquestionably others which are real manifestations from the spirit side of life. Pay just a little attention and you can easily tell the difference. I once had an end table in my living room that was made something like a box, open in front but closed on the back and sides. Every night around bedtime, one of our spirit friends told us "good night" by sounding three quick raps, one on each side and one on the back of this little end table. We enjoyed him immensely, but you would be amazed at the unnerving effect it had on some of our visiting earth friends. There is no reason to be frightened of this friendly manifestation from the spirit world. They will give you stronger raps if you get in the habit of saying "hello" to them.

2. Aura Vision.

In the chapter on spiritual healing we discussed the human aura and its relation to the health of your body. As you work to develop your aura vision, you will begin to occasionally notice an aura that is not attached to a living human body. This is not a trick of your tired eyes! You are privileged to look at the aura of a visiting spirit entity. Again a friendly greeting will help the spirit to better manifest to you. Here is a wonderful chance to use your developing clairaudience or clairsentience to enter a more direct communication with the world of spirit.

We are often visited in our living room by such spirit manifestations. They remain anywhere from a minute or two to a couple of hours, and we often manage very interesting conversations. It's just as much fun to be visited by a spirit friend as by one who still has a body. Why not enjoy both? Nothing can help you achieve this more than your own relaxed awareness and a friendly attitude toward those gracious spirits who come visiting.

3. *Automatic Writing.*

Some well meaning spiritualists will warn you of the dangers of automatic writing, but they are dangers only to the emotionally unbalanced. With your inner strength born of the mystic's understanding of the universe, there is nothing to fear at all. If you care to give it a try, it is best to set a regular time either once a day or once a week, and announce this to your spirit teachers. Then on your schedule, sit down in the comfortable place you have chosen, armed with pencil and paper. Relax for a moment and call on your spirit teachers for protection and assistance. Then ask if they have anyone who wishes to write through you. Next hold the pencil in your normal writing position on the paper and let spirit move your hand, causing it to write. It may take more than one sitting before anything happens, but almost everybody will get some results within a reasonable time.

It is when you start getting results that you need to keep your judgement and reason about you. You can often get real words of wisdom and good spiritual advice by this technique, but sometimes it is possible to contact a lesser evolved entity who will flatter you, lie to you, or even direct you to do something ridiculous or criminal. If the writing begins telling you that you are a great avatar or a reincarnation of Napoleon, or asks you to go shoot Joe Doaks down the street; break off the contact and ask your spirit teachers to assist the offending spirit to find light. Like most other spirit manifestations, this technique works very well for some, not so well for others, and not at all for those who tense up and refuse to let spirit move their hands. It is well worth a try for any spiritually oriented person.

4. *Inspirational Writing.*

A useful variation of automatic writing is known as inspirational writing. Again you sit with pencil and paper (or as in my case with a typewriter) and call on your teachers to be with you. Tell them that you are ready to write under their inspiration, then relax. Very soon you will be impressed with an idea. Write it down in your own words, and likely as not another will come to you while you are still writing the first. Whether consciously or not, most authors use this technique for virtually all of their writings.

Though I will certainly accept the responsibility for any errors which have crept in, I must confess that both this book and the previous one, *The Miraculous Laws of Universal Dynamics*, were produced by inspirational writing.[1] It is truly amazing how much you learn when you sit down to work for spirit through this medium. One teacher in particular handles a great deal of this work through me; I call him Professor Rienhardt. While handling some of the more difficult ideas, we will often seem to "write ourselves into a corner," and I instinctively stop and look up laughingly with the question, "O.K., Rienhardt, how are we going to get out of this one?"

Instantly there will come an intuitive flash that clearly shows it was me in the corner, not the spirit helper whose higher vision had it all planned from the beginning. Anyone who will take the trouble to develop some degree of sensitivity can become an effective messenger of spirit through this simple technique. Experiment with a little automatic writing first to get the feel of the thing, then try this. You will be glad you did.

---

[1] Al G. Manning, *The Miraculous Laws of Universal Dynamics*. Englewood Cliffs, N.J.: Prentice-Hall, Inc.

5. *Inspirational Lecturing.*

Quite similar to inspirational writing is the phenomenon of inspirational lecturing. Certainly the whole world would agree that the best speakers don't simply read a previously written speech. They may use a set of notes to chart the course, but the real meat of the lecture comes through more or less spontaneously. I was privileged to attend regular Sunday lectures by one of the most powerful religious speakers in the country. His voice literally filled the large auditorium with guidance, inspiration and a lively wit. Experiencing the man in this manner built a mental image of him as almost 10 feet tall and a virtual human dynamo. When I finally met him in the flesh, he turned out to be short (about 5'5") and mild mannered almost to the point of being retiring. But every time he walked out on that platform, he was transformed by the spiritual light and turned into a fantastic showman as well as an inspiration to all within earshot.

Not everyone gets the chance to speak before a group regularly, but it will be good for you to accept any and all invitations to do so. Prepare by calling on your spirit teachers for inspiration and specific help. Then choose your subject and make a short outline—stick to subjects that are familiar to you so you can keep your poise and confidence. When your turn comes, stand up and speak! The first three times are the hardest. After that it honestly gets to be fun, and you can bring much solid inspiration to many people. Never refuse an invitation! Your spirit teachers want to work through you.

6. *Psychometry.*

There is a vibratory essence in any object which picks up the happenings and moods of its surroundings and the people who handle it. With a little practice, you can hold someone's watch or ring and tell him how he feels today, what he has been thinking about; who gave him the object and under what circumstances; and countless little things that have occurred while he was wearing or carrying it.

This practice is called psychometry, and extensions of the technique are manifold in the psychic world. There is some argument as to whether the object merely forms a convenient point of concentration for reading the mental aura of the subject, or actually carries the vibrations itself. Your mystical *knowledge* will tell you that there is much more to the world than the simple three dimensions we see, and there is a way in which both arguments are true.

Try some simple experiments in psychometry yourself. Hold any object in your hand and ask it questions about its history and the events that have taken place in its presence. Expect your answer to come through one of your normal channels of intuition, clairvoyance, clairaudience, or clairsentience. This is one of the first steps to useful *mediumship* for many students. You could well be one of them.

7. *Precognition.*

The Bible makes quite a thing out of Pharaoh's dream which Joseph interpreted as predicting seven years of plenty followed by seven years of famine. Joseph's future seemed to be made by his interpretation, but it was *Pharaoh's dream* which we would classify as the precognitive experience. Any feeling, vision, word or symbol that accurately foretells of a coming event is a manifestation of precognition. Your common sense can often extrapolate from a set of known facts and accurately predict the outcome without your claiming occult powers, but there is a vast gray area beyond the usual bounds of common sense where your ESP can be extremely practical.

Immediately some eager beaver will say, "O.K., tell us who is going to win the feature race at Santa Anita tomorrow." A disinterested medium might be right half of the time, which is excellent in a field of ten or more horses but there is a joker if you plan to use it for personal profit! When the *something for nothing* motive enters in, we get so bound up in the anxiety born of greed that we block our receipt of the very information we seek.

Nevertheless there is much good guidance and help for yourself and others to be gained from learning to recognize precognitive tips from spirit. Pay careful attention to your outstanding dreams and the other normal symbols which reach you through your ESP. Try to interpret their meaning, but temper your judgement with down to earth prudence.

8. *Spirit Photography.*

There are many examples of spirit entities having their pictures taken beside an unsuspecting member of the family. Such manifestations are classed under the general heading of spirit photography. Some people strive consciously to photograph spirits and consider it a form of mediumship, while others get the manifestations completely by accident. It is definitely true that spirit entities are occasionally photographed.

At one time I tried some simple research in spirit photography, using infra red film in the hope of getting better manifestations. However, it turned out that I got more clearly recognizable results by accident while taking regular pictures of some friends. Now with the power of hindsight, I think I understand the reason. Infra red film is specially sensitive to electromagnetic radiations of lower frequency than visible light bordering on the range of radiant heat, but spirit manifestations must lie in the range of the spectrum on the other side of visible light—somewhere beyond ultra violet. Therefore it is easier for them to step down their vibrations to the upper end of the visible spectrum than to further step them down to affect infra red film.

It costs very little to try your hand at spirit photography. Almost everyone has a camera. Ask your spirit friends and teachers to pose for you, then take some pictures. After they are developed, examine the prints carefully for faces or whole bodies that were not physically present during the festivities. You might also examine your old pictures with this thought in mind. A spirit face may have been clearly visible for years, yet ignored because no one had the insight to notice.

9. *Independent Voice.*

As opposed to clairaudience which is heard only by the medium, there is a phenomenon called independent voice which can be heard by all those present. As you work to develop your psychic centers thus, providing a better instrument for the use of your spirit friends, you may be treated to some interesting bits of this fascinating phenomenon.

A whistle or a simple hello out of nowhere could be the beginning of your new ability. If it appeals to you, ask your teachers for help, and keep your ears open. Be sure to respond to spirit greetings of this nature and encourage more. If you should be fortunate enough to combine this with good aura vision, you may talk to visiting spirits just like you talk to your earthly friends when they come to call.

10. *Spontaneous Psychokinesis.*

This somewhat menacing title is the name given to that class of phenomenon which involves spirit forces lifting or moving physical objects. It is basic human nature to accuse spirits of moving or hiding things. During World War II we were treated to numerous stories of groups of gremlins whose mischievous antics helped relieve the tensions of the day. But what we are talking about is the physical movement of objects while one or more people are watching.

Obviously things of this nature require better conditions and more spiritual development of the medium than simple clairsentience or intuition, but they are possible if you are willing to work for them.

11. *Trumpet.*

A fascinating combination of psychokinesis and independent voice results in the phenomenon called trumpet mediumship. The instrument is generally a conical shaped aluminum tube which resembles a trumpet like the ones used during the Middle Ages. In the presence of the medium, the spirit forces cause the trumpet to levitate and, from the raised position, voices of those from the other side of life speak through the trumpet for all to hear.

Few things give us the appreciation of the power of the spirit world as that which comes from a good trumpet demonstration. Not many people develop these things on their own, and not too many succeed even in good development classes, but this is just as real as the egg you ate for breakfast.

12. *Trance.*

Many spectacular psychic occurrences come from the simple phenomenon, trance. Basically, trance is the temporary surrender of part or all control of your physical organism so it can be used for the manifestation of a spirit entity. Spirits control the body of the medium so that the voice quality and mannerisms exhibited are like the ones they displayed while still living on earth, and carry on "normal" conversations with those present. One should never try to develop trance mediumship without the presence of a good teacher from the earth life who is familiar with the work, because you will not normally remember what takes place while you are in trance.

The story of a prominent medium is replete with examples of the danger of a good trance medium being exploited by unscrupulous assistants who direct the manifestations to achieve their own selfish ends. This story is beautifully told by Gina Cerminara in her book *Many Mansions.*

A big advantage of trance to the earnest student is the possibility of receiving lectures directly from highly developed teachers on the spirit side of life. Naturally the trancing medium will not be able to hear the message first-hand, but modern tape recorders can easily catch the lectures for convenient replay.

13. *Platform Mediumship.*

Although it isn't a truly separate type of phenomenon, platform mediumship deserves a brief word here. To stand before a group and bring spirit messages of meaning to each one in turn is an excellent demonstration of the existence of another dimension beyond the door men call death. When this work is done sincerely and without pretense, it is one of the better ways of introducing new students to the work.

Probably no two platform mediums work in exactly the same way, but they all use some combination of their basic senses of clairvoyance, clairaudience, and clairsentience. If there is a secret to this work, it is becoming so used to working with the spirit world and so confident they will never let you down, that you completely relax on the platform and let all anxiety or stage fright dissolve in the thrill of loving service to mankind. I have been called upon to give messages in this manner occasionally and, though I don't consider myself really good at it, I feel we should always try to serve. One of my greatest rewards from this activity was the look of bright happiness that appeared on a complete stranger's face the first time I was able to bring through a spirit by name and relationship. When I said, "I am touched by a spirit I feel was your father and I believe his name was Harry," the look on her face was enough living proof of the reality of spirit contact to last us both a lifetime.

Since I had started to study ESP and spirit contact only a few short years before this occurrence, it is my personal opinion that *anyone can develop some degree of this ability,* by the simple art of application of the self with a deep desire to succeed.

14. *Billet Reading.*

Closely akin to platform mediumship is the more spectacular art of blindfold billet reading. Here the members of the audience are requested to write the name of a person in spirit, a question that the spirit should be able to answer, and their name on a small piece of paper generally called a billet. The billets are collected in a basket in plain sight of the audience and deposited on a table in front of the medium. Meanwhile, the medium has been thoroughly blindfolded.

The demonstration starts by the medium picking up a billet and through psychometry and spirit help, calling out the names and answering the questions. Meetings of this nature are also good for opening up the minds of new students to the tremendous power of the spirit world and the advantages we may gain by learning to work with it.

15. *Astral Travel.*

I made several references earlier to out-of-the-body experiences. It is not uncommon for students to leave their physical bodies in some form of a trance or sleep state and travel with the conscious part of themselves to distant places on earth or into the spirit realms. The most common name for this is astral travel. What part of you actually travels? It is generally agreed that the emotional body of light, most often called the astral body, is the vehicle which carries the seat of your consciousness on these journeys.

Many of your most vivid dreams are in reality astral experiences, but it is also possible to deliberately leave the body and go to some predetermined place. Think of the time to be saved by attending classes in the spirit world while your physical body lies in bed getting the rest it needs. It would be like recapturing a whole third of your life! Don't scoff. It is within the realm of possibility for all.

16. Apports.

Spirit has the power to transport physical objects over great distances, virtually instantaneously. Naturally there is as yet no scientific explanation for the process, but it has happened to many people of good integrity. When spirit brings you an object, you have little knowledge of whether it was manufactured in the spirit world or merely brought to you from some distant storage place. In either case we call the object an *apport*. Leland Stanford, the noted patron of Stanford University, collected many apports during his years of serious personal investigation of psychic phenomena. This is a startling, but controversial manifestation which probably does much more for the faith of the medium than for the audience. After all, it is only the medium who can be absolutely sure that there was no fraud or trickery. Therefore these demonstrations should be reserved for very carefully screened groups of believers.

17. Spirit Materialization.

Under the proper conditions, a well developed medium can furnish the physical energy necessary for spirits to manifest in apparently physical bodies. The spirits come in the shape and physical characteristics best known to the person they wish to contact. They can carry on a normal conversation, and may even allow you to touch them on occasion. Once you have seen a spirit aura visiting your home, it is no great stretch of the imagination to visualize this aura forming a force field around which the energy drawn from the medium's body congeals to produce the manifestation. This too, is a form of phenomenon that has been subject to fraudulent duplication in the past, and it is apt to antagonize those who are not yet ready to understand. It should be demonstrated only to the spiritually prepared few, and then its real purpose should be to serve the spirits who are longing to contact their loved ones directly.

18. *Other Phenomena.*

We could go on and on and on, but this is hardly the place for it. There are things like levitation of the human body, independent spirit writings on paper or slate, spirit painting and sculpture, and many more. As yet there may be no scientific proof of any of these, but they happen in the daily lives of many sincere students. There is a legend about a lady who asked Edison: "What is electricity?" The great man's answer is said to have been: "Madam, electricity *is,* use it." Certainly this is excellent advice for us. Psychic phenomenon *is,* use it.

How to discover your own advanced phenomena

Now let's come back to you. What does all this mean to you personally? And what might you be doing about it? Let's start way back at the beginning for a moment. The most realistic view of this life is that it is like a day or perhaps a semester in school. You have certain lessons to learn and special tasks to accomplish along the way. Your achievements during this session of life-school will benefit you both now and in future classes to come. Like earthly children in grammar school, we can make it hard or easy for ourselves by our attitude and the extent of application of our efforts to the tasks at hand.

Now as regards the subject of psychic phenomena, the proper use of some phases will undoubtedly help you in your life's mission. The better your working knowledge, the better you will be equipped to learn and grow. You entered this life with definite natural aptitudes for handling the specific types of phenomena which will be most useful in accomplishing your mission. Some of us may develop a great many variations while others will seem limited to just a few; but there is something for everybody. Certainly the more you open your mind, the more useful these things will become to you. Your sincere, open attitude can help lift up the consciousness of all mankind.

How shall you look for your hidden talents in this field? First, as always, is your developing sensitivity to notice the tiny or subtle manifestations of spirit that take place all around you every day. In simple words, *pay attention!* We can't put enough emphasis on this simple technique—*pay attention*. A basic law of nature is that attention always elicits response, and this is greatly amplified in the psychic fields. As you notice the little knocks on your wall say, "Hi, you're very welcome here," to the spirit and you will be amazed at how much more frequently they will come. Be on the lookout for spirit auras and greet them all. You wouldn't ignore a physical body coming to call on you, and your spirit friends are equally real. Why snub them?

It has been said in every major religion, "As you turn to God, God turns to you." This is another manifestation of the law of response. Your spirit teachers are the angelic ambassadors of God, sent to help you. Certainly the more attention you give them, the greater response you can expect. Take your earnest desire into your quiet place and ask your teachers to help you continually improve your contact with them. React with a thank you to their exhilarating touch or the small symbol of greeting that is certain to reach you. Then ask for guidance and help in unfolding your psychic abilities.

Begin a campaign to open your mind. Get books on ESP and the psychic world from your library and *study* them. Visit as many different types of psychic demonstrations as you can find, and seek to fully understand the principles behind each. You will naturally meet people who like to talk about these things, and you can learn a great deal in this manner. You may be invited to join a development class which can be an important step in achieving things like trance, trumpet, and platform mediumship. But here your down to earth good judgement is necessary. There are many deeply spiritual people teaching in this field, but unfortunately there are also quacks and pirates. Know what you are getting into *before you do it.* Particularly if you are contemplating trance, or any phenomenon where you surrender temporary control of your physical organism, be sure that all sessions are attended by a close friend or relative who can tell you exactly what happened while you were gone.

Do everything possible to put yourself at ease while you are seeking, whether it be in your own quiet place or in a good class. Nothing drives your demonstrations away like your own anxiety. One student was in a development class working for trumpet. For nine weeks she had some interesting visions and guidance, but no physical manifestations. Then toward the end of the tenth meeting, her trumpet raised slightly and seemed to emit a low growl. She became so excited that she jumped up, grabbed the instrument, and looked inside. This anxious action completely broke the vibration, and for many weeks the trumpet remained still and silent.

The same relaxed awareness that gave you the first glimpse of the world of your spirit teachers is the catalyst for any advanced development you may desire. Take it with you, wherever you go!

Concentrate your efforts on one simple phenomenon at a time

It seems that all spiritual work is a lesson in patience. We are like children in these matters, doing silly things like standing back to back to compare heights as we grow, and always wishing we had achieved everything already. This is the point to pause and renew your oneness with the Infinity of Creation. To the Infinite Being divisions of time and space are meaningless nonsense since He is all time and all space already. The better your feeling of oneness, the easier it will be to control your impatience. But here in our finite world, it is best to tackle one job at a time, even in the realm of spirit manifestations.

A little communion with your teachers in quiet meditation will help you choose the particular type of manifestation which is most likely to come to you in the beginning. Then really try to develop it. Ask your spirit teachers for help, and regularly apply your psychic energies and conscious attention to a development program.

One student decided that she would do best by striving for the development of aura vision. In her quiet place, she asked for advice as to method, and help in unfolding this psychic faculty. Quickly the idea came to look for her own aura first. She brought a large mirror into her meditation area with the idea that she might stare at the area around her head, then close her eyes and possibly get an after image of her aura. The process got slightly short-circuited when she stared at her head for a few moments and noticed a faint fringe of light around it. At first the light seemed to come and go, and she wondered if her eyes were playing tricks on her. But a few days' practice taught her that the trick was in the *way* she looked at herself in the mirror. If she kept her eyes focused right on the center of her forehead while she looked at the area around the edges, her aura seemed to stand out very clearly.

The beauty of aura vision is that it can be practiced almost anytime and anywhere. Our student soon found that she could spot the aura of people clear across a big room, or even walking down the street. Alone without a mirror, she could practice looking at the aura around her fingers, arms, and feet. There is a whole new science of human aura waiting to be unfolded for the healing and educational benefit of mankind. Dedicated students like this one will one day bring it forth to the world.

The degree of *application* to your development work makes all the difference. We still live in a material world that makes its special demands on our time for the earning of our keep and for the fulfillment of our previously contracted earthly obligations. To shirk any of these is to fall backwards spiritually as well as materially. Seek your own point of balance that does a good job of satisfying the world's demands but leaves you the maximum time for spiritual striving.

The recapture of just half the time you usually waste or fritter away will give you progress that is richly rewarding. An excellent period for affirmative prayer is the time spent driving or riding to work. Many psychic exercises lend themselves to practice while you are actually working. There is plenty of time to handle everything without neglecting your family *if you want it that way.* There is an old saying that if you want a job accomplished quickly, give it to a busy person to perform. You will always accomplish just as much as you honestly set out to do—no more, and certainly no less. Do it!

How to seek spontaneous phenomena

The idea of *seeking* something *spontaneous* contains a seemingly intellectual conflict quite similar to some of the basics of Zen Buddhism. From the lessons of Zen we may also find the help we seek. Anyone who claims to understand it doesn't! Zen is not capable of comprehension by the mind because it is an experience completely outside the realm of finite thought. Thus in seeking Satori, the intellect plays a very subordinate role, much like a servant preparing the master's house to receive a welcome guest. This servant knows not when the guest will come, or what he looks like, but he perseveres and is eventually rewarded with the privilege of serving the guest personally.

So it is with spontaneous phenomena. We can play the role of the servant and prepare for its coming to the best of our ability, but we cannot of ourselves bring it to pass. The Zen monk doesn't refuse to work for Satori just because his intellect and physical body are not able to control it. He knows that the experience is worth all the perseverance he can muster. Similarly, we should never refuse or give up our seeking of the truly spontaneous phenomena. But how shall we seek?

Once again you must start with your steadily developing relaxed awareness. Take it to your quiet place and talk the matter over with your teachers. *Ask* for spontaneous psychic manifestations to be directed to you by the spirit world. Earnestly desire an ever improving rapport with spirit, and communicate it to your teachers as the reason you are interested in phenomena. Check your attitude carefully and often. Are you still looking for something for nothing? Are you seeking thrills or parlor game type entertainment? Work to purge your being of any traces of such negative attitudes.

There are only two good reasons to seek spirit phenomena, and both should be present before you can expect results. First is simple friendship, the warm love that makes people want to enjoy each other's company; and the other is a desire for that cooperation which encourages mutual spiritual growth. The side-show artists may always be with us, but their shallow results fall infinitely short of the product of friendship and cooperation. Constant policing of your attitude, and maintenance of your relaxed awareness are your contributions as the humble servant waiting for the arrival of the invited guest.

As little demonstrations begin to take place around you, consciously direct your mental and psychic powers to amplify the spirit signals. It is normal and necessary for your spirit friends to borrow physical energy from you in order to produce their manifestations. Your relaxed and willing cooperation will materially assist the development of regular and frequent demonstrations of the presence of spirit entities.

A small group of seekers gathered in their host's living room one warm Sunday afternoon. During a lull in the conversation, someone said, "Gee, it's hot! Why don't we open a window?"

Before anyone could move a window opened by itself, and no physical body was within six feet of it at the time! Though startled, the host said, "Thank you, good spirit, now please join us in our discussions." Then each person, in turn, was touched by a spirit hand in greeting; and the conversation continued, much uplifted by this simple spirit manifestation.

Children are often richly blessed by spirit companionship, and we should be alert to avoid the adult tendency to teach them that such things are impossible. A spiritually minded young mother thought she heard an unusual amount of laughter coming from her small son's room. She walked softly to the door and peaked in. He seemed to be playing ball with something or somebody his mother couldn't see, so she walked quietly back to her kitchen. Presently the boy came looking for his mother. *To her question,* "What were you doing in there that was so much fun?" *he answered,* "Oh, I was just playing with one of my friends." Because she accepted this answer with understanding, it was a beautiful experience for both mother and son.

A young couple became acquainted with these manifestations through spirit activation of a little joke. One night at bedtime, instead of getting up to turn out the lamp, the husband waved his hand at it and said, "Poof." Instantly the light went out, and they laughed at the coincidence. But next morning the lamp worked perfectly and the bulb was not burned out. On the second night the wife said, "Let me try it this time. Poof." And sure enough the light went out again. They laughed and agreed the light must be burned out this time. But again the next morning the light burned and the switch worked perfectly. On the third night the poof worked again, so they decided to take the hint and begin a serious study of psychic phenomena. The lamp functioned quite normally for years afterwards, but their seeking led them on to many interesting experiences.

How to approach the direction of
phenomena

The slightest taste of spontaneous psychic phenomena seems to whet one's appetite for more, and very quickly there grows up a desire to produce it at will. In other words, you suddenly realize that you urgently desire the ability to produce at least some form of phenomena whenever it seems appropriate. Before there is much chance for real progress along these lines, it is again necessary to police your motivations. The question is, why do you want to produce phenomena? When and where would you want to use them?

We are quick to rationalize our inner motives and tell ourselves that these desires are purely for the spiritual advancement of mankind. But are they really? Earlier I mentioned my first out of the body experience wherein I seemed to have the power of levitation. My reaction the next morning was: Wow, if I can only learn to do that in the flesh, I can fill the Hollywood Bowl with people and really open their eyes! What's wrong with such a well meaning attitude? Simply that the statement was a good rationalization of a not so good desire for fame and fortune by creating a sensation. It's very hard to get rid of the selfishness and little ego that would willingly exploit the psychic for personal gain. That sort of sensationalism would close more minds than it opened, and create all sorts of wild controversy and skepticism. There is certainly a place for the more startling phenomena, but that is in small classes of truly dedicated students who will understand the real meaning of such things; give thanks; and talk about it only among people who will not be affronted. Be sure you understand the reasons back of your desires, and purify them before you seek.

O.K., now you are convinced you have cleansed your attitude of all selfishness. How do we start? First it is necessary to provide some reasonably appropriate physical facilities. For some time you have been using a favorite quiet place. Let's examine it in detail to see if it can also be suitable for a place to develop phenomena. An ideal place would meet these special requirements:

1. It will be absolutely quiet while you are using it.
2. It can be locked from the inside to prevent your being interrupted.
3. It is equipped with some sort of blackout curtains so you can exclude all light when necessary.
4. It is supplied with a comfortable chair and a small table which can be used as an altar. The altar may contain two candles in holders, incense, incense burner, a mirror, and anything else that appeals to your esthetic sense.

Let's call this place your *meditation chamber* to distinguish it from any convenient location you may use for a quiet place. Prepare your meditation chamber for use by lighting the candles and incense, then lock the door to insure against interruptions. It is good to open with the *Lord's Prayer*, the 23rd *Psalm*, or both; then call on your spirit teachers and ask for their presence, their protection, and their help. Now tell your teachers the specific purpose of your meditation. Let's say you want to develop automatic writing and promise to join them regularly for this purpose. All that remains is to mentally direct your subconscious faculties to assist in the phenomenon, pick up your pencil and assume a comfortable writing position, then remain relaxed and patient until you get results.

Directed phenomena in the darkness

If you want a seed to sprout and grow, it is normal to plant it in carefully prepared soil. There in the darkness of the loving mother earth, something triggers the growth process and the seed comes to active life, putting down roots and soon sending a sprout upwards to seek the sunlight. For some reason not yet clearly understood by the human mind, the development of many forms of psychic phenomena must also begin in a complete darkness, symbolic of the little seed planted in mother earth.

Trumpet, trance, spirit materializations, apports and the like specifically require nearly total darkness during your development period. If you have any inclination or tendency toward trance, you should arrange to be accompanied in your chamber by someone you trust implicitly. Also a tape recorder would be very useful so you can carefully review the discourses which come through your physical organism while you are away in trance.

Now let's go back to your meditation chamber, light the candles and incense, lock the door, and adjust the blackout curtains to exclude all light from the outside. It is probably a good idea to have a trumpet on hand whether that is your primary interest or not. These little instruments are advertised at very nominal prices in any psychic periodical. Anyway, open with a prayer, then call your teachers and tell them that this is your regular period to sit for psychic development. Then extinguish the candles and sit quietly in the darkness.

This is not the time to be so insistent on one special phenomenon that you reject others which may begin to come. You will probably be visited by tiny lights, and often by a whistle or the calling of your name. This is also an excellent place for the further unfoldment of your clairvoyance, clairaudience, and clairsentience. Be receptive to whatever manifestations your teachers are able to bring, and respond with thanksgiving for each one. Sincerity, patience, and perseverance are your contribution to this development process. Your spirit teachers will furnish the rest.

A woman sat in the dark for psychic development and was taken on an out-of-the-body trip to a classroom in the spirit world. She attended a fascinating lecture on reincarnation, and at its conclusion she was shown a small silver cross that was to be a spirit gift as a memento of the experience. When she returned to her body she was delighted to find a small silver cross on her altar, exactly like the one she had been shown by the spirit teacher.

You will never be fully aware of the fantastic power of the spirit world until you experience it personally. Start sitting for psychic development now.

Directed phenomena in the light

It will be a time of great happiness when you are able to bring your newly developed psychic abilities out of the darkness into the world of light. You can't help but derive real satisfaction from demonstrating psychic and spirit contact to the little groups of believers you contact along the way. Our civilization needs many more dedicated workers to help in the task of opening the collective mind to the true relationship of our physical world, to the world of spirit, and to the universal scheme of things.

There is much new philosophy waiting for the time when man can open his heart to its teachings of the *reality of the brotherhood of all beings* and our direct relationship to the Creator. As you become more adept at demonstrating psychic phenomena, it is important that you understand the responsibility that comes with it. Because you can demonstrate the truth of principles which the average individual only vaguely suspects, you have become a special ambassador of God to everyone you contact. From now on, it is not just your psychic demonstrations that will be observed, but the sum total of *everything that is you.*

It is imperative that you accept your new responsibility and strive to live a life of true inspiration to all. Yes, you are still a human being with human faults and weaknesses, but those within your sphere of influence will be apt to forget that fact. To them you are an ambassador of God and the spirit world, and their concept of God will be greatly influenced by everything you seem to stand for. As a practical matter, there remains much pettiness and bigotry in our world, and more than your share will undoubtedly come your way. Accept your responsibility as a spiritual leader and rise above such things.

Our Master Teacher left us the simple ground rules: resist not evil, turn the other cheek, and *If thy brother trespass against thee, rebuke him; and if he repent, forgive him.* How many times? *Forgive him unto seventy times seven!* This is not to suggest that you become a spineless jellyfish who is afraid to stand up for what he believes, but it is an effective way of minimizing the strife and vexation around you. It is clearly a matter of good judgement of the importance of a problem to the spiritual well being of you, the group, and the community; whether you shall grab a whip and drive the money changers out of the temple, or smile and turn the other cheek.

You are here to be about your Father's business. As you seek to live your life in that manner, you will receive all the guidance and help necessary to your effectiveness. *Let your light so shine before men that they may see your good works, and glorify your Father which is in heaven.*

Points to Remember

I. The humility born of deep mystical understanding is a practical prerequisite to advanced psychic phenomena.

II. You may expect many different types of phenomena. For example: Knocks and raps, aura vision, automatic writing, inspirational writing, inspirational lecturing, psychometry, precognition, spirit photography, independent voice, spontaneous psychokinesis, trumpet, trance, platform mediumship, billet reading, astral travel, apports, spirit materializations, and many more.

III. Seek to unfold your own advanced phenomena as part of your over-all spiritual development program.

IV. Phenomena are not for thrills or parlor games.

V. It is useful to prepare a meditation chamber that can be locked from the inside to be certain you are not disturbed during your development work.

VI. You will become an ambassador of God to all mankind. Accept your responsibility.

how to

Insure Your New Growth

Those who have read my book, *The Miraculous Laws of Universal Dynamics*, already understand that this book is really *Volume II* of a series, and it constitutes our third trip around the evolutionary spiral. We closed *Volume I* with a suggested method of beginning your new growth by scientific prayer for the manifestation of an organization to fill the gaping void between science and religion.

Throughout life we see evidence of the spiral of evolution. Radio is a simple illustration. It began by the use of a plain little gadget, the old-fashioned crystal, until it was replaced by the more complicated vacuum tube. Less than half a century later we returned to the use of the crystal, now renamed transistor in honor of its greatly increased effectiveness. We returned to the old concept, but a whole revolution higher on the evolutionary spiral. From technology to dress styles to morals, things seem to progress in a spiral rather than a straight line, and the same is true of our spiritual progress. We continually return to the old ways, but with deeper understanding born of our more extensive experience. Even the apparently unresolvable conflict between modern science and religion will melt away as we travel the spiral onward to a new living religion based not on blind dogmatic faith, but on enlightened understanding of the inner meaning of the old teachings. We will approach God with a fuller measure of knowledge than the generations who were asked to accept on blind faith. In our time, faith can come to mean *certainty*, not merely hope or wavering trust. Let's take a better look at the apparent conflict.

Science vs. religion

Blind faith may have been a good vehicle for the population of 2,000 years ago, but our contemporary society has taught us to prize something else. The scientific method is the vogue, and its tool is the intellect. But we must manage to view science in its proper perspective. Just what is it? What are its limitations? And why should we worship the intellect more than some other tool like a hammer or a saw?

A high school teacher might open his elementary class by defining science as the systematic classification of knowledge obtained by study, experimentation, and practice. This is a good working definition, *if* you understand that *knowledge* is neither static nor sacred. Science constantly seeks new knowledge, and reclassifies the old in the light of that which comes later. But isn't this just another form of growth? Isn't today's knowledge merely yesterday's speculative ideas proved true? And aren't today's truths often discovered to be but special cases of greater truths?

A good example of unfolding knowledge lies in the history of geometry. It started with Euclidian plane geometry. Here were evolved the basic concepts of the point, the line, the plane, and the various plane figures such as the triangle, circle, and polygon. Then came the addition of another dimension. Plane geometry was conceived to be merely a special case of spherical geometry, still true but only as it approximates a point on a sphere. Then a whole new set of higher principles evolved to explain the world more nearly as it is. Thus it made possible theories of navigation which *practically benefited* travel of all kinds. In the same way, Professor Einstein showed that physics as it was known is true, but only at relative speeds which are insignificant with respect to the speed of light.

Not all concepts of science stand the test of time as well as Euclidian geometry and elementary physics. The batting average is pretty good because the theories are based on the observation of actual phenomena, but scientists are quite human and capable of making mistakes. Even the collective group of specialists referred to as science is capable of making whopping big mistakes!

Less than five centuries ago the majority of the scientific community still believed our world to be flat. True, the Greek civilization, B.C., knew the world to be a sphere but that would be small comfort to Columbus if Queen Isabella had refused to back him. There have been many more recently accepted theories which seem utterly absurd by the measure of late twentieth century knowledge. We won't belabor the point, but a couple of good examples are worth laughing about.

Less than three centuries ago Georg Ernst Stahl expounded a theory of combustion which was generally accepted by the scientific community for nearly a hundred years. In this conception a material of fire, which Stahl named *phlogiston,* is lost by every combustible in the process of burning. Phlogiston plausibly, but quite inaccurately, explained the process now called *oxidation and reduction,* as well as the heat given off by the animal body and its restoration by food. The discovery of the element, oxygen, ultimately led to the abandonment of the phlogiston concept; but the theory was so firmly established that oxygen was first called "dephlogisticated air." How many bright and shiny scientific theories of today will vanish with phlogiston into the archives of the dead past? Only time will tell, but we can be sure the number is greater than most people realize.

From the time of the death of phlogiston, well into the twentieth century, the theory of *ether* has waxed and waned in scientific popularity. Ether was a hypothetical substance occupying all space including that filled by solid matter, and serving to transmit any of the forces which one material object exerts upon another from a *distance*. As sound is propagated by vibrations in the air; so light, gravity and magnetism were theorized to be propagated by vibrations in ether. Stated in its simplest form; sound is to air as light, gravity, and magnetism are to ether. For the whole of the nineteenth century and well into our own time, ether reigned as the best explanation of the related phenomena. It was not until Albert Einstein showed that many of the properties ascribed to ether could just as well be attributed to empty space and time, that the theory was seriously challenged. Ether is generally in disrepute today, but that whole realm of science is in a state of flux and it wouldn't seriously stretch the imagination to see the old theory return to prominence—but with the term ether replaced by a fancy new name like transistor instead of crystal.

This discussion is not intended as a slap at either science or religion. It is simply an attempt to provide some historical perspective. In the short run, science can be as dogmatic as the most intolerant religion, but time has its ways of bringing out truth. It is logical to respect both science and religion for the good that they accomplish, but it's also prudent to keep each in the best possible perspective.

Science and religion look at matter

The ancient Greeks conceived of matter as composed of tiny solid particles; reasoning that if you start to divide a piece of any substance, you can continue to divide it into smaller and smaller parts until finally you will reach the smallest particle, which will prove indivisible. They named this hypothetical smallest particle the *atom*.

Antedating the Greeks, but persisting in an unbroken line to this day, some *mystery schools* and religious orders taught that matter is merely a specialized form of energy. They were laughed at by scientists for many centuries. The discovery of radium with its curious property of radiation gave a faint inkling that these way out people might have a point. But it took the atom bomb to prove them right.

Even in the 1930's, an atom was a relatively simple thing made up of arrangements of only three basic particles: the very light, fast moving, negatively charged *electron;* the dense, positively charged *proton;* and the dense, electrically neutral *neutron.* However, a little stranger soon began to make himself known in atomic circles. He was light and fast like an electron, but he carried a positive charge. He didn't fit very well into their neat little atoms, so the scientists politely labeled him a *positron* and hoped that if they ignored him he would go away. But instead of going, he brought along his whole family; so today the number of recognized atomic particles is well over a dozen and threatening to continue the increase.

Of special interest to the layman is the concept of anti-particles and anti-matter. Modern physics now tells us that each atomic particle has an exactly opposite counterpart. It seems conceivable to our scientists that an atom of regular matter could collide with an atom of anti-matter and the result would be some sort of explosion, with the two atoms cancelling each other out, leaving nothing, as in algebraic addition. There has even been scientific speculation of whole galaxies of anti-matter in outer space, and the possible results of their collision with regular galaxies.

A recent article on anti-matter provokes me to a little tongue in cheek scientific speculation. If we look upon *nothing* as being made up of equal parts of matter and un-matter (a more convenient term than anti-matter), we are able to produce the first completely scientific explanation of the miracle of the loaves and fishes:

Jesus stood on the mountainside wishing to feed the hungry multitude, but he had *nothing* except a few scrawny fish with which to supply them. Being a man of great understanding, He used a fish for a pattern and divided his *nothing* into equal parts of fish and un-fish. Having no particular use for the un-fish, He threw them away and fed the multitude with the regular fish; and so also with the bread. Facetious? Of course, but it still leaves much food for thought.

Only as man uses his creative imagination, does he gain new insight into the true nature of the world around him. This imagination has built excellent machines and devices to extend the useful range of our senses; but we must take care not to let them restrict our thinking to the dead part of our objective environment.

Your new beginning is your contribution to the world's future

The promise of the future is always evolution of man's knowledge; the continuing improvement of scientific techniques and gadgetry leading to ever greater scientific understanding of the universe. Even scientific history has a way of repeating itself, like the spiral from crystal to vacuum tube to transistor. Where is this scientific spiral of growth leading us? Eventually and inevitably back to God at a wonderful new level of understanding.

Enough progress has been made that we are nearing a major breakthrough toward the union of science and religion. Out of this union will grow the new beginning of peace and cooperation between all beings of the earth. Right now there is a significant opportunity for a few people to make a very special contribution to this important phase of the progress of man. The breakthrough is inevitable. It is bound to happen sooner or later. But think of the untold suffering and anguish that could be spared many millions of our brother beings if this union of science and religion can be achieved fifty or a hundred years sooner than by accidental fallout from our space and defense programs.

This brings us back to the conclusion of *The Miraculous Laws of Universal Dynamics* where I suggested the need for a new kind of organization, "a living, vibrant group unhampered by the rigors of academic pressure and the strict scientific approach or the doctrines and dogma of traditional religion."

We briefly sketched the mission of such a group, and I invited the reader to join in prayer for his own progress and the birth of the group. It concluded with this suggested twice daily affirmation: "I trust in God with all my heart and He directs my growth in the Christ Idea. He is giving birth to an effective organization to unite science and religion into a living, vibrant organism, now. Thank you, Heavenly Father, for this perfect gift to mankind."

Your new beginning of spiritual accomplishment in ESP

Balance is necessary even for spiritual growth and achievement. The ancient occult teachings tell us that we should strive in three specific areas if we would attain balanced growth. They are (1) work for personal growth and progress, (2) work for the progress of your school, and (3) work for the progress of all mankind. Your progress is inextricably bound up with the progress of all life on this planet. You provide the best spiritual growth for yourself when you strive also for the good of mankind through the vehicle of some organization whose aims and beliefs are consistent with your own.

Note that number one is always your personal growth. Nothing will ever relieve you of the basic responsibility for developing the potential of your own individuality! That must ever be your underlying goal. In a very practical sense, the submergence of your individual goal in earnest work for the good of all mankind is the best path to personal attainment. Naturally the sensible way to work for the advancement of mankind is through an organization. There are many worthwhile schools through which you can serve. Choose any one that appeals to you, but *do work with one or more of them!* It will be to your own greatest advantage.

Your prayers are important!

The great wall of China stands as a magnificent example of what can be accomplished by group perseverance. It was fashioned out of determination, stick-to-it-iveness, guts, and very little else. But it will live forever as a monument to the potential of *group effort*. No member of any group or school can ever be more important than you, because it is only the accumulated efforts of everyone that adds up to results.

Points to Remember

I. All life is a spiral of evolution.

II. The apparent conflict of science and religion is the result of lack of historical perspective.

III. Creative imagination is the source of all material progress.

IV. The promise of the future is a breakthrough which will unite science and religion into one vibrant, spiritual organism.

V. Balanced growth comes from working for the progress of yourself, your school, and all mankind.

Chapter 18

Melissa looked at her calendar and realized that she was seven months pregnant on that day. She wished she could rewind the hands of time to reverse everything that she was going through. Fingering the bottle of wine, and then looking back at the calendar she cursed herself and the day she allowed the devil to pop up with the likes of Nathaniel Jackson. Ever since he'd found out about the condition of baby he'd surprised her by stepping up, and what was even more shocking to her is that Serena hadn't interfered one time.

Melissa hadn't stopped drinking, and she'd recently increased her intake by indulging with a glass of wine in the mornings before leaving for the salon. She became dependent on the elixir to help her make it through her days, and recently, she started keeping a secret stash of Moët in her office at work. Her excuse for drinking even more was to numb the pain of having created a harder life for herself than what she'd bargained for. Instead of continuing to show up at church, Melissa had fallen into a deep depression. She felt like such a fool, flaunting into Crystal's office ready to reveal Nathaniel's sin as if she'd been justified in engaging in the affair with him.

Business was down due to the salon opening later than advertised, and Melissa's clients had seen a change in the care she took of their hair, which caused them to go straight to her competitors. Melissa ended up losing two of the stylists in the shop due to one of the girls catching her slipping one day in her office with a flask and bottle. When the stylist questioned Melissa about what she was doing, Melissa had forgotten who she was and laid the stylist out. It was only a matter of time before Melissa snapped on anyone who looked at her the wrong way. One stylist told the other, and within two weeks after the incident, her help was no longer willing to help her, and they went ghost on her.

It didn't take long for the word to get out that Melissa was drinking on the job, which meant she was slipping. The clientele that she'd built up was quickly disappearing right before her eyes. Before she had begun drinking and cursing folks out, there was always an aspiring hairstylist coming to work at the upscale establishment. Once life happened and Melissa began losing her battle to alcohol, she couldn't find anyone to give a job to.

Shame had become Melissa's stronghold, and depression followed quickly. The bottle was slowly replacing Trina as her best friend. Melissa couldn't believe that her life was turning out the way it was. She didn't care about anything anymore, and she didn't care about herself either. Her cell phone buzzed and danced around on the table. Melissa glanced over to see that Trina was on the other end of the phone.

"Trina, what's up?" Melissa's words were slurred *again*. She picked up her glass of Moscato that she'd been nursing and took another sip.

"Bestie, are you drunk?" Trina asked, fearing that Melissa wasn't handling her business in a healthy manner. She sat in her car not waiting for Melissa to answer before exiting and heading up to Melissa's door. She pulled out her spare key that she'd had made just in case Melissa had shut down on the world again.

"I'm not drunk. I only had a few drinks since I've been home from work. Guess what, Bestie, today is the first day of the rest of my life, and I'm celebrating." Melissa faked a laugh but stopped as she looked over at her door when she heard someone trying to enter. "Lord, someone is trying to come up in here on me."

Trina opened the door with a scowl on her face and cell phone still glued to her ear. She entered and closed the door with her leg. "It's me, fool," Trina said, hitting the END button on the phone and throwing it in her pocketbook. She made a beeline over to the dining area where Melissa had bottles of wine on deck. Her hands flew to her hips, and she immediately went in on Melissa. "What are you doing? You have enough issues going on as it is, and now you're contributing to the baby's issues."

Trina didn't wait for Melissa to reply before going in again. "By the way, do you care to tell me why you sent a text to me about my god-baby's sex instead of calling me like normal people do? I mean, do you even care that God opened your womb so that you would be able to carry a baby? There are many people who would kill to be in your . . ." Trina's voice trailed off when Melissa put her hand up to intervene.

"Why are you talking to me like my baby is going to be healthy when he's born? God is punishing me for being hardheaded, and He's allowing my child to need surgery as soon as he comes from my womb. The doctors are sure of the spina bifida, and they've done other tests to check the fluids in the amniotic sac to determine that my baby is carrying some sort of bacteria which will only make things more difficult.

"I've had the hardest time with all of this, so as you know, I've turned to drinking. It helps to relax me, and it makes it possible for me to not think. Thinking has become one of my worst enemies. They've made it clear that they will need to close the hole in my baby's back because his spine will be affected with little to no recovery if not done successfully. I've been having dreams about giving birth to a baby boy, and the doctors flip him over only to see his insides protruding outside of his little body. Waking up sweating and screaming until I realize it's only a dream is getting old. I don't know how I'm supposed to take care of a special needs or handicapped child." Melissa flounced around the room.

Trina was about to rebut Melissa's tirade with a scripture, but she thought better of it because Melissa had already caught her second wind and continued to vent.

"Normal people, you ask? There's nothing normal about me, I mean, *look* at me. I took the world by storm by opening and maintaining my clientele in the worst economic downturn of the last few years. I've been able to remain aboveground and prosper when others were going bankrupt." Melissa stood and swayed from side to side. "And now look at me. My—"

Trina rushed over to Melissa, afraid that she would fall to the floor and injure the baby, and grabbed her by the arm, guiding Melissa to her sofa in the living room. "Calm down. Your going off on the deep end isn't going to change what is happening right now. You need to snap out of it and get it together."

Trina walked back over to the table and snatched up one of the wine bottles and shoved it in Melissa's face. "*This* has got to stop. You just said that God has been good to you, showed you favor, and all because of what the doctors have said, you're going to lose what little faith you built up?" Trina fumed before dropping down beside Melissa on the couch.

"I'm a failure, Trina." Melissa's temperament had gone from being delirious and angry to sad and vulnerable.

"Girl, you aren't a failure. I know you are going through a rough time right now, but you've sulked long enough. You've blamed God and Nathaniel long enough; now it's time that you take some responsibility for all that's happened. Have you ever thought about all of the drinking you've been doing which isn't making the baby's condition any better? Do I need to give you statistics?" Trina concentrated on not sounding condemning, but hoped that her tone exuded compassion for her best friend, even though she wanted to wring her neck.

Melissa broke down with her best friend at her side. She couldn't believe that she'd allowed her disappointments of the choices she'd made to convince her that her unborn baby wasn't worth giving the best of her. For the first time, Melissa felt true remorse about the woman she'd become in the last year. Even though Trina told her some hard truths, they were just that . . . true. She couldn't stop the tears from flowing from her eyes as she allowed herself to really feel the pain she'd been trying to mask with the alcohol. The truth was that she'd been broken, and because of her acknowledgment of that revelation, deliverance would come.

Chapter 19

Nathaniel and Serena had promised Crystal that they would be in church that Sunday morning. Crystal had been relentless in calling and coming by to check on them ever since the afternoon when she showed up at their home unannounced to let her know that Melissa had met with her and told her everything. Serena battled an internal war between her pride and the shame she'd felt because of Nathaniel's infidelity and Melissa's pregnancy.

Nathaniel pulled up into the church parking lot and rushed around to assist Serena out of the car. They hurried into the church right before the doors closed to the sanctuary. She tried not to think of all of the eyes that would be on them now that the gossip had begun and the rumors of divorce ran through the congregation. Before going in, she took a deep breath and hoped for the best. Nathaniel grabbed her hand from behind him and pulled her to the front of him as he followed her lead. They were ushered down to the front of the sanctuary to the pews reserved for the pastor's family.

Serena mentally reminded herself that she had no reason to be ashamed or self-conscious about what anyone in the church would say. That was one burden that she refused to carry; she left it to Nathaniel to deal with his truth of what he'd done. Serena slid down the pew to where Amina and James already were sitting. She smiled stiffly at her niece and gave a nod to James who returned a smile before she turned her attention toward the pulpit.

Nathaniel felt the eyes of those watching boring holes into his back. He'd caught Trina's eye before heading down to the front and taking his seat. He couldn't deny the relief he experienced when he discerned that Melissa wasn't in church. His eyes traveled slowly around the church in case he'd missed her and she'd decided to sit someplace else. Nathaniel tried to play off his search for Melissa by throwing his arm around Serena's shoulders and scooting closer to her while he checked out the amen corner.

Serena could feel Nathaniel tense up, and she was sure that it was because it was the first time he'd returned to church since the news broke about Melissa's pregnancy. She dared not look around, afraid that all eyes would be on her. Serena tried focusing on the praise team. It seemed like one part of the service melted into the next part, and before she knew it, the benediction was being given.

Nathaniel barely sat still through the service. He was jittery and continued looking over his shoulder as if someone was after him. If anyone had asked him or Serena what the sermon was about, neither one of them would have been able to give an intelligent answer. Nathaniel almost broke out in a sweat as he tried to rush to the door, oblivious to everyone around him as he made a beeline for the side door to escape from the church.

Trina had been watching Serena and Nathaniel throughout the service. She felt sorry for Serena because it seemed that every time things seem to be getting better for her, up pops the devil. He was always someplace, trying to destroy the most effective warriors of God, and Trina believed that Serena's anointing and mandate were even greater than Crystal's. She knew that her thoughts weren't God's thoughts or His ways her ways, but she'd had a hard time with all that was going on around her. Trina couldn't help but wonder what God was doing and why Serena was the chosen one to have to deal with all of what she was faced with.

Nathaniel bumped into Trina, almost knocking her to the floor. Instinct kicked in, and he threw his arm out to catch her fall. Thankfully, mostly everyone had moved to the front of the church to get their last words and hugs from Crystal. "Oh, I'm so sorry. Are you all right?" Nathaniel pulled Trina over to the pews so that she could get her bearings.

Trina tried to catch her breath and threw her hand up to her chest as she tried to calm herself down. She didn't speak right away, but she held up one finger and nodded her head to let Nathaniel know that she was okay. After catching her breath and a few additional moments of silence, she was able to speak. Eying him warily, she said, "What in the world were you flying for? You blew through here like you were the quarterback on your way to the end zone to make that final touchdown during the Super Bowl."

"Well, I believe I'm in the line of enemy fire ever since the gossip began about Melissa and me." Nathaniel huffed and said, "I didn't want Serena to be any more embarrassed than she already is due to my foolishness. I mean, look around; this is *her* family church, and I'm an outsider. The allegiance will always be to Serena and her family, and rightly so, but I don't know . . ."

Trina sat and listened to Nathaniel crying over spilt milk. She puckered her lips in disdain, thinking that it was too late for that. She squinted her eyes as if she'd eaten something sour. "Look, Nathaniel, the only innocent party in all of this is Serena. I mean, really, how do you think that *she* feels having to come into her church where you proposed to her? It's bad enough that you've disrespected her family, but to make matters worse, you chose to lay up with the very woman who hates your wife, *annnddd* now she's pregnant with *your* child." Trina let *that* resonate within Nathaniel.

Nathaniel's head hung down as he continued to be hit with his shortcomings. He knew that someone would eventually lay into him, and he didn't have an argument or a comeback for what was the truth of the damage he'd caused.

"I looked up to you as one of the good ones." Trina watched his body language, but felt like she could keep on going throwing fiery darts, and she did just that. "When I saw you propose to Prophetess Serena, the adoration in your eyes was evident as you got down on bended knee. It gave many of us single women hope that there was still someone out there who could do the right thing by us and put a ring on it." Trina dropped her head in disappointment.

The conviction fell from above, and Nathaniel winced from the pain he felt hammering him on his head. He became choked up and swallowed as the lump in his throat threatened to cut off his air supply. His breathing became labored as emotion rose up, and he had to clear his throat in order to keep his feelings in check. He had to find the words to say to Trina, but he just didn't know what would change her outlook. "Trina, wow, I'd always heard that someone else was watching your life, but I didn't really believe it until now. Can I share something with you?" Nathaniel asked, no longer concerned about quickly getting out of church.

"Yes, you can," Trina said, nodding her head.

"I owe you an apology, and actually, I owe this whole congregation an apology for my actions." he confessed, "I have sinned against God and my wife, but hearing you say what you just shared has given me cause to make a public announcement. I never thought that I would turn out to be one of those guys that everyone wanted to stay away from because I was a known heartbreaker. I didn't intentionally set out to hurt Melissa or Serena."

Nathaniel looked around at the custodians milling about, cleaning and picking up around the sanctuary. He knew that he needed to hurry up and meet Serena at the car before she came back inside. Instead of cutting his conversation short, however, he continued baring his soul to Trina. "I realize now that I've become a stumbling block, not only for you ladies, but for my brothers in Christ as well. Somehow, some way, I'll do what I can to help clean up what I've messed up." Nathaniel took Trina's hand in his and said, "I hope that you can accept my apology. I know I've allowed my emotions to speak for me during those times you were trying to stand up for your girl, and so I want you to hear my heart today." He looked into Trina's eyes, hoping for a sign that she'd forgiven him.

Trina thought about what Nathaniel had said. She realized that everyone made mistakes, even the good guys. Regardless of what happened between Melissa and him, Trina still believed that Nathaniel was one of the good guys. She could tell by the sincerity in his tone, and she could see it in his eyes that he was remorseful. "Yes, I can forgive you, and I do forgive you." Trina stood signifying to Nathaniel that the conversation was over.

Nathaniel gave Trina a light church hug and smiled before making his way to the door. He was feeling much more relaxed than when he entered the church. He could have smacked himself in the head for not asking about Melissa's whereabouts. Nathaniel wanted to blame her for the issues their child would have to endure upon coming into the world. He held her accountable for the state his son was in. She'd been drinking constantly ever since she found out that she was pregnant. Trina didn't hesitate to let him know that Melissa had begun drinking more since she'd received the bad news about the baby.

Serena raised her head and looked over at Nathaniel when she heard the lock click on the door. She'd dozed off while he was still inside the church. "What took you so long?" she asked before turning to put her seat belt on.

Nathaniel snapped his seat belt, and then hit the button on the key chain to crank the car. Sighing, he said, "I got stopped by Trina." He glanced over to his right to look at his wife. "She just wanted to talk about what was going on. She even said some things that got me to thinking." Nathaniel stopped there, not wanting to make Serena feel too uncomfortable with talking too much.

"Hmm, I'm listening. What did she say that was so profound?" Serena asked with her eyes closed. She didn't want to look at Nathaniel and begin feeling unbalanced again. Serena was just getting her balance back emotionally, and she couldn't afford to be knocked off again.

"Baby, it's something that's important for me to have heard today. I plan to be a better man and to take a step in correcting my mistakes. I learned today that I don't want to be the example that other young men use to dishonor their commitments to their girlfriends, fiancées, or wives. Thanks to Trina, I realize that when women think of a man who had his house in order and wouldn't be that guy to let their women down, they thought of me. I know that there's no good in crying over spilt milk, but I've got to try to rectify my shortcomings," Nathaniel said more to himself than to Serena.

"Hmm, okay." Serena sighed with relief and turned her head to look out the window. Gratefulness flooded her heart as her heartbeat slowed back down and she relaxed. The baby kicked, and Serena's hand flew to her stomach to rub it. At six months pregnant, the baby's kicks were finally feeling stronger, and that made Serena glad. The doctors were monitoring her now once every two weeks. They drew plenty of blood each time to make sure that she didn't have any deficiencies that would help her to fight off sickness. Serena's medical team let her know that due to the late stage of her cancer recurrence that she wouldn't be able to have chemotherapy treatments. They were concerned about the risks the medicine would cause her unborn child. Although Serena wasn't on a treatment plan, she needed to take better care of herself since the baby would take up to half of her calcium and vitamins A through K.

A wave of sadness marred her face momentarily, and then it was gone in a flash. The greatest news she could have gotten was that the cancer she was diagnosed with wouldn't pass down to her baby. The close monitoring with ultrasounds have allowed the obstetrician to see how healthy the baby was while in utero. Pulling down thoughts of worry, Serena laughed as she looked at her belly. It looked like something was moving around under her suit top. Serena finally had to break down and buy some maternity clothes, even though she was against it. She felt like it was just a waste of money since she'd only be able to wear those outfits for a few months.

Nathaniel looked over at his wife, seeing a huge smile on her face as he allowed his eyes to travel to where her hand lay. "Baby, are you okay?" he asked, grinning.

Without speaking, Serena reached over and grabbed Nathaniel's hand from the steering wheel and placed it on her stomach. "Do you feel your baby flipping and flopping around inside of me?" Serena looked at Nathaniel as he almost wrecked the car. She sat up stiffly, her heart pounding in her chest. "What is it?" she screamed.

Nathaniel hadn't felt the baby moving underneath his hand that way before. He was only used to a little flicker underneath his hand, where he had to concentrate to make sure he could detect the baby's movement. It both scared and excited him at the same time. Instead of trying to contain his happiness, he pulled over to the side of the road and hit the emergency flashers.

"Serena, do you know how blessed we are? The little bundle of joy that's growing inside of you . . . God restoring us so that I can be what you need . . . and now the pending birth of our baby reminds me that we have some work to do."

He leaned over and caressed the back of Serena's hand and smiled at her. "Baby, do you realize that our little crumb snatcher will be here in three months? Just in time for Christmas. We have so much to do." Nathaniel smiled lovingly at his wife.

Serena had forgotten about the fact that the baby would need the bedroom to be set up, and since they still didn't know what they were having, her mind was picturing what color the room should be. Mentally, light pastels flooded her mind. She decided on light yellow and lime green. "What do you think about yellow and lime green?" she asked. "You know whatever colors we decide on will need to be done quickly. Time is ticking away. We need to clean out the bedroom to turn it into a nursery."

Chapter 20

Serena had received a call from Amina, asking her to meet her at The Homestead in Bahama, North Carolina. She loved the country-style restaurant, but hated the fact that it was always packed. She couldn't get too upset considering the fact that she ate there at least twice a month. Serena pulled Nathaniel's ivory-white Dodge Charger into a parking space away from the crowded parking lot. Looking in her rearview mirror, she allowed the car to idle while she checked her makeup. She needed some work done to her car, and even though Nathaniel had offered to drive her, Serena declined. She didn't want to have to wait on him to come back and pick her up once they'd finished their dinner.

It was cold outside, and Serena sang Nathaniel's praises for making sure he had that very important feature in the car: seat warmers. The heat spread throughout the leather seat and enveloped her backside before wrapping around the front side of her. Listening to her favorite song, "Peace," by her favorite prophetess, Serena hummed along while she primped and rubbed her hair down. The song vibrated throughout the car and Serena went into full worship mode.

Throwing her hands up in the air, she prayed for Amina and that whatever was going on that God would bring peace in the midst of her storm. During their brief phone conversation, although Amina didn't share too many details, Serena detected in Amina's voice that something

was amiss. She couldn't put her finger on what seemed
to be troubling her niece, but she didn't want to press
the issue. Instead, Serena prayed that whatever news she
was sure to come out at dinner that God would help them
all through it. Serena didn't think that she could take on
anything else for anyone. She was in prayer as the song
ended and the next song, "Morning Glory," followed,
causing her to shout and bob her head.

The song caressed the emotions and mind-set of Serena.
She lay her head back on the headrest and allowed the
melodies to soothe her anxieties, insecurities, and van-
quish her fears. She believed that God knew what was best,
and that above all else, that He loved her unconditionally
and would never leave her. It had been awhile since she
was able to reconnect with the joy of loving the Lord and
accepting His plan for her life. She concentrated on the
music and in her silence, she was able to confess that God
had a bigger plan, and that His expectation of her was to
be a strong soldier with an expected end.

Amina spotted her uncle's car and couldn't find a
spot right beside it. She parked on the other side of the
parking lot. She'd been trying to collect her thoughts ever
since she'd received the phone call. Her eyes were puffy
from crying on and off for the past three days. She'd kept
it to herself long enough; she needed to call her family in
for their help. Jumping out of her car, she noticed that
the windows on Nathaniel's car were foggy. When Amina
reached the car, she heard the smooth idle, and she
knocked on the window.

Serena was startled out of her fellowship with God when
she heard the knock on the car window. She couldn't see
out of it due to the heavy fog on both sides of the window.
She hit the button on the steering wheel in order to roll the
window down. "Oh my goodness, how long have you been
standing out there?" Serena used her right hand to turn
the music down.

"Auntie, I just got here and saw the foggy windows. I thought to myself, I know she's in there breathing all hard and whatnot," Amina laughed.

"Let me turn the car off. I'll be ready in a moment. If you want to go ahead in, that's fine," Serena said working to get the car turned off and secured.

"Nah, I don't mind waiting. The temperature is really shaping up for a blustery winter, though, isn't it?" Amina asked.

"That's for sure," Serena said. "This summer was more like two seasons of spring. It's been considerably cooler this year." She straightened her back and pulled her cape over her seven-month baby bump. Amina covered her mouth giggling at Serena's duck walk as she trailed behind her into the restaurant. Before she could reach the door, someone called out to Amina as Serena disappeared into the eatery.

Turning around, Amina walked back toward the voice. "Hello," she said.

"Wow, you look just like me. I can't believe I made something as beautiful as you. You're the one thing that I did correctly," the stranger said to her.

"What are you doing here?" Amina asked, ignoring the woman's comments.

"I followed you here because I needed to talk with you. Can't you give your mother a few minutes of your time?"

"You are *not* my mother. I don't *know* you, and I don't *want* to know you. Why are you following me? Didn't you get the memo when I told you that I didn't want to have anything to do with you when you showed up at my job the other day? How did you know that I was here?" Amina was near tears again.

"Well, little girl, you *are* going to hear me out. I'm not going anywhere until we have a conversation. So what's it going to be? I have some contacts here, and they have been giving me information on how to find you. Oh, and I know where you stay too," her mother said snidely.

"Hmm, up pops the devil. Look at what the cat drug in from God knows where. You heard my daughter." Crystal fumed as she walked up to them. She stood toe to toe with Sherry and locked her hands to her hips. "Now don't start none, won't be none. I'm quite sure that you are able to hear well, so if I were you, I'd get to moseying on down to the next trash stop." Crystal stood flat footed and eyeballed Sherry down.

"Now, look here, Ms. Sampson, this don't involve you. Leave me alone while I talk to Amina, and then I'll be on my way." Sherry stood her ground.

"Sherry Paxton! Step away from my niece *now*," Crystal demanded before giving Sherry the verbal lashing that she'd always wanted to give her. "Amina's not a little girl anymore, and she can make her own decisions now, unlike when she was a baby. I heard you say that you're her mother, but I beg to disagree. If you were *ever* a mother, you wouldn't have left this child for someone else to raise." Crystal hated to have to say such things in front of Amina, but some things just needed to be said.

"You don't know everything, *Pastor*," Sherry said with her words dripping with sarcasm.

Crystal ignored Sherry and continued setting the record straight. "Not once in all of the years you conveniently up and walked out of her life and broke my son's heart have you tried to contact them. So let's be clear, *you* gave up those rights *long ago*." Crystal walked up into Sherry's face and stood toe to toe. "Now, I'm going to ask you politely to leave. If that doesn't work, I'll be calling nine-one-one to take care of you," Crystal barked at Sherry.

Serena emerged from the restaurant with a confused look on her face. She got worried when Amina wasn't behind her when it was time for them to be seated. Serena waddled closer to the two women who were having the shouting match in front of the esteemed establishment. When she realized that it was Sherry Paxton standing there in the flesh, she gasped loudly.

"Oh, looky here. Serena's going to be a mommy," Sherry antagonized. "Is this your first pregnancy?" Sherry stepped toward Serena, unfazed by Crystal's threat to call the police on her.

"Don't you dare come closer to me and don't worry about what's going on in our lives," Serena said, trying to keep her temper in check. She had a lot of built-up aggression and was more than ready to unleash on anyone who was an enemy.

"Or what, *Auntie Serena*? What are you going to do? I'm sure not too much since you look tired, like you'll go in labor any moment now," Sherry spat back. "Look, I didn't come for any trouble. I'm just here because I need to talk to my daughter." She softened her tone and glanced at Amina.

Amina didn't know what to say. Once again she was on an emotional roller coaster. She felt powerless, so she just stood there and cried. Serena walked over to her and wrapped her arms around Amina to try to comfort her. After giving Amina a few moments to collect herself, Serena escorted her into the building and to the nearest restroom.

"Baby girl, are you okay?" Serena wiped Amina's face with a damp paper towel. She had removed her cape due to the heat she'd felt due to the arrival of Sherry.

"Auntie, she's the reason I wanted to meet with you and Gran today. I am so glad that Gran walked up when she did. I don't want you stressing over me, especially when you have so much going on in your life. The last thing I want do is contribute to your hardships."

"Shhh, baby, this is not your fault. I love you and want what's best for you; always have and always will," Serena said.

"I just can't believe that she's doing this." Amina slammed her fists down on the countertop in the bathroom and stared at herself in the mirror. "Why, after all of these years, does she want to talk to me? I just don't understand."

"Well, baby, the only way to find out is to talk to her and see where her head is. I never thought in a million years that your birth mother would ever pop up. I wonder if your dad knows that she's in town." Serena slapped her hand up against her forehead. "Ugh, I remember how heartbroken he was when Sherry told him that she didn't want to marry him or be a mother to you. You were only a few months old when she disappeared. Gran and I decided to keep you with us because your dad was in no shape to take care of you by himself. Did you go looking for her or did she come looking for you, baby?" Before Amina could respond, Crystal blew into the bathroom huffing. "Oh, there you two are. I've been looking for y'all. Are we going to break bread or is this meeting confined to the ladies' room?" Crystal inquired as she looked into the mirror. She pressed her hair down and wiped eyeliner from the bottom of her eyelids before washing her hands.

The ladies filed out of the bathroom, and Serena signaled to the waitress by holding up three fingers over her head. Moments later, they were being led past the Christmas decorations and the many trees that stood over eight feet tall. Christmas lights gave the restaurant the feel of serenity. The atmosphere was always beautifully decorated, and it didn't matter that Christmas was still two months away. The Homestead never decorated for Halloween, which suited the trio just fine. They smiled as they walked through the festive aisles feeling better about the evening that lay ahead.

They chose a booth to sit in for the intimacy and privacy they felt they needed to get to the heart of the matter of things. Serena was hungry, and for that she was glad. Instead of gaining weight during her pregnancy, she'd been losing weight due to her illness. She felt the baby kicking around inside of her and wondered if it were possible that the aroma of food was the cause.

A young lady came over to their table to take their drink orders and brought a hot basket of bread with cinnamon butter on the side. She walked away to get their drinks and returned within a couple of minutes. Serena knew what she'd wanted before she got to the restaurant so she went ahead and ordered her entrée. She ordered more than enough food, and by the time she'd completed her order, Amina and Crystal were ready to order as well. The waitress smiled and informed them that their food would be out shortly.

"Now that we've got the ordering out of the way, Amina, did you bring us here to discuss your mother?" Crystal asked as she buttered a piece of bread.

Amina had butterflies in her belly, and they seemed to be working overtime in keeping her on edge. "Gran-Gran, I didn't know what else to do. When I got to work on Wednesday, I was buzzed in my office and my admin said that I had a visitor downstairs. She never told me who it was, and since I assumed it was James, I didn't think to ask who it was." Amina pulled a napkin from the holder and dabbed at her eyes.

"It's okay, baby, you know you're safe with us. If you need to cry, get it out, and once you're done, we can continue this conversation." Crystal had a faraway look in her eyes, as if she was ready to beat anyone down who dared to cross her.

Serena didn't know what to think about what had transpired ever since she'd arrived at the restaurant.

Time after time, the hounds of hell were let loose to cause havoc in their lives. She wondered how long they would be tested, if they could endure being in the wilderness, and how did God expect to get the glory from their individual situations?

"Auntie, can you pray? I don't feel confident that I am equipped to handle this. And what about my father? How is he going to receive this information when I share it with him? I don't want to be the reason he relapses back into drinking alcohol. He's told me how much my mother meant to him and how he had self-destructed after she left us. How do I tell him that she's back and that she wants access to me?" Amina's voice trembled.

Serena grabbed the hands of her mother and niece before praying. She'd become emotional as she prayed, knowing that the situation would get worse before it got better. She prayed with fervor as she called out to God, and her baby leapt in her belly. The prayer was cut short by their food arriving. They all said amen in unison.

"I'm sorry to interrupt, ladies, but well, your food is here," the waitress announced.

Crystal smiled at the lady who had returned and begun serving their dishes. Her smile was strained as she thought about Jonathan and what the recent events would do to him. By the time all of the plates had been served, Amina's appetite left when the waitress walked away. Serena took a bite of her chicken cordon bleu and chewed slowly.

"Mm, this is good," Serena said through bites of food. "Y'all haven't touched your food yet. I know we didn't just come out for me to feed this baby. Come on, your plates look appetizing, so if you don't want to eat I'll be happy to take the load off of you." Serena was ravenous so she dipped her fork into Crystal's shrimp scampi and slid the food into her mouth. Her eyes bulged in her head. "Oh,

Mommy, this is sooo good! I don't know what it is, but this is the best food I've tasted in a long time. Hey, y'all, I can eat all of your food if you don't show some signs that you are even interested in eating tonight."

"Well, I can't tell you how happy it makes me to see you feeding my grandchild. Yes, I'm going to eat my meal and worry about what's to come of this foolishness later." Crystal nodded her head and unwrapped her eating utensils. Eyeballing the fork she could see the spots despite the dimness in the room. "Humph, you know I hate these public establishments when it comes to the eating utensils. Every time I go someplace, I have to check these things. You never know what goes on with them dishwashers, and you know everybody isn't as clean as they should be."

Amina was finally coming out of her funk. She didn't want to ruin dinner by being antisocial. She'd have to figure out what to do about Sherry later, but for now, she'd force herself to eat, even if she didn't feel like it. "Gran-Gran, you always say that every time we go out to eat. I'm sure we can get a glass of hot water for you to sterilize your fork and knife in. I'd better get started chowing down now, or else Auntie and the baby are going to eat me up under the table," Amina said before digging into her chicken Caesar salad. She picked all of the croutons out of the salad. She'd been so preoccupied that she'd forgotten to tell the waitress to leave them out.

"Chile, why are you emasculating that salad that way? You're taking out all of the good stuff." Shaking her head, Crystal picked the morsels up with her fork and slid them onto her plate.

"Mommy, how did you get Cruella to leave? I mean, she looked a hot mess, didn't she?" Serena laughed in between bites of food.

Amina sat stiff with a stoic look on her face, letting Serena know that her joking around was in bad taste. Sherry didn't look that bad. She actually looked pretty good, like she'd come into some money. Amina reminisced about Sherry's first appearance when she showed up at her job and how she couldn't believe how much she looked like her birth mother. The more Amina thought about the two occurrences, she thought that it was crazy that she didn't seem to have any of Jonathan's features.

A frown covered Amina's face, and Crystal noticed it. "What's wrong, baby? Your food . . . How is it? I don't know how they could have messed up a salad."

"Gran-Gran, I was just thinking, that's all," Amina said with sadness in her voice.

"A penny for your thoughts, baby girl," Serena offered. She'd finished her plate and was gawking at Amina, hoping that she'd be able to finish off her salad too.

Twirling her fork around in the bowl, Amina exhaled. Never taking her eyes off of her plate, she said, "Now that I think about it, I really don't see any physical resemblance to my father in me. When I looked at Sherry the two times we've been in each other's presence, I can see myself in her a whole lot."

Crystal always thought the day would come when Sherry would try to come find Amina and expose the truth to what she'd believed all of those years ago. The day of reckoning was going to come sooner than later.

"Oh, baby girl, you have mannerisms like your dad. You also have his height," Serena said trying to convince Amina that nothing was amiss. "It happens all the time where the child will favor one parent more than the other. I guess it just depends on who has the more dominant genes. Don't worry about that now; you know who you're daddy is." Serena slurped her tea, seemingly nonchalant to the conversation at hand.

"Auntie, something is definitely amiss when it comes to my looks. I couldn't deny it if I wanted to that I inherited Sherry's physical makeup. I'm beginning to think that she showed up here after all of these years because she feels guilty about leaving me all of those years ago. I mean, there has to be some type of explanation, don't you think?" Amina had placed her fork down, her mind fully on trying to find out why her mother just suddenly showed up out of nowhere. And the thing that caused Amina the most stress was . . . Why she'd decided to return *now*?

Chapter 21

The phone at the church had been ringing all day, and Edna, the multitasking church administrator of Abiding Savior, was exhausted. Her desk was cluttered with papers and financial information that needed to be filed, but she couldn't get anything done with all of the interruptions. Before she could begin filing, she needed to make a few more calls to remind the ministry leaders of their commitments to bless Crystal before the holidays, but suddenly, there was a knock on the door.

Crystal was blowing on her hands when the door opened. "Brr . . . It's freezing out here. Didn't you hear me knocking before now?" Crystal brushed into the church and waited for Edna to lock the church door.

"I'm sorry, Pastor. The phone has been ringing all morning and well . . ."

"It's fine. I appreciate your hard work." Crystal leaned over and hugged Edna to show her appreciation. "Jonathan will be here soon. I'm just going to go into my office and remove some of these layers of clothing. Do you mind coming into my study and preparing the Keurig for some hot tea? Whew, it's cold out there," Crystal said as Edna walked behind her toward her office.

Finally, Edna was able to get some work done after she attended to Crystal's needs. She knew that her pastor wouldn't need anything anytime soon since Jonathan showed up a few minutes later. Upon his arrival, he headed straight to Crystal's office. Edna had the Gospel music flowing, and she was in her zone when the ringing phone startled her. "Abiding Savior where Jesus is the center of our lives, this is Sister Edna, administrative assistant. How can I be of assistance to you?"

"Uh-huh," she said as she listened to the caller and worked on the word document for the announcements for Sunday morning. "Well, the amount is $100 per ministry, and if everyone does their part, then we should be able to bless the pastor and her family for Thanksgiving and Christmas," Edna whispered into the mouthpiece. "Please have it ready to turn in no later than two Sundays from today. It's our hopes that the trustee board can present the gift during the morning service." Edna tapped away at the computer keys as she tried to concentrate on what the caller was saying before saying goodbye and disconnecting the call.

The intercom buzzed just as Edna was cleaning up her desk. She appreciated the moments of solace to get her work done, and by four o'clock, she couldn't type another word, deal with another clueless leader whom she'd given the same information to over and over again, nor did she want to be summoned again for one or two more menial tasks that day. Despite the way she was feeling, she exhaled, hit the button on the intercom, and chirped, "Yes, Pastor?"

"Sister Edna, are you finished for the day?" Crystal asked.

"I'm wrapping up now, Pastor." She rolled her eyes up in her head, mentally kicking herself for the words she was about to say. "Did you need for me to handle something else for you before I leave for the day?"

"Did you remember to send out the invitations to Prophetess Serena's surprise baby shower?" Crystal asked.

Edna slapped herself on the forehead and snapped her neck back. "Oh, Pastor, I totally forgot to order the invitations, and I am sorry. I can place the order now since I still have the Post-it notes with the details on my computer monitor." She hoped that Crystal wouldn't become impatient with her, because her job had many moving parts and she was already stretched to the limit.

"Well, you know that the date is quickly approaching. I suppose that since you haven't even ordered the invitations that you haven't begun working with a caterer or event planner to get the ball rolling too, right?" The annoyance was evident in Crystal's, tone and she didn't try to hide it either.

Edna didn't know what to say. Clearly, she'd dropped the ball in the planning of Serena's baby shower. She felt totally responsible because instead of telling Crystal that she needed help planning the event, she had made her believe that she could handle the extra load. "Pastor, please don't worry. I've got everything under control, and I know who I'm using to make the day a special one indeed for Prophetess Serena and Brother Nathaniel. I'll get started putting things together tomorrow and will update you when all of the tasks have been completed. I'll also have the menu ready for tomorrow so that we can go over it."

"Please make sure that you jump on planning that first thing in the morning. Jonathan and I are here discussing how we can make this party and celebration of my second grandchild's entry into the world. Now, if you need some help or can't handle the assignment, let me know right now, and I can get a committee together to pull this thing off." Crystal's tone was laced in disdain.

Edna walked in front of the window of her office and looked out. Sometimes she wished that she could be like the leaves that were being chased by the wind. She wanted to be as free as the leaves that flew up and down the street. She knew she'd better get her tone in check before answering her leader because regardless of how she was feeling, she didn't want to come off as disrespectful to the woman who'd served her as much, if not more, than anything Edna had done for the ministry.

She pulled her chest in and said, "Pastor, I'm sure that I can handle everything. If I find that I am incapable of getting things together, I will be sure to reach out. One thing's for sure, and that is, you don't have to worry about a thing."

Having moved around to her desk, Edna began scribbling some information down in shorthand and stuck the Post-it note to her keyboard so that she wouldn't miss it when she arrived at work the next morning.

Crystal had calmed down a bit and said, "I trust that if anyone can do it, then the woman for the job is you. However, I would feel much more at ease once you get the ball rolling and the invitations in the mail due it being so close to the holidays." She leaned back in her chair, ready to wrap the conversation up as she needed to speak with Jonathan about something important.

"Your confidence in my ability to take care of everything is much appreciated. I'm going to head on out and will lock up. Please remember that the alarm will be prepared and all you will need to do upon leaving is to hit the code and arm it. You will have about thirty seconds to get out of the building before the cops are alerted. I hope that you all have a blessed evening, Pastor, and I love you." Edna moved around the office straightening up and tucking papers everywhere she could find an empty space as to not leave any confidential information out in the open.

"Thanks so much, Sister Edna. Be safe getting home, and I hope that you know that your pastor loves you and appreciates all that you do."

"Yes, ma'am, thank you, and please get home safely as well. I hope that you will not leave the building alone, but that you will leave when Brother Jonathan leaves. Please let me know that you returned home safely. Good night, and as always, please call me if you need anything."

Crystal disconnected the intercom and turned to Jonathan. Swiveling around in her chair to face her son, she was happy to hear that he'd been meeting with his probation officer regularly and that things seemed to be going well for him. She figured that they'd had enough small talk and that she needed to get to the reason why she called him in for the meeting that day.

"Son, have you talked with Amina lately?" She drummed her freshly manicured nails on her desktop waiting for his response so that she would know how to proceed.

"It's been about a week or so since I've heard from her. Is there something going on that I don't know about?" he asked. "The last time I spoke with her over the phone, she sounded strained, as if she didn't really have too much to say. It was like pulling teeth to get her to talk to me, and I wasn't sure if I'd done something wrong or what." Jonathan adjusted his lean body in the leather wing-backed chair, trying to get comfortable.

"Well, did she share anything with you that would explain her behavior?" Crystal picked her son for more information.

"No, Mom, even after I asked her over and over again what was bothering her she just seemed so distant."

Crystal knew that she needed to let Jonathan know about Sherry showing up in Amina's life and what she suspected the reason was for her abrupt reappearance. Wiggling her legs underneath the desk, she leaned forward and braced herself for the next words she would say that would change the course of all of their lives. Tears welled in her eyes as she looked at her son with guilt and regret.

After seeing Crystal's eyes filling with tears an uncomfortable feeling swept over him. Shifting in his chair, Jonathan said, "Okay, spill it. There's obviously something that you're keeping from me, and I'm starting to get nervous. She isn't pregnant, is she? I know I can't tell her what to do; however, I told her that I believed that she was moving too fast with James." Jonathan slammed his fist on the desk while fury and tension took over the calm peace he'd felt just moments before.

"Calm down, she's *not* pregnant. You getting all hyped up, and I haven't told you a thing yet. Get yourself together before you leave from here the same way you came in—*clueless*." Crystal rolled her eyes at him.

"Now, I need for you to listen and listen closely to me, son. Okay?" She shivered as a chill ran through her which calmed her down and made her nervous at the same time. She watched him until she saw the fire go out of his eyes, and then spoke.

"Your sister, Amina, and I met for dinner about two weeks ago. I wanted to give her the opportunity to have this conversation with you, but since she didn't . . ." Crystal's words ran off of her tongue, and she dropped her eyes downward.

"Come on, Mom, tell me what's going on with my daughter." Jonathan felt himself getting uptight again as he moved closer to the edge of his seat.

Crystal exhaled, clasping her hands together before releasing them. Nervous energy wouldn't allow her to sit still, so she got up and walked over to the table that held all of her snacks and teas. She turned the Keurig on again and turned to Jonathan. "Son, can I get you some tea or a bottle of water?" Seeing the glare in his eyes made her uneasy. Crystal turned back to making her tea and grabbing some peanut butter and cheese crackers. Extending her arm to offer the crackers to Jonathan, she smiled.

"Nah, I'm good. The only thing I need is for you to quit beating around the bush and tell me what's going on with Amina. The way you're acting has got me turned up, and you know I don't handle stress well, Momma."

"Okay, son, I'm going to do just that as soon as I finish making my tea. Just give me a minute more." Crystal wished that she didn't have to be the one to break the news to Jonathan, but she knew that she had to tell him everything.

The sounds of dripping water finally came to an end, and Crystal knew that the appointed time had come. She took her time getting back to her desk, aware that Jonathan watched her every move. Instead of going back to her chair, she placed her cup down and walked back over to where Jonathan sat perched anxiously at the end of his chair.

Lifting his hands into hers, Crystal motioned for Jonathan to follow her to the couch where they would be more comfortable. Sitting side by side, she suggested that they pray. Jonathan was hesitant, but he bowed his head in prayer. "Amen," they said in unison when Crystal had closed out the prayer.

"Amina had a visitor a few weeks ago and . . ." She struggled with what she needed to say.

"And *who* was this visitor?" Jonathan asked warily. He was already tired of the cat-and-mouse conversation that seemed to never progress.

"Sherry." Crystal waited for Jonathan's response, but the only response that came was his pupils increasing in size and his hands instinctively had a clammy feeling.

He broke out in a sweat and jumped up from the couch, snatching his hands from Crystal's.

"Sherry's back and *no one* told me?" he shouted as he paced around the office pouting. Jonathan was upset, and his heart was pounding like a lovesick pup. It was hard for him to hear that the mother of his child who'd left him so many years ago was back in town. The pain from yesteryear resurfaced when Jonathan reminisced on the evening Sherry came to his mother's house and told him that she didn't want to marry him and that she was leaving Amina with him to raise alone. "I can't believe that Sherry is back." Jonathan grabbed his head. "Sherry . . ."

Crystal's heart broke for her son again. It didn't take a rocket scientist to know that he was taking Sherry's return hard, and rightfully so. She didn't have the strength to go to him, hold him and kiss him, or tell him that everything would be all right the way she did when he was a little boy. It wouldn't work so she mentally rubbed his back and whispered into his ear that she was sorry that he'd never healed from the hurt of Sherry Paxton. Tears of regret and sorrow fell from her eyes as she saw his shoulders slump, and then jerk up and down. Jonathan allowed himself to break down, not caring that his mother was watching him from behind.

"Jonathan, I have something else to tell you." Crystal wrung her hands together as the tears fell freely from her eyes and her cheeks onto her suit.

Jonathan never turned around to acknowledge Crystal speaking to him. Memories came rushing back of how things were when he thought that Sherry loved him and planned to marry him once Amina was born. Visions of what was and the outcome of his existence was based on her leaving him. He blamed Sherry for his gay lifestyle, certain that he never would have gone that way if she'd stayed with him and followed through the way they planned.

"Son, please come over here so that I can finish telling you what's going on with Amina. We have to talk about this because we need to all be there for her." Crystal walked over to Jonathan and stood next to him.

"Mom, what is Sherry doing here? Does Amina know that she's in town? What's really going on?" Jonathan reached out to hug Crystal.

"Son, come on over and let's sit down so we can discuss this." Crystal hoped that she would get the words needed to be able to speak openly. She fixed him a cup of tea and grabbed the box of Kleenex off of her desk. Once she was settled on the couch, she took a deep breath.

"Well, as I was saying, your sister, Amina, and I went to dinner." Crystal tried handing the steaming cup of tea to Jonathan, who declined it by waving his hand away. She got up and placed the cup on her table before returning to where he was sitting. "Now where was I? Oh, yes, when I walked up, Sherry was trying to get Amina to go someplace and talk with her about something, but when I asked what she wanted, things got a little out of hand," Crystal told him and went back to wringing her hands together.

"I wonder how she knew where Amina was going to be. Is she stalking my daughter?" Jonathan asked angrily.

"Well, I was surprised to see Sherry standing there. I believe that I know why she was so adamant about talking to Amina that night." Crystal took a couple of deep breaths before continuing because she knew that once she got started that there would be no turning back.

"Son, have you always believed that you were Amina's biological father?" Crystal leaned away from Jonathan just in case he blew up.

"What in the world are you talking about, Mom? I've always believed that I'm Amina's father. I may not have been the best father to her by leaving her here with you, but nonetheless, I've always trusted that she's mine. I can't believe you're asking me this." Jonathan tried containing himself, but found it difficult to do so.

"Jonathan, you remember how I told you about the rumors concerning Sherry being seen out with other guys late at night when you were home taking care of Serena?" Crystal asked gently.

"Yes, Mom, what about the rumors? I sure do hope that you know that you don't have to throw more dirt on her to deter me from trying to talk to her or win her back. So please, Mom, save it." Jonathan shook his head as he rocked back and forth before springing up from the couch.

"Son, I'm not trying to make her look any worse than she has made herself look. Think about it, baby. Why would she just up and leave with no forwarding address, never trying to contact Amina or me. She knew where we lived for many years, and yet, no one has heard from her. I even tried to contact her through her mother many times, but, of course, her mother denied knowing where Sherry was."

"So you're sitting here telling me that the reason Sherry left town and left me with our child is because I'm not Amina's daddy? Sheesh, that just doesn't make any sense—nor does it sit well with me."

"Whether you like it or not, and as ugly as it seems right now, I'm suggesting that you get a DNA test done to see if those rumors were true. I can't lie to you, son, I've always been skeptical that Amina was yours."

"You mean to sit here and tell me that you expect for me to go downtown like some deadbeat dad and get some doctor to tell me what I already know? Amina *is* mine, and that's all there is to it. Do you understand, Mom? She's *my* daughter, *my* flesh and blood. I can't believe that after all the years we raised her . . ." Jonathan jumped up again and began punching the air. "And now, after all of these years, Sherry has decided that she's going to push her way back into Amina's life and take her away from me?"

Crystal wanted to get up and slap Jonathan upside the head due to his sudden case of amnesia, but she let him vent and empty himself of his emotions. The hurt on his face caused her heart to soften, not sure that his life as he knew it with his daughter was coming to an end. She bowed her head and prayed again . . .

Chapter 22

Jonathan sat in his apartment wishing that he could have a drink. He was glad that Crystal encouraged him to stay at his place. She assured him that the loneliness would eventually go away once he'd gotten used to being on his own. Now, more than ever, Jonathan needed to be alone because his mind was still reeling from the news that Crystal had given to him last week.

Ever since she'd told him that he may not be Amina's father, he'd been calling her nonstop. He needed to find out where to find Sherry because he'd lost his peace of mind, sleep at night, and his appetite. His apartment was dark and closed up, just the way he needed it to be. He'd been living in a bubble for the last week, only leaving his apartment to go to work, and then come back home.

Flipping through the channels on his television set, Jonathan wasn't interested in watching anything that was on. He hit the off button on the remote control before tossing it onto the wooden table in front of him. Jonathan lay back and closed his eyes. He dozed on and off when the phone started to ring. He hesitated before answering the call. "Hello?" he said.

"I know you thought you'd never hear from me again, lover," Sedric laughed into the phone.

Jonathan pulled the phone away from his face and looked at it in disbelief. His heart raced as a sweat broke out across his forehead and his hands felt clammy. He threw the phone away from him onto the floor as if it

were a snake. "Ah, man, I knew that I was tired, but geesh
. . . Sedric?" Jonathan whispered into the vast emptiness
of the room as he allowed his former lover's name to linger on his lips. It was a struggle for him to keep his mind
from running away with thoughts of yesterdays gone by.
It was times like those that Jonathan wished he was still
in New York with Sedric.

When the phone rang again, Jonathan jumped straight
up from the couch where he had dozed off. He placed
his hand over his thumping heart and looked over at
the phone. Realizing that he was asleep and that Sedric
hadn't really called didn't sit well with him. Snatching,
the phone up from the couch, he clicked the talk button
on and blasted into the mouthpiece.

"How did you get my number? In case you didn't know,
I haven't contacted you because I don't *want* to talk to
you," Jonathan fumed thinking that maybe he hadn't
been dreaming at all and Sedric had called back.

"Hello to you, Jonathan," a female huffed into the
phone.

"Who is this?" Jonathan shook his head not sure if
someone was punking him or just what.

"Well, I'm obviously not who you thought I was. It's
Sherry, and we need to talk," she said.

Jonathan almost lost all control as he struggled not to
unleash on Sherry. At first he couldn't believe that she
called him, but he recovered quickly and was ready for
her. "How did you get this number? Is there something
that you need to be telling me?"

"No hello, no how are you doing, no long time no see?
How have you been, Jonathan?" Sherry asked. "And, by
the way, your phone number is listed in the phone direc-
tory." She laughed.

"I don't have time for the niceties. There's a question on
the table." Jonathan paced around his living room burning with anger.

"I'm calling to talk to you about Amina," Sherry said ignoring what he said.

"Is Amina my daughter?" Jonathan spat.

"Well, that's what I've been trying to talk to Amina about. I needed to let her know that . . ." Sherry stuttered.

"What do you need to tell Amina that you don't need to tell me considering the fact that I'm her daddy?"

"Um, Jonathan—"

"Jonathan *what?* Just tell me what's going on, Sherry. You left me all those years ago and somehow you just wanted to come back here and tear our worlds apart— *again?*" Jonathan's voice quivered.

"I've had my reasons of why I left all those years ago. I'm sorry, but I've gotta let Amina know that you are *not* her father. I mean, when we were together, we only had sex once. The truth of the matter is that you were always tied to your house, never being able to go out and treat me like your girlfriend. I didn't feel like I had a boy-friend." Sherry tried to defend her actions.

Jonathan had heard enough. "What do you mean you have to let Amina know that I may not be her father? What about talking to me first before you go around stalking my family with this great revelation that you have? I can't believe what I'm hearing right now. Where's your respect for my family's sacrifices that were made for Amina's well-being all of these years?" Jonathan ran his hand over his head.

"Jonathan, I'm grateful for all that your family has done for my daughter while I was away, but I'm back now. I'm trying to clean up what I've messed up, and truly, I'm sorry that I hurt you back then. We were young, and I have to admit that I was a little fast and loved partying." Sherry started baring her soul, yet Jonathan cut her off.

"This can't be happening. My mother *was* right about you," Jonathan cried. He plopped back down on his couch after circling it about twenty times.

"Pastor never liked me anyway. She told me I had shifty eyes and couldn't be trusted after I gave birth to Amina. That's one of the reasons I couldn't marry you. She was always talking about how I was no good for you, and it was obvious that she didn't like me. Do you remember all of those times you would tell me that your mom didn't approve of me?" Sherry's tone turned from arrogant to sad, as if she'd had a glimpse of yesterdays gone by.

"You were supposed to love me enough to fight for us like I was prepared to fight for a life with you and my daughter. We talked about getting married, Sherry, and you just flipped the script on me. And now after all of these years, you have the nerve to tell me that Amina isn't mine." Jonathan dropped his head and cried. "I'm the only daddy that she knows, and now you're ripping that away from me too. Our lives, our existence has been nothing more than a lie."

Sherry listened intently to what Jonathan was saying, but she couldn't turn back the hands of time for him or for them. She'd always wondered throughout the years how Amina was doing or if she had looked anything like her biological father who was in the bathroom taking a shower at the moment. Sherry heard Alvin cut off the water in the bathroom, and she panicked. She'd been quiet for so long, Jonathan wondered if she were still on the line.

"Hello, are you still there, Sherry?" Jonathan had come down from his tirade and was depleted of all energy and feeling.

When Sherry responded it was almost impossible for him to hear her. "Yes, I'm here," she whispered with the reality of her wrongdoing crashing down around her for the first time in almost twenty-three years.

"I have to know one thing. How do you know that Amina isn't my daughter? I mean, do you *really* know, or are you grasping for straws to tear my family up? Are you on some vindictive kind of ish to destroy the one thing I've always believed in, and that's my daughter's life? Really, you destroyed mine the day you came to my mother's home and told me that you didn't want to marry me or be Amina's mother." Jonathan felt anger's slow burn begin to reignite within him, and he was ready for round two.

"Look, Jonathan, the truth is you and I slept together one time, but I was sleeping with Alvin Bass for months before you, and then after you. We've been together ever since, and while I know that this hurts, I had just had my period when you and I had relations. So there's no way that Amina can be your biological daughter. I know it's jacked up of me to bring this out after all of this time, but Alvin wants to be in his daughter's life now. We're both recovering drug addicts. We left long ago because Alvin had gotten into some trouble with the law because of his addiction, and, well, my love for him plus my drug dependence had me chasing behind him."

Jonathan sat and listened to all that Sherry had to say, and the wheels in his mind began to turn. "So everything my mother told me about you was true? Alvin? Alvin from high school, the same dude that was a troublemaker, you fell for *him*? I loved you with all of me and you were just playing with my heart. I was on the road to self-destruction after you broke things off with me, and now the truth comes out. That's why your mother continued telling my family that she didn't know where you were or hadn't spoken with you. Did she know that Amina wasn't my daughter too? Did she know that you were into drugs?" Jonathan shook his head so hard, hoping that he could erase everything from his past.

"When I first saw Amina, I knew that she was Alvin's daughter because aside from the features that she and I share, she's the spitting image of her father. And to answer your question, Mommy knew nothing about any of this. My intent was to come here and try to make things right with the people I care about, and that included coming clean to my mother. I don't think that she'll ever forgive me; she pretty much told me as much. I'm hoping that you will forgive me one day, and that Amina doesn't hate me forever. Jonathan, I promise that I'm only here to give Amina a choice that I had never given her in the past, and that's a chance to know her mother and father." Sherry was in tears.

Not able to sit still, Jonathan couldn't listen to anymore. Standing up, he hit the END button on the phone and allowed it to drop to the floor. Running into his bedroom, he pulled out his suitcases and began throwing clothes into the bags. Not caring if they were folded or not, he just filled up each piece of luggage and zipped it shut. Tears flowed like a river from his eyes as he said to himself, "And to think that I was just beginning to change my mind about God . . . I don't care anymore about anything." He stopped what he was doing and dropped to his knees feeling as if his heart would cave in at any moment. Then he released earth-shattering wails into the atmosphere.

Chapter 23

The hot and muggy summer days melted into a cooler-than-usual fall season. Melissa welcomed the turning of the leaves on the trees. During her alone time and after doing lots of thinking, she had finally begun to take responsibility for her actions and pregnancy. She'd shut the world off the last few weeks and had become a recluse, only leaving home for doctor's visits and grocery store runs. Trina checked in every couple of days and would try to encourage her.

After giving out assignments to her remaining stylists to take over and handle all business matters until further notice, Melissa exhaled. She had mixed emotions, but at that moment, she was happy, glad that her pregnancy would be over within the next month if her baby met his due date. Melissa couldn't deny that she was also stricken with moments of guilt and sadness about her unborn son's condition.

The sun shone through her curtains in her bedroom giving an orange glow throughout the room. Kicking the sheets off of her feet, Melissa was way past finding any comfort lying down. For the last few months, she had to resort to lying on her side, or in a fetal position with pillows between her legs. Her internal alarm clock buzzed at seven a.m., as if she was going into the salon, and she willed it to shut off in her mind. Sticky goo coated her eyelids, and instinctively she rubbed her eyes trying to wipe away the sleep.

Moaning, Melissa rolled over to the side and glanced at the bright red numbers on the alarm clock. Her belly ached, and when she looked down, she could see that the baby was balled up to the left side. "What are you doing in there, Shalimar?" Melissa talked to the baby while rubbing her belly, trying to get him to move around and stop causing her so much discomfort.

After putting a halt to the drinking and self-medicating, Melissa was actually able to bond with the baby. She no longer felt ashamed of her son, nor did she feel like she couldn't make it. Determination replaced her doubt each time she felt her baby kicking and moving around inside of her. Melissa didn't know when it happened, but her mind was changing, and she had faith to know that because God had blessed her womb, that He could still turn the situation around.

Instead of hitting the snooze button on the clock, Melissa turned it off altogether. "Hmm, don't need to be on anyone's schedule anytime soon. It's just you and me, li'l man. You wanna help Mommy clean up the house? We've got to get your room ready, baby boy. I hope that your daddy will be able to come over here and play house for a while." Melissa laughed, doubting that Nathaniel was interested in playing house or anything else with her. Not that it mattered, but she'd been calling and leaving messages most of the week, and if he didn't respond soon, Melissa knew what *would* get results.

The phone rang, and she knew who was on the other end by the ringtone. She skipped to her bed where she heard the phone ringing, but didn't see it. The phone continued to sing out, "Pieces of Me." By the time Melissa had torn the bed up to retrieve the phone, he had hung up. "Ughh, I hate that I missed his call, and I hope that he left a message." She rubbed her baby bump and talked in a calmer tone when she spoke to her belly.

"Shalimar, Mommy's li'l baby boy." Melissa rocked him from side to side as she waddled to the living room and sat down in her rocking/recliner chair. She pressed the number and placed the phone to the side of her head. Melissa cradled the phone between her shoulder and chin. Frowning at the phone upon seeing that Nathaniel hadn't left a message, she called him. His phone rang and rang until Melissa had to leave yet another voice mail for him. "Ughh, why can't he just answer the phone? I mean, he *just* called." She tossed the phone onto the floor, instantly regretting it because that meant she would be the one who'd have to pick the phone up at some point.

Melissa had taken a shower and even fixed a little breakfast when she heard honking horns outside. It sounded like someone was going to drive straight into her house. She scurried to the back of the house since it sounded like the front of the house would be taken down by the vehicles approaching. Next, the doorbell began ringing, and Melissa had to catch her breath before peeping out the window to see what was going on. What she saw brought tears to her eyes.

The sun nearly blinded Melissa when she opened the door to see a shiny pickup truck with baby furniture tied down and covered with plastic. She shielded her eyes in order to be able to make out the face of the person standing on the front porch. "Hi, Melissa, I hope that you don't mind me coming over here with Nathaniel to help you set up your nursery," Serena said with a small smile on her face.

Melissa couldn't hide her shock. "Why are you here?"

Serena looked taken aback, and Melissa didn't miss the dark hue that covered Serena's eyes for a moment until she blinked it away. They stood there just looking at each other with their pregnant bellies reminding them of why they would always be connected. In the nick of time, Nathaniel and Trina showed up. There was an awkward silence hanging in the air until Trina spoke up.

"Girl, what are we going to have to do to get inside and get this baby nursery together?" Trina snapped her neck in Melissa's direction with a smile filling her face. "You know I ain't got all day. My standing appointment at Spa Nails is next on my to-do list, so I need to get in and out of here, chile. Now move over so that the guys can begin moving this stuff in here. You're wasting valuable time. If there's something you two need to discuss, you can do it inside and out of harm's way." Trina moved Melissa out of the way and shouted to the movers, "Come on in, guys; this way."

"Melissa, I'm sorry I wasn't able to get ahold of you before now. I tried to warn you that we would be coming over." Nathaniel was uncomfortable to have to see his wife standing in the presence of his sin once again. There was nothing he could do but to bring Serena along because he wanted her to trust him again. He took the limits off to make that happen.

"Yeah, you should have made sure you talked to me before having your *wife* come to my home," Melissa responded tersely. Her eyes were near crossed, but what could she do? Serena should have been kicking her tail for plotting on her husband, but instead of anger, Serena was trying to offer an olive branch. The problem was that Melissa was still a woman scorned, and she didn't want to become buddy-buddy with them, regardless of the fact that their kids would be related.

Nathaniel stepped up and asked, "What's it going to be, Melissa? All of this was Serena's idea." He swooped his arms in a circling motion to show that the furniture was his wife's idea and not his. "Are you prepared for

Shalimar's arrival into the world?" His facial expression said that he doubted it.

Serena felt a kick when she heard Nathaniel say his son's name. His voice had dropped an octave or two lower, and there it was . . . love and tenderness. The blood in her body seemed to drain right down to her feet, and it took her down with it. "Oh my goodness, Serena!" Nathaniel screamed and jumped toward her, and, as always, he caught her fall. Looking at her with fear in his eyes, tears instantly fell. He felt so bad for bringing her, but she wouldn't have it any other way. "Can I take her inside? I need to lay her down," Nathaniel yelled at Melissa who stood stark still as if she'd seen a ghost.

Snapping out of it, Melissa answered saying, "Sure, take her into the living room and lay her down on the couch. Do I need to do anything? Is there anything I can do to help?" Melissa felt her iciness melting as she thought about all she'd done to try to hurt Serena . . . and regret was left.

Trina heard Nathaniel's loud screams, and she almost bumped into the mover to get back to the front of the house with frantic thoughts of what could have happened. When she reached the living room, she saw that Melissa was standing over Nathaniel, holding out a wet cloth to him. He was perched on his knees checking Serena's pulse.

"Do I need to call nine-one-one?" Melissa asked after Serena still hadn't come to.

"I need to get these movers out of here." Trina went to the back room and explained to the movers that there was a medical emergency and that they would be called later to return and put the furniture together within the week. She took their card and escorted them to the front of the house where they could finish unloading the truck and putting things into the garage.

"Serena? Serena, baby, please wake up." Nathaniel hovered over her.

Melissa called for an ambulance. Her nerves were frayed, and she actually felt a blanket of shame of how she'd acted toward Serena all of those times. It wasn't Serena who had hurt her or broke her heart; it was Nathaniel, yet, she took it out on Serena. She'd known that the cancer had come back, and instead of praying for Serena or even offering her an apology for her part in what she'd done, she continued to spew hatred and jealousy.

Trina came back into the house to see Melissa crying quietly as she watched for the arrival of the emergency squad through the living-room window. Although Trina wasn't sure why her best friend was crying, she felt that this time her tears weren't for herself, but for Serena. She may never know how right she was. It seemed like an eternity for the paramedics to arrive, but when they did, they worked expediently and efficiently, taking Serena's vital signs and loading her up to rush her to Chapel Hill to try to save her life.

Chapter 24

Crystal had taken a leave from church matters while Serena recovered at home. She cooked, cleaned, and tried to make Serena as comfortable as could be expected. The pregnancy and the cancer were wreaking havoc on Serena, and she'd begun to lose weight again. Teary-eyed, Crystal thought about the day they all went to eat and Serena was eating off of each of their plates, including her own food. She wondered if she'd ever be afforded another opportunity to see her daughter indulging in a good meal.

Time waited for no one, and Crystal was determined to take any time given to remain by her daughter's side. It provided her some comfort being able to be there since she'd neglected to give her kids enough of her while they were growing up. She was always busy, running the church and making sure the lives of others were intact, yet leaving her own home in shambles. Her kids felt as if they were at the bottom of her to-do list, and she knew that it was hard on them losing their father when they were young.

Emotional turmoil was the space Crystal dwelled in since she hadn't heard from Jonathan after their meeting at the church. He'd left her there after blaming her for keeping her suspicions to herself instead of telling him, like she'd done everything else. He went off on a rampage as he hurled words at her that stabbed liked daggers. It had taken her back to the time before he'd been in the accident, almost killing himself.

Hours had passed by before Crystal left the church. She was inside alone crying and praying to God. She walked the expanse of the church and ended up in the sanctuary down at the altar. Her fears of Jonathan returning to the alcohol had crept up inside of her psyche. Her praying and travailing in the presence of God was the result in her behind-the-veil experience, where she was able to receive spiritual foresight on what was to come concerning her son.

Nathaniel entered into the kitchen and saw Crystal sitting there looking afar off. His heart burst with love for her as he stood by watching and thanking God for her. He knew that she was fully aware of what he'd done. Standing in her presence made him feel less than a man because she was his pastor, spiritual leader, and mother-in-law, and he knew that his actions cut her deeply. He'd made a decision to have the talk with her about all of his issues because he felt that he owed her an apology as well.

"Hey, Mom," Nathaniel said strolling into the kitchen. He knew that something was heavy on her mind, and while he didn't want to disturb that, he had some things on his mind also.

Crystal jumped as she heard her name being called and turned around to see her son-in-law leaning on the island watching her intently. Sadness laced her face, and she gave him a lopsided smile. Looking past Nathaniel, Crystal got up and moved around, attempting to calm her nerves as Jonathan lingered on her mind and in her spirit. She was able to look at her son-in-law with love despite the mistakes he had made. She admired his quiet strength, which spoke volumes to her spirit.

"Oh, I'm sorry to scare you. I needed to talk to you if you care to." Nathaniel rubbed his bald head, and the stubble that pricked his fingers reminded him of the need for a visit to his barber soon. He peeked up at Crystal as he waited for her to either come back to the table or tell him that it wasn't a good time. When she smiled, he relaxed and walked over to the table and sat down.

"Do you want something to drink before I join you at the table?" Crystal asked, pulling out two glasses from the cabinet.

Nathaniel stood to head to the refrigerator, but Crystal held him at bay saying, "Sit, son, I got this."

"Sure, if you don't mind. I'd like some of your famous iced tea," he smiled.

Once she was seated and Nathaniel had her undivided attention, he grabbed her hands and dropped his head. When he raised his eyes to hers, there were tears in his, and when she saw him, tears sprang up in her eyes as well. Silently, Nathaniel poured out his heart to Crystal, and after the silence became overwhelming he spoke. He never heard Serena come into the kitchen and hear his confessions about what had broken him down and pushed him out. How he was going through the difficulties too, but he felt alienated by Serena.

"Mom, I'm so sorry." He shook his head at himself. "I'm so ashamed that I fell so short of the glory of God. I never wanted to hurt Him, Serena, or any of you by my selfishness. Had I come to you and trusted you with what I was going through, then maybe none of this would have happened."

Crystal almost felt sorry for Nathaniel. She couldn't help but to forgive him and love him unconditionally. If Serena could forgive him, then surely she had to. She preached forgiveness constantly in her ministry, and she'd had to be forgiven of some stuff many times herself. She didn't respond verbally to Nathaniel, but she stood up and went to him. He stood, and she gave him the biggest hug and told him, "It is well."

Serena sat on the stool near her, tired from eavesdropping. She cried silent tears and rubbed her belly. The baby leaped around inside of her stomach, growing, and no doubt, smelling the chicken gumbo that Crystal had made. To see two of the people she loved the most sharing an intimate moment of reconciliation did Serena's heart good. Tears welled up in her eyes as she felt compelled to sit quietly watching her mother and husband as they shared their moment of reconciliation. They stood and hugged with tears of joy rolling down their faces. When Crystal lifted her eyes to see Serena sitting there, she winked at her daughter.

Chapter 25

The audio system was on, and the whole church had been invited to Serena's surprise baby shower. Music poured from the speakers, and Sister Edna and the rest of the baby shower committee danced around one another putting the last touches on the fellowship hall. Edna stood back to admire the handiwork of the little elves who worked to make sure that everything was in order for the joyous occasion.

"Sister Edna, the photographer is here and wants to know where he can set up." Sister Felisha flitted around in a rush.

"Um, just tell Mr. Drake that he can set up back near the rear of the hall. The guest of honor will be seated there in her royal chair for the duration of the shower. Now, is there anything else, because I need to go into the kitchen and check on the caterers?" Edna didn't have time to waste since they only had three hours to set the party up before the Jacksons arrived. Her first priority was that Crystal never doubted her ability again.

"Okay, that's what I needed to know," Felisha said before walking back toward the photographer. She admired his height and his golden brown face that housed a cleft in his chin. Mentally, Felisha sized him up and thought to herself that he looked like a good catch. She grinned as she wondered where she'd seen him before.

"Mr. Drake, thanks for waiting for me to find out where you could set up shop. If you will follow me this way, I'll be more than happy to show you where you will be today." Felisha flashed him the biggest smile.

"Please call me Damien." He extended his hand out to shake Felisha's.

"Oh, okay, Damien, please forgive me for my lack of manners. I'm Sister Felisha Green, but you can just call me Sister Felisha," she said with a dreamy look on her face. She smelled a heavenly fragrance coming from Damien as his arm swooshed in front of her.

"After you, my lady, I'm right behind you." Damien moved to the side so that she could lead the way. He had a huge grin on his face.

Felisha felt like she was in the movie, *Waiting to Exhale,* when Gloria was walking away from Marvin. She added an extra twist to her walk, knowing that he was watching her. She giggled to herself, blushing and hoping that the fine man would be interested in her.

Damien was ecstatic that he didn't have all of his extra photo equipment to lug around because he wanted to stay close to the sister. Her silent flirtation wasn't missed, and he was determined to get her phone number before leaving the function. Damien was happy that he'd already been to the church to scope it out the week before when he had attended Sunday services. He loved everything about the ministry, and he was totally impressed with the pastor.

"Here you are." Felisha turned 180 degrees to face the handsome photographer. "Is this spot good enough for you?" she asked. "We need you in this area because the guest of honor will be here." Felisha pointed to the chair that was decorated in silver for Serena.

Damien almost bumped into Felisha when she abruptly stopped walking. He was mesmerized by her beauty and had gotten caught up. He stopped before stepping on the back of her ivory slingbacks. "Oh, I'm sorry that

I almost ran you over." Embarrassment colored his cheeks, and he smiled sheepishly. "I was just admiring the view, and I can tell you that what I've seen looks good." Damien turned 360 degrees, seemingly taking in the scene. "I mean, the fellowship hall is decorated beautifully. I'm confident that I will have some good shots by the end of the day."

"I'm happy to hear that you like what you see. It just means that we took great care in preparing all of this." Felisha swung her arms around in a circular motion. "If you need anything, please don't hesitate to let me know. I hope that you don't mind me appointing myself as your point of contact for the afternoon and evening. But now, I've got to get moving. There are some things that need my attention. Make yourself at home, and there's a chair right behind you if you want to rest yourself." Felisha flashed her pearly whites at Damien before walking away.

Tables were decorated with assorted candies, cookies, cupcakes, and ribbons with big plastic safety pins laid out. Everything pointed to Baby Jackson being a blessed and well taken care of little bundle of joy. The musician showed up and began to play his saxophone. Since the shower was happening in the fellowship hall, the anointed instrument player played many of the old R&B songs from back in the day, beginning with the seventies, and then moved up by decade.

It was a beautiful day outside. The sun shone brightly but provided little warmth, which was evident when the guests filing into the building came bundled up. And those who weren't dressed for the cold were rubbing their hands together trying to ward off the chill. By late that afternoon the festivities were set to begin. The hall at Abiding Savior was brimming with ladies, and even some of their husbands were there to support Nathaniel and Serena.

Some came because they truly cared for their pastor and her family, while many others were there just to be seen and for their own guilty pleasures, seeking drama. Not that any of that mattered because they all received the wish list that was provided by Amina, and in order to get into the soiree, everyone had to present a gift. Edna had outdone herself, and she could finally exhale when Serena and family showed up.

Chapter 26

Serena was getting dressed in the beautiful maternity outfit that Nathaniel had presented her with earlier that day. She was surprised because she didn't believe that she had anyplace to wear the fuchsia-colored top with flowing sleeves that stopped midarm and the black palazzo pants with the flare leg. It was times like those that Serena wished that the cancer had never returned. She wanted to be able to watch her baby grow into a beautiful little girl or handsome little boy. It was the toughest decision for her to make, but she didn't think twice about giving her unborn baby a chance at life.

Dr. Sinclair wanted to see her in the clinic every week. They'd recently come up with the plan to induce Serena's labor on December the fifteenth in hopes of having a healthy baby despite the expected early arrival. Serena was pretty comfortable with the plan, but she couldn't help but to worry about how much time she would have with her child. Not knowing the length of time she had left had robbed Serena of her peace.

Nathaniel sat on the edge of their bed feeling good for the first time in months. He stared at Serena in awe, just as he did every time he laid eyes on her. In his mind, he traveled back in time to when they were standing at the altar. He cried unashamedly because he'd never known a love like that before. In the beginning, Serena played hard to get, but Nathaniel knew why and was determined not to make the same mistakes so many men made concerning their wives. Despite all of his good intentions, however, he'd become just like those men. Nathaniel's mind was still boggled trying to figure out why they would leave home for something out in the streets.

"Baby, you are so beautiful. Please tell me you are going to wear your outfit this afternoon," Nathaniel said, alluding to an outing someplace, but not saying where to.

"Honey, I don't have any plans to leave the house today. You know I have to reserve my energy for around the house, and all I want to do is lie around and enjoy our little one." Serena smiled placing her hand on her belly. She walked over to Nathaniel's opened arms and placed a kiss on his lips.

"Come on, I want to take you out. We need a break from the monotony of our mundane existence. I'm tired of sitting in the house, and I want to take my favorite girl out to show her how special she is." Nathaniel smiled, hoping that his tactics were working.

"Nathaniel, look at my hair. It's a mess, and I can't get an appointment on such short notice." Serena looked hopeless.

"Mami, your hair is fine. You have no reason to be self-conscious, because everything about you is still fine to me. Unless you're worried about what the other fellas will think when they see you." He smiled at his wife, taking in the physical changes she was going through. She may have looked as fragile as a porcelain doll, but she was the strongest woman he'd ever met.

"Boy, please, ain't nobody checking for me," she laughed.

"Nobody needs to be checking for you because I've got that covered." Nathaniel stood and swept Serena up in his arms. "Baby, I need you, is that all right? I promise that I'll be gentle." His eyes pleaded with her.

Serena may have been tired, but she smiled at Nathaniel. Peering into his eyes, she could see his need, and she nodded her head before wrapping her arms around his neck and giving him a kiss. She wanted to be there for him in whatever way he needed her since she needed him too. That moment was just what the doctor ordered. The glow that flowed over Serena made her look almost angelic.

Afterward, Nathaniel finally talked her into getting dressed and going out. She had no idea of the baby shower planned for her. He felt like he could walk on air, he was so happy.

An hour later, Nathaniel, fully dressed, waited on Serena to get ready. He watched his wife primping in the mirror and said, "Serena, I'm going out to the car to check the oil and make sure that it's clean before we leave. I need for you to put some pep in your step so that we can get on out of here. I have reservations, and I'd hate to lose out because you're being the diva." Nathaniel tapped his watch on his wrist before leaving the room. He needed to call the church while he was checking the car to make sure that there was nothing in the trunk that didn't need to be there so that he could load it down with gifts.

Turning his phone on with one hand, he blew on the other due to the frigid chill. He opened the trunk of the car and leaned in to rearrange some files, which were the only things in there. His phone vibrated, and he looked at his phone to see who it was. He snapped his neck up and banged his head on the trunk door. "Ouch!" he muttered. Nathaniel grabbed his head and rubbed it. "Oh my God, this can't be happening. Not today, Lord, not today. Please! What a cruel joke . . ."

Nathaniel's phone screen read, I'm in labor. Please be here when your son comes into this world. He's going to need the support of both parents as he will be fighting for his life. We're at Duke Hospital, and the baby's going to be prepped for surgery after he's born. His phone continued to vibrate in his hand, but he couldn't get his thoughts together. He calculated in his mind that Shalimar's due date was still a few weeks away. Nathaniel's heart raced as he wondered if Shalimar's early birth would cause more harm to his life. Despite the cold air that whipped past Nathaniel's body just a moment ago, his hands grew sweaty.

The ringing of his cell phone brought him out of his trance. He didn't look at the caller ID before answering. "Hello?" His voice shook.

"Is everything all right, son?" Crystal asked fearfully, reacting to the strange sound in Nathaniel's voice.

"Mom, I don't know what to do," Nathaniel said.

"What's going on? Is it Serena? You all didn't get into a fight, did you? Is she feeling okay? What is it?"

"It's not Serena, and we're fine. Well, we were before I came out to prep the car before we head to the church. It's Melissa. She's in labor, and she needs for me to be there. I don't know what to do. The baby is in real danger of not surviving and has to have immediate surgery to determine what form of spina bifida Shalimar has. I need to get Serena to the church, but I can't be in two places at the same time." Nathaniel rubbed his head and paced back and forth near the rear of the car.

"Have you spoken to Melissa yet?" Crystal rolled her eyes up into her head. She was determined that nothing would ruin Serena's day. It seemed like every time she turned around, Melissa was in the midst of something. On the other hand, she felt sad for Melissa. Crystal knew that she had a responsibility to Melissa as her spiritual head. It would be a shame and disgrace if Crystal allowed what Melissa plotted to stand in the way of what's right in the eyesight of God.

"I haven't spoken to her yet." Nathaniel continued to pace. "I'm going to reach out to her to see if she can talk. I'm hoping that Trina is there with her because she doesn't need to be alone during this." The high that Nathaniel was feeling before leaving the house left him feeling deflated, nervous, and sad. His mind was boggled with thoughts of becoming a father within the next few hours.

"You just get Serena to the church. It's almost five o'clock. I'll call Sister Edna to let her know you all are on the way."

"Mom, I would feel terrible if something happens to my son, and I'm not there for Melissa. I know she's been foul in the past, but I believe that she's ready to move past all of this. I know that she's afraid that our son won't have a fighting chance. I'm partly to blame for all of this turmoil, so I need to stand up and be accountable." Nathaniel looked around in a daze.

"Nothing and no one is going to ruin this day for my baby. Now, I'm sorry that Melissa is going through this, but your place is to be with your wife first. Please, son, help Serena to celebrate as if she was the only one on your mind today. I will go to the hospital to check on Melissa, and then will go to the church. Is she at UNC?"

"No, ma'am." Nathaniel sighed, feeling defeated. He was stuck in between a rock and a hard place. "She's at Duke. You know they have a great specialty hospital for children there, so she opted to go there instead."

"Okay, I'll go over there to get a report, pray with her, and then I'll head on over to the church for the shower. And, son?"

Nathaniel couldn't help but to feel like his world was coming to an end. He couldn't enjoy the fact that he had a child coming into the world. A son who would carry on the Jackson name and legacy was all he'd ever wanted. He tried to combat the sound in his spirit saying, *Ishmael is not the promise*, by inhaling loudly, and then exhaling. "Yes, ma'am," he said.

"Just remember that God is in control and has the last say. Now, please, get in there and talk to her about what's going on. You should make the decision together on whether you go to the shower. I will be praying that whatever happens, that the baby won't come into this world until you arrive. I love you, son. Talk with you soon." Crystal disconnected the call without awaiting a reply.

"Honey, you've been out here a long time. Is everything all right with the car?" Serena asked standing at the opened front door.

"Sweetie, are you ready to go yet?" Nathaniel asked, sounding strange even to himself. He had since moved around to the front of the car and was stooped inside.

"I thought you were coming back inside before we leave for dinner. It's getting late, and I'd hate for us to lose out on the reservation that you were so adamant about earlier." Serena stood there discerning that something was amiss but couldn't put her finger on it. Instead of pressing him about it, she went back into the house and gathered her things. "Lord, please don't let anything else be going on. I pray that whatever it is, if anything, that you will reveal it quickly. Amen."

Nathaniel still hadn't gone back into the house by the time Serena reached the car. It was as if when she put her hand on the door handle to let herself into the car, Nathaniel sprang out of the other side of the car. She watched his movements and focused on his body language since it seemed as if he'd purposely shielded his face from her by cupping his hands to his mouth and dipping his head down into them.

Nathaniel sprinted into the house and began walking through the house in a panic. "Lord what do I do now? I can't disappoint Serena, and I can't just leave Melissa to have our baby all alone."

He could feel his heart breaking as he was torn in two. He didn't know what it would do to Serena if he went back out there and told her what was going on.

The blowing car horn alerted him to Serena's impatience of being left outside in the car for too long. "Now she's really going to be suspicious, and I'm going to have to tell her." Fear gripped him, and he grabbed for his chest as pain shot through it. Not sure if he wanted to live or die at that moment, he figured the latter may be better than him having to ruin Serena's day. It was supposed to be her day, but once again, everything was all messed up.

"What Love," the ring tone sounded from inside of Nathaniel's pants pocket. He fished his hand around in his pocket and pulled the phone out. Without looking at the caller ID, he pressed the talk button. It was Serena's favorite song and Nathaniel had assigned that song to her contact number. At that moment, he wished that he'd already made his phone call to Melissa to at least check on her, and then to the church. But before Nathaniel could say anything, Serena's voice blared through his earpiece.

"Nathaniel, *what* is going on with you? First, you leave me in the house for God knows how long, and then you're acting all strange when I come outside. Now, *you're* inside, and it doesn't look like you're coming out anytime soon," she fumed into his earpiece.

"Baby, I'm so sorry. I'm coming, and then I'll need to talk to you about something," he said with sadness in his voice.

Serena heard the heaviness in his words, and it frightened her. She knew something was up when she was waiting on him to come back in, but his delay bothered her. She had looked out the window to see him pacing and hovering down in the car with his phone glued to his face.

Melissa. "Um, well, okay. How long will you be?" she asked, hoping that his delay would give her time to get herself together. Anxiety transferred to the baby as it began to move around, kicking her in her ribs and balling up on one side, then the other.

Nathaniel shook the feeling of fear that threatened to paralyze him. He gulped before speaking, "I should be out in five minutes or less," he answered nervously.

Disconnecting the call, Serena's phone fell from her limp fingers, hitting her stomach, and she hollered. "Ouch," she hissed into the empty car, rubbing the spot that the cell phone landed. She wanted to pray, but the words wouldn't come. Serena hit the buttons on the stereo looking for some holiday music, which was her favorite. She hoped listening to it would calm her nerves since nothing else was working at the time.

Nathaniel rushed back to the car, knowing that they were super late to the shower.

Nervousness coursed through his being as he thought about Melissa. Not hearing back from Crystal about Melissa's condition made him extremely nervous. He couldn't stall any longer, but at least he'd called the church and spoken with Edna briefly to let her know that they were on the way.

"Baby, I'm sorry that I've kept you waiting." Nathaniel looked at Serena apologetically.

Serena just looked at him as if he'd lost his mind. She was almost ready to go back into the house, lock him out of her room again, and jump back into the bed where she had wanted to be anyway. However, she needed to know what was going on with Melissa. Serena was very intuitive and sure of what she'd felt drop in her spirit. All she needed was the confirmation, and it was going to come by way of Nathaniel.

"You said that there was something that you needed to talk to me about," Serena said trying to remain calm.

Nathaniel kept his eyes on the steering wheel as he backed out of the driveway. He avoided her gaze for as long as possible, and when he pulled out into the oncoming traffic, he slowly let out a long sigh.

"Nathaniel, are you going to tell me what's going on, or must I guess?" Serena shifted sideways in her seat in order to look at him before continuing. "Because if I were a betting woman, I'd say that whatever has got you so rattled has something to do with Melissa."

"I didn't want to ruin this day for you." Nathaniel couldn't look at Serena, so he gazed out the window in front of him. "When I woke up this morning, my plans were to surprise you and take you someplace special. That's what I'm doing, and I promise as soon as you have had your moment, then I will let you know what's going on." He patted her leg and turned, driving quietly toward the church.

"Why are going to the church? And what are all of these cars doing here? Are we having a service that I didn't know about? I really wanted to stay in today, and now I'm really not up to being all up in folks' faces." Serena's mind was still on what the big secret was about Melissa, but before she knew it, Nathaniel had the car parked, and she was being ushered inside for her baby shower.

Upon entering the fellowship hall, the *oohs* and *ahhs* began as the surprised Serena stopped at the threshold in shock. She looked around at the sea of faces and examined the exquisite ambiance of the room. It finally dawned on her that the celebration was for her. Tears streamed down her face as Nathaniel escorted her behind Edna to her royal chair which was decorated in silver.

Edna called everyone to attention, and the celebration began. There was an array of colorful foods and desserts. Serena sat in awe of the outpouring of love and support from so many in the church. Everyone seemed to be having the best time and presents were lined from wall to wall in all shapes and sizes.

Nathaniel sat alongside of Serena trying to get his mind off of Melissa and the baby, but he couldn't. Crystal hadn't arrived yet, and he had been checking his phone every few minutes to see if she had at least called. He knew that he wouldn't be able to sit still much longer and so when the food was being served, he pulled up to Serena. She felt him come close and exhaled, waiting for the news he'd been wanting to share.

Amid all of the people coming by with well wishes for the couple, Serena wished that they would go somewhere else and sit down so that Nathaniel could tell her what was going on. The more she thought about it, she'd wondered where her family was. Something didn't seem right, and she hoped that he'd hurry up and fill her in.

"Baby, remember on the way here I told you there was something that I needed to talk to you about?" Nathaniel rubbed his sweaty palms together.

Serena's lopsided smile sat on the corners of her mouth, but looked more like she'd tasted something sour. "Yes, I remember. I haven't been able to fully enjoy myself in anticipation of what's going on with you and Melissa," she said tersely.

Felisha walked up to them and asked, "Prophetess, would you like for me to fix you a plate? Brother Nathaniel, can I get you anything?" she asked respectfully, feeling a tinge of sorrow for all that Serena had to go through.

"Nothing for me," Serena said, smiling misty-eyed. She was glad that her rumbling stomach couldn't be heard over the laughter and music. Nerves wouldn't allow her to eat a thing. She hoped that she wouldn't have to keep up the façade much longer.

Nathaniel shook his head no and smiled at Felisha who took that as her cue to leave.

"I know you're wondering what's going on, and, well, while I was outside preparing to make this day all about you, I was going to call the church to let Sister Edna know we were on the way, but instead, I had a message from Melissa saying that she's in labor and needed me to be there with her." Nathaniel took Serena's hand in his, hoping that she didn't pull away.

Serena knew that her gut feelings were correct, and it saddened her that this is how things would be for the rest of her days. Melissa would always be a part of their lives. She thought she had made her peace about it, but sitting here at her own baby shower, the realization of knowing that she wouldn't really ever get over what happened slapped her in the face.

"I know you're wondering why Mom isn't here. She called me to check on us before heading to the church, and I told her what was going on. She offered to go to the hospital and pray with Melissa. I'm assuming that Amina is with her. I'm aware that this isn't the best time for me to pick up and leave, but I have got to be there to support her. She's going through a lot right now, and I would never be able to forgive myself if something happens to my son, and I'm not there," Nathaniel said solemnly.

"Then you should go. If you can just take me home first, I'll wait until you can call me with an update on what's going on."

Nathaniel couldn't look into Serena's eyes because he was afraid that he would see pain in them. He rubbed her hands and held onto her ring finger. Fingering her wedding band, he bit his bottom lip to hold back his emotion. "Baby, I need you to come with me. I want you there. I don't think I can do this without you."

Serena was surprised at Nathaniel's public display of emotion. A tear fell from her eye onto their joined hands. She wanted to be with him, but she was afraid.

Oblivious of the stares of those who sat around them, Serena kissed Nathaniel and said, "Let's go."

Nathaniel pulled Edna over to him and told her that they hated to have to leave, but a family emergency came up and asked if she would let everyone know that they appreciated the love, gifts, and would be sending a thank-you card later. As Edna made the announcement to their guests that an emergency had occurred and that Nathaniel and Serena would have to leave, Nathaniel helped Serena get up and back to the car, and then they headed to the hospital.

Chapter 27

Nurses were hustling in and out of the hospital room when Nathaniel got to Melissa's room and his heart raced. As he walked down the shiny floors of the hospital ward with his shoes clacking against the tiles, he hurried into the room where Crystal, Trina, and Amina stood off to the side. He nodded to them without speaking.

"And you are . . .?" a nurse stepped to Nathaniel when he entered with a bewildered look on his face.

"I'm the baby's father, Nathaniel Jackson." He held his hand out to shake hers.

"Awesome, I'm Nurse Denise and you, sir, got here just in time. We're about to take Melissa in for surgery. Did you want to scrub in? I'm sure that Ms. Wright will need your support. If you don't mind walking over here with me for a moment, there are some things that I need to let you know beforehand," Denise rushed on.

"Well, can you give me a moment to go over and speak to my family and my son's mother?" Nathaniel didn't wait for a reply as he moved over to speak to his mother-in-law, niece, and Trina. "How is she?" He nodded his head in Melissa's direction. The beeping machines gave him flashbacks of when Serena was in the hospital, and it gave him the eeriest of feelings.

Crystal was the first to speak, "She's been trying to hold on to the baby, but he's in distress, and unfortunately, she's going to need to have an emergency C-section. I let her know that you would be here as soon as possible. Do you need me here any longer?" Crystal asked.

Running his hands over his smooth baldness, Nathaniel exhaled with jitters in his belly once again. "Well, Serena is in the waiting room, so if you all will excuse Melissa and me, we can talk with the nurse and get this thing over with." Nathaniel turned toward Crystal and said, "Mom, Amina, thanks so much for standing in for me until I could get here." Turning to address Trina for the first time, he said, "Thank you for being the best godmother in the world and Melissa's best friend." He leaned over and hugged her lightly. "I'd like for you all to stay if you can, but right now, I need to speak with Melissa and the nurse alone."

Moments later, Nathaniel stood at Melissa's bedside as the nurse filled him in on the precarious situation that the baby was in. Once she left the room, he looked at Melissa's teary face and squeezed her shoulder. "How are you holding up?" he asked with sincerity in his eyes.

"Nathaniel, I'm scared. What if our son doesn't make it? What if I have to go home alone without my baby?" she asked hysterically.

"Shhh, that's not going to be the case. We have to think positively." He reached over to rub her hair down. Her disheveled look painted a picture of wariness and fear.

"Nathaniel, this situation is my fault. Had I not tried to pursue you after you married Serena, we wouldn't be here right now. I was foolish enough to think that having your child would bring you to me. When that didn't work out in my favor, I tried drinking myself to death, knowing that our son's life was already in jeopardy," she cried.

"Look at me." Nathaniel turned Melissa's face toward him so that he could be sure that she heard everything that he needed to say in the last crucial moments before their child made his entrance into the world.

Melissa struggled to focus on Nathaniel's face through the tears that profusely spilled from her eyes. She was so afraid of what was getting ready to happen that she started snatching the covers from her body, exposing her swollen belly and worn blue and grey hospital gown.

"Whoa, hold on. Where do you think you're going?" Nathaniel asked as the machines began beeping out of control.

Melissa pulled the monitor from her belly and left it lying on the bed. It didn't take her long to begin snatching at the IV tubes that were taped securely to her arm. She would have succeeded, but a labor pain crippled her, and Nathaniel caught her as she toppled face forward. "Ughh!" she screamed from the pain.

The nurse came dashing back into the room, followed by a tall black man dressed in all-white. "What's going on in here?" Denise asked, rushing toward Melissa and Nathaniel. The scene frightened her.

Nathaniel helped Melissa back to the bed. "Nurse Denise, Melissa is having some anxiety about the pending procedure, and she was ready to walk out of here until she had a contraction. I was just about to hit the nurse's button once I got her back to the bed safely."

Denise went to work getting Melissa hooked back up to the monitors, and Nathaniel went to talk to the doctor. The realization of the fact that his son would be born into the world within a few moments unnerved him, and he felt vulnerable because of the unknown. Bracing himself, Nathaniel stepped to the doctor to introduce himself.

The doctor was busy looking at Melissa's files and checking her vital signs. Wrinkles creased his forehead as he wondered how this would all turn out. He wasn't as optimistic as he'd originally had been, but he still had a job to do.

"Doc, can I talk to you for a second?" Nathaniel asked.

The tall chocolate brother turned around slowly so that he could fix his face to greet Nathaniel. He stuck his hand out and shook Nathaniel's. "Hi, I'm Doctor Seth Crosby, and you are . . .?"

"I'm Nathaniel Jackson, the baby's father." Nathaniel returned the handshake. "So, Doc, what's the deal? Is my son going to be all right?" He looked past the doctor at Melissa whose face was pale and ashy.

"Well, I like to be honest with my patients and clients, so I'll give you the short version. The baby is a few weeks early, which poses an immediate threat to his life. That, coupled with the spina bifida, just compounds our issues once he's born. I don't want to sound so grim, but there are no guarantees here." Dr. Crosby pointed over to the fetal monitor and continued to explain his findings.

"When Ms. Wright came in, we did everything we could to slow down her contractions, but she delayed in reacting when the pains initially started. She reported that her contractions were coming between four and five minutes apart consistently. We allowed her to labor on her own until the fetal monitor showed that the baby was in distress, and we realized that her temperature shot up as well as her blood pressure. The only thing we've had time to do was to give her some meds to try to stall the labor, but as you can see, those lines going up and up shows that the baby isn't going to wait too much longer. My job is to get him here as safely as possible."

Nathaniel had barely breathed while the doctor was talking. The more Dr. Crosby laid it on the line for him, the sadder he became. He rubbed his hands together and rocked on the back of his heels. "So, Doctor, what will happen once the baby's born?"

"Well, Mr. Jackson, the first thing we need to do is get the baby out, and then we will know better what needs to happen next. We will conduct one more ultrasound before delivering him, and since we can do it right here in the room, you will know everything as I'm checking things out." The doctor patted Nathaniel on the back and left the room.

Finally alone, Nathaniel walked over to the window that looked out over the north side of the hospital. The sun had set, and darkness had settled in. He gazed up at the stars in the clear sky and began to pray in his spirit for strength to make it through this. He then prayed for the baby, Melissa, and Serena. He shoved his hands in his pockets to keep them from shaking. He hadn't heard Serena come into the room.

Serena peeked into the room after listening to Crystal give her an update on the status of the baby. She wanted to be there for her husband and for Melissa too. She swallowed her pride again and tiptoed into the room where the curtain covered the entrance. Pushing the heavy, colored curtain back in order to gain entry, her eyes went directly to Nathaniel. Then she looked over her shoulder at Melissa, who had her eyes closed and an arm thrown over her forehead.

Gently wrapping her arms around Nathaniel's waist, she whispered to him. "Baby, I'm here, and we will get through this together." Serena held on to him, hoping that a measure of strength she was feeling would transfer to him. Relief swept over her when he wrapped his arms around her and held onto her.

Kissing the top of her head, he said, "Thank you, baby. I admire your strength, and I thank you for loving me more than hating what I've done to you. If I could take it all back today . . ." Nathaniel felt like he was on the brink of an emotional breakdown as he realized that God still favored him.

"No more feeling guilty, no more placing and casting blame. We are here now, and God is still with us." Serena felt a spirit of peace overcome her, but she wasn't fooled; it was for her to operate in the presence of Nathaniel and

Melissa. She was ready for what could be one of her last earthly assignments.

The door flew open, and the doctor and the nurse rushed back into the room with the ultrasound machine. They scurried around to Melissa's beside to prep her for the ultrasound. Serena smiled at Nathaniel and squeezed his hand before walking over to a groggy Melissa.

Serena reached out to touch Melissa's arm. "Hey, I just wanted you to know that no matter what happens next, God has got you, and He will never leave you. I don't know what the end result will be, but I hope that right now, you will place all of your trust in Him."

To her surprise, Melissa reached out to touch Serena's hand that lay on the bedside and conjured up a small smile. She mouthed, "Thank you," pulled her hand back unto herself, and turned away as a tear slid down her cheek.

Chapter 28

"It's going to be okay, just breathe," Nathaniel said, leaning over to rub Melissa's hair as she cried.

The doctors were busy working on getting Shalimar out of her. Although there was a white sheet that separated her face from seeing what the doctors were doing, she shivered as she felt the tugging in her abdomen. Gratefulness settled in her soul as she heard the cries of her baby. Denise rushed the baby up to Melissa's face and leaned him over into Nathaniel's direction for them both to kiss his little face before he was whisked away for emergency surgery.

"My baby!" Melissa screamed.

"Shh, he's going to be all right. Let the doctors worry about helping him now, and we will concentrate on you getting cared for and in a room to relax." Nathaniel rubbed his finger across her eyebrows. Sadness overwhelmed him; however, he knew that being strong for Melissa and the possible outcome of Shalimar's procedure was paramount.

Doctor Crosby came around to her bedside and stood near her face. "Congratulations on a safe delivery. I must tell you that little Shalimar has a long road ahead. He should be going into surgery first thing in the morning, but for the night we must keep him in the Pediatric Intensive Care Unit. There he will get moment-by-moment monitoring and be kept in isolation since before birth, testing detected that parts of his spinal cord were pressed through an opening in his spine. "Another thing, I'd advise a word of caution. I've seen many cases such as these come in and out of our hospital, but we've lost more than what we were able to save. If you have a relationship with God, it would behoove you to begin praying now. You're all sutured up and will be moved into a private room within the hour. Your pressure is higher than we'd like so we are also going to be keeping a close eye on you tonight." Dr. Crosby squeezed Melissa's arm, gave her and Nathaniel a gentle smile, and left the operating room.

"See, I told you," Melissa began to jerk around in the bed. "I need to see my son! I need someone to help me!" She clutched her throat as if she couldn't breathe.

"I need for you to calm down. Did you forget that you just had major surgery?" Nathaniel panicked, slapping the nurse's button on the bed rail. While he struggled to hold Melissa still, he missed the button over and over again. Grabbing her arms, he shouted, "Stop it, nowww! Get it together." As he shouted, sweat poured down his forehead and onto the face mask he'd pushed up onto his forehead.

Finally, it was like Melissa had finally heard him snap through her manic attempts of escape. She'd calmed down so much that it frightened Nathaniel. Her once rigid body full of fight had gone limp, and she wasn't conscious. Reaching over her unmoving body, Nathaniel was able to hit the nurse's button, and when he started, he didn't stop until he was sure that someone was on the way. He'd even reached over Melissa's head and pushed the emergency button on the wall, and the loud sounds caused everyone dressed in a white suit and colorful scrubs to come flying into the room.

Nathaniel moved backward in a daze. He didn't know what was going on or what the outcome of the situation would be. The frenzy of hospital officials asked him what happened, and he tried his best to explain, but nothing would come out of his mouth. Leaving them to their work, he snatched off the hospital garb he was wearing and went to find his strength. Serena.

Serena saw Nathaniel coming down the hall with a distraught look on his face and tension in his body. He wasn't walking upright with his usual confidence or swag, and that scared her. She was glad to see him but afraid of the story behind his look of defeat. Without thinking, she opened her arms for him to walk into them. Love burst within her and admiration for his inner strength.

Nathaniel rubbed his hands together as he trudged down the corridor to the waiting room. It was evident that he carried the weight of his world on his shoulders, and all he could do to not collapse was just to keep walking. He picked his head up to see Serena standing at the end of the hall with her arms open wide. Speeding up his pace, Nathaniel hurried into her arms. There he felt safe, as if the troubles of the world couldn't touch him and that anchor alone kept him holding onto her until he felt Serena's arms loosen.

Stepping back, Serena wanted to give Nathaniel some space to get himself together before she started drilling him for answers. Standing with her arms locked behind her back, she waited and she waited. Watching him with sorrow in her heart, Serena began to pray for him. No longer praying in her head, she prayed with her heart. Anything that caused Nathaniel distress, sadness, or pain caused the same for her, yet it made her want to keep holding onto him. She knew that it wasn't possible that she could shield him from the process of the pain he was going through, but it didn't stop her from wanting to take it all away.

Nathaniel began talking fast. He hadn't really had an opportunity to process what was going on; however, the pensive look on Serena's face reminded him that she was waiting on some news.

"Baby, things have gotten way out of hand. I'm not sure what happened after Shalimar was delivered. The nurses were ready to rush him away for vital checks and preparation for surgery in the morning. Then the doctor says that if we knew God, we should pray because many more babies have lost their lives versus the number they've been able to save with his condition. Obviously, my son had more of his spinal cord exposed than what the doctors saw on the ultrasounds." He paced the floor.

Serena's hands flew to her mouth, yet she refused to break down in front of Nathaniel. She knew that it wouldn't do any good for her to react just yet so she followed his lead. "Honey, we know the power of prayer, and whatever the outcome may be, we have to trust that God makes no mistakes."

"I don't know, Serena. I'm starting to feel as if God is allowing this to happen to me again. Why would my son's life be in jeopardy when the good Lord has already taken my *father* and my *mother*?" he asked sarcastically. "And you know the worst part of it? I'm out here not knowing what's going on with either Melissa or Shalimar!"

Serena felt some kind of way when Nathaniel put emphasis on *his son*. But instead of going off, she shook off the chilled feeling that snaked its way up her legs to her arms. "What did you say about Melissa? Did I miss something? Is she all right?" she asked with genuine concern.

"She had gotten hysterical after the doctors left the room, and the next thing I knew, she was lying there unconscious. I panicked and hit every button I could find. I was afraid to leave her alone in the room while I went for help. The doctor mentioned that her blood pressure was high and that she would need to be watched throughout the night. Shalimar's condition worried her the most.

I don't know what's going on with her now since I'm out here." Nathaniel walked into the waiting room and flopped down on the leather couch, almost causing the other end to fly up due to his weight.

If she ever needed her mother, she needed her at that moment. She'd have to intercede alone because Crystal and Amina had gone home, but not before Serena assured them that she would be fine and promised to call them as soon as she heard something. The most important thing that Serena could do was to pray for the baby's and Melissa's lives. Walking slowly through the halls, she got on the elevator and traveled up to the fifth floor to where the baby was being kept.

Serena was met with an aquarium full of colorful fish and lots of pictures that were obviously the handiwork of children. After stepping off of the elevator, she felt compelled to stop and look at each picture, down to the writing on them. She fingered the writing in crayon that held numbers on them. Looking up at the marquee on the wall which displayed the room number ranges let her know that she was correct. She prayed for every child represented on the wall in pictures of sunny days, kids playing outside, riding bikes, and the one that had a little boy playing with his turtle.

The realization of what could be with her own unborn child brought tears to her eyes. Unashamedly, Serena allowed them to flow. She sat down on the bench which had shapes carved in them to suit children and looked around at the wagons stationed along the colorful walls. She bowed her head and prayed not only for Shalimar, but for every child on the ward.

Chapter 29

Throughout the night, Melissa's condition was touch-and-go. She'd been under twenty-four-hour watch and seemed to finally cross over the mountain. When she awoke, she placed her hands on her belly, remembering that she'd already had Shalimar. The pain kicked in, and she winced in pain and snatched her hands off of her sore stomach. Looking around, she tried to gain some sense of where she was, what had happened, and where her son was. Melissa felt as if she'd been run over by a Mack truck as she tried lifting her head, but the pounding forced her head back onto her pillow.

Trina sat watching as Melissa had come out of her sleep. She wished she'd never left the hospital the other day, but she needed to run some errands and handle her home life. By the time she'd gotten back, Nathaniel was talking to the doctor, and she'd overheard pretty much the whole conversation. Melissa had developed a fever and had a seizure after having the baby. There was blood work done, and an infection was found to be the culprit in her becoming sick, and thus, two days had passed and she was now finally waking up.

The room was dark and conducive for good rest. Melissa had been so out of it that she didn't know how worrisome the nurses had been, whipping in and out of her room at least three times a night checking her vitals, taking blood, and changing her saline IVs to keep her hydrated. Trina thought that it was a good idea to open the blinds in the room so that she could have a much-needed conversation with her best friend.

Melissa saw Trina walk across the room, which didn't take long since the room was the size of a match box. Her eyes followed Trina's every move, wondering why she hadn't spoken to her. "Trina? How long have I been here, and where is Shalimar?" She had to whisper because her head was hurting so bad. "Where's the nurse? My head is killing me." Melissa screwed her face up at Trina.

"Girl, let me get the nurse for you." Trina walked over and pressed the nurse's button.

"Nurse's station," the lady on the intercom said.

"Yes, the patient is awake now and needs something for a headache." Trina released the call button and walked over to where Melissa watched her with a wild look in her eyes.

"The nurse will be right in," the lady advised.

"Girl, you've been asleep for two days." Trina exclaimed. "I wasn't sure if you'd ever wake up, but I've been praying. Prophetess Serena has been praying along with the church family." Trina glanced at Melissa to see how she felt about that.

Melissa shrugged her shoulders. "What are they praying for me about, and where is my son? The last I remember, he was having surgery to close the hole over his spine, so I should be able to see him now, right?" Melissa's eyes watered with a doomed feeling in the pit of stomach. Her tear-filled eyes desperately searched Trina's eyes for a glimmer of hope that everything was okay.

Trina stood in front of Melissa trying to hold back her tears of the news she needed to share with Melissa before the nurse walked in. "Bestie, like I said, you've been sick for the last two days and—"

"I don't care about me; tell me the whereabouts of my son before I turn this place out." Melissa's adrenaline raced as the blood rushed to her head.

Afraid for Melissa's safety, Trina stood to the side hoping that she could go through with telling Melissa about what had happened. Hearing a knock on the door, Trina took take a deep breath and released it when she heard Nathaniel's voice. Happy for a lifesaver, she quickly spoke up. "Come on in, Melissa's awake now."

Nathaniel pushed the heavy curtain back and walked into the room. He wasn't sure if Melissa had been told about Shalimar, but he'd find out shortly.

"Wow, you're awake, sleepyhead. How are you feeling?" He walked to the other side of the bed to check Melissa out for himself. He'd been worried about her ever since she had passed out, and then it seemed like the bad news just kept coming.

"I'm hurting all over and I want—no—I *need* to know where Shalimar is. I want to know how long it will be before someone brings him to see me. Can you make that happen, Nathaniel?" Melissa was getting irritated with the lack of answers she seemed to be getting, which only fueled more fears.

Nathaniel grabbed her hand and sighed. Holding his head back, he realized that he'd have to be the one to break the news to her. He blew a breath of hot air out through his nostrils before meeting Melissa's eyes again. "Melissa, Shalimar . . ." Nathaniel felt like his tongue had gotten swollen in his mouth, keeping him from having the much-needed conversation.

"Well, spit it out! Please, what is it?" Melissa looked from Trina to Nathaniel, and they were both overcome with emotion. She started to scream. "Nooooo! Not my baby, why me, whyyyyy? I trusted you, Nathaniel . . . Again! I should never have listened when you were selling me false dreams and hopes about Shalimar being okay." Melissa cried and wailed for the loss of her baby.

As if on cue, the nurse came into the room and upon hearing the cries of her patient she knew that the news had been given to her. She did an about-face and left the room to get something stronger than the ibuprofen she had in her hands.

Trina reached over into the bed to grab Melissa to give her a shoulder to cry on. Melissa held onto her best friend, while her heart burst into a million pieces. The debris from her despair rained upon her, cloaked in guilt, selfishness, and stubbornness. She wished that she could die with her child. She'd have nothing left to live for and therefore couldn't deal with anything else. She shut down.

Nathaniel struggled to tell Melissa the story of how the surgery was more involved than the doctors estimated. He went on to explain that because of Shalimar's premature lungs and heart, he expired on the operating table. His little heart just stopped beating and just like he'd come, he was gone just as quickly. Nathaniel cried harder with each word that came out of his mouth, but he had to keep on talking even if Melissa didn't hear him because he didn't think he'd make it through by having to repeat what happened ever again.

"Serena sends her condolences as well as Pastor Sampson. She will be coming by to see you today or tomorrow." Nathaniel had hoped that God could see how He continued to wreak havoc in the lives of those He supposedly loved. Nathaniel shook his head in silence.

Melissa felt the hair on her skin rise at the sound of Serena's name. Anger coursed through her veins, causing her blood to rush to her face, forcing her words out of her mouth. "Serena! I don't ever want to hear her name again. I don't need her prayers, or anyone's for that matter. She's probably laughing at me and talking about me like the rest of the church." Melissa went off on a tangent, and she was just beginning.

Trina tried to calm Melissa down, but to no avail. No one would have ever known that she was as sick as she'd been, not the way she was turned up at the moment. Trina tried holding her close, but Melissa wasn't having it.

"Get off of me, Trina." Melissa winced in pain as she snatched her arm from Trina's grasp. "I know you'd better not be taking up for the precious *Serena*. *I'm* the one who's lying here without her baby. I'm the one who only had a glimpse of my son before he was taken away from me moments after he was yanked from my womb. *Me . . . not* Serena! When is someone going to stop and feel something other than contempt for me? I've admitted my wrong, repented, and yet and still, God is ripping me apart. Shred by shred, He's stripping me, and I can't handle this pain I'm feeling, the void I've been left with. What about *me?*" She cried from a place of brokenness.

The nurse quickly returned after hearing all of the commotion coming from Melissa's room. She balanced two needles of some type of medicine. She gazed at the three people in the room, and then addressed them. "I brought Ms. Wright something to relax her, and I'll need for you both to leave due to the agitation caused." She dismissed Nathaniel and Trina, turned her back on them, and began working on trying to calm Melissa down.

"I'm not leaving, I don't care what she says." Trina turned to Nathaniel. "It may be best that you leave now, and I'll be sure to call you or text you to let you know when the tide has turned here."

Melissa must have heard Trina because she hollered at her to get out. Trina didn't know what else to do but to honor her best friend's request. She'd be sure to call the hospital periodically to check on Melissa. Nathaniel and Trina walked out of the hospital with a defeated look on their faces.

Chapter 30

The sounds of music permeated through the church walls and out of the front door at Abiding Savior on Sunday morning. Crystal sat in her study for as long as possible before taking calculated steps toward the sanctuary. Her spirit was troubled, and she hadn't slept soundly the night before. With everything going on with Amina, Jonathan, Serena, Nathaniel, and Melissa, the only thing she really had to smile about was Tremaine.

He'd been a constant in her life when everything else was going haywire. She gained comfort in knowing that he'd be in service that morning, and she needed to feel the peace of God before standing before His people. Jalisa walked behind Crystal until they reached the door that led into the sanctuary. Crystal moved back to allow Jalisa to open the door for her to walk through to the backside of the pulpit.

With each step Crystal took her legs felt heavier and heavier. She wasn't sure how she would be able to deliver a word with so much going on in her own life. She'd been in the gospel game a long time, yet this was the first time she was at a loss of what to tell the people of God. Crystal wondered what she could relay to the sheep when she herself was having a hard time hanging on to her faith.

Instead of looking out into the congregation to gauge the crowd as she usually would, Crystal kneeled down in front of her chair and prayed to God for an answer. Blocking the music out from the choir and music ministry,

Crystal was able to become one with God. The peace of God was being poured out over her head and permeated throughout her body until her legs and feet felt lighter.

With the assistance of the pulpit members, Crystal was able to stand and take the pulpit.

She held her head up high and smiled out into the waiting congregation. "Praise the Lord, everybody!"

Shouts of praise erupted in different sections of the congregation. Amens rang out and hallelujah shouts could be heard echoing in the background. Crystal heard the minister of music getting turned up, and she welcomed it. She needed just a few more moments to get herself together. The minipraise fest was the perfect distraction that Crystal needed in order to peer out into the congregation to see which one of her family members was seated down on the front row.

Her soul was lifted to see her family in full effect. Suddenly, there was a little igging feeling that gnawed at Crystal's spirit. She snapped her neck back when the sight of Sherry caught her eye. She fumed inside wondering what she was doing there. She thought that she might not be able to preach after all seeing that heathen up in her church. Crystal's eyes scanned the crowd to see if Jonathan had come out of hiding and showed up today for service.

A sweat broke out on her neck and traveled down Crystal's back giving her chills. She gripped the sides of the podium so tight that her knuckles hurt. Glancing down, Crystal tapped her foot, not to the music but to try to calm herself down before addressing the children of God. Crystal was no novice, and she was used to being in uncomfortable situations, yet not where her family was concerned.

Holding her hand up to quiet the music ministry, Crystal inhaled, sucked in her bottom lip, and released it slowly before speaking. She turned the microphone on, put on her happy face, and belted out, "I will bless the Lord at all times. His praises shall continually be in my mouth." She noticed that there was a spirit of heaviness that had taken the place of praise. Starting again, Crystal sang out, "I will bless the Lord, at all times. His praises shall continu-ally be in my mouth. Bless His ho-lyyyy name." Suddenly, she realized that it was she who was carrying the heavy spirit, not the church.

Amina sat out in the congregation looking at Crystal, and sensed that something deeper was going on. Their family had been in the storm for so long that Amina was sure that Crystal was growing weary in well-doing. She began to pray for her grandmother's strength, not realizing why Crystal kept looking out over her head. Curiosity had finally gotten the best of her. She turned around to see what had Crystal's attention, and that's when she came face-to-face with her birth mother.

Sherry sat as quiet and still as a church mouse while her nerves caused her knees to knock. She'd debated with herself and the man who she had believed was Amina's true birth father about showing up again. However, she needed to speak with Amina and felt like the church was the only option since she'd almost had to fight Crystal the last time she just showed up. It took every ounce of strength she could muster up to walk through those church doors. Sherry was afraid that everyone from her past would come out of the woodwork to condemn her for her mistakes.

Amina's eyes bore into Sherry's and she hissed between clenched teeth, "What are you doing here?" Pain pierced Amina's soul, and she became indignant. Standing up in the midst of every eye in the place, she shouted at Sherry, "Why won't you just go back to where you came from? You don't have a clue of all of the turmoil you showing up has brought into my life and my family's."

Serena had been in a daze with her mind traveling a thousand miles per minute. Her health had been declining, and she was bombarded with thoughts of the pending induction of her unborn child. She heard the commotion going on down the row from her and snapped out of her preoccupation. The stress of baby Shalimar's death caused her the most fear and trying to make sure that Nathaniel was okay from moment to moment resulted in her not resting or eating well.

Amina's loud voice jerked Serena back to the present, and she jumped up as if on instinct. Looking around, the members seemed to be sitting on the edge of their seats ready for the jump off. Crystal had already come down from the pulpit with two of the Men of Valor flanked at her sides.

Sherry stood up and took cover, not expecting to be ambushed by the family. Tears sprang up in her eyes, but she had no place to retreat to. The row where she'd been sitting was packed to capacity. "I'm only here to talk to my daughter, and I thought that coming to church would be the best place to have the conversation with Amina." Tears flooded Sherry's eyes as she stood face-to-face with her past.

Serena stood at attention, watching quietly. She felt a smidgen of sympathy for Sherry in light of the recent events of Melissa losing her son. Any feelings of sorrow Serena was feeling, however, instantly evaporated into the air when she saw Amina's tears. Wanting to shake Sherry so that she could see what she left behind, something inside of Serena snapped. No one had time to react when Serena lunged forward and grabbed Sherry by the neck.

The congregants went wild as they watched the dramedy unfold. Those who were up in the balcony watched the melee on the big screen. Downstairs, some were scrambling to get out of harm's way, yet there were others recording the scene on their cell phones. No doubt they would use the footage to post on Facebook or Twitter later that day. The pulpit members and every leader had assumed their position and were standing at attention crowded around the family ready to take action to keep the first family safe.

No one paid attention to Sister Edna who had to fight her way through the throngs of people as she mounted the pulpit. Taking the microphone in her hand, she prepared herself to speak. "Attention, church, I will need for everyone to vacate the church immediately. Worship service has been cancelled, and I ask that you . . ." Edna stopped talking when she saw some teenagers recording what was going on and switched tracks.

"Hey, DeMarkus, what are you doing? I had better not see nor hear about what's going on here today being posted online anywhere or I will tell your mother. As a matter of fact, where *is* Sister Debra?" Edna called the youth out and put him on blast in front of his friends. She couldn't believe her eyes, and if someone had told her what was happening without her being able to see if for herself, she would have never have believed it.

Seeing the members show out in front of the visitors, Edna knew that the fallout would bring big repercussions to Abiding Savior. What bothered Edna the most was the fact that when things calmed down once again, she knew that Crystal wouldn't be able to keep the situation hush-hush. More members might possibly leave the ministry, and surely the foolishness would give the visitors something to talk about. She'd need to provide a statement of apology to her church family as well as the city if the news reporters showed up. Edna stood holding her breath and waited while droves of people exited the church.

Chapter 31

"Oh, no, baby, what were you thinking? I can't believe that you put yourself and our child at risk. I can't lose another baby," Nathaniel said after he'd taken Serena home.

"Ahhh! Just take me to the hospital. I believe that I'm in labor, and I need to get to the hospital *now*. Ughh!" Serena screamed in agony. "Honey, I don't know what happened to me. Clearly, I blacked out. Standing there watching that woman come up into our church demanding to talk to Amina when the girl had made it perfectly clear that she didn't want to speak to her, I don't know—I just lost it. *Ahhh . . .*" Serena clutched at her swollen belly. "This pain is excruciating. It's sharp, like someone is stabbing me in the back, and then the pressure radiates around to the front.

"I mean, think about it, Sherry has interrupted our lives at the worst time. Jonathan has gone into hiding ever since he found out about the possibility of Amina not being his. I've called Ariane time after time, and she's just as worried about him as I am. We think that he's gone back to drinking, and you know the trouble he's caused due to his drinking in the past. I'm sure that he blames me too for not telling him, but *I'm* the innocent one here. He's disappeared just like before when things get too hard to deal with. I sure hope that Jonathan doesn't do anything to jeopardize his freedom . . ." Serena rubbed her achy back.

"Will you call Dr. Sinclair and see what she says?" Serena asked. In deep thought she revisited what had happened earlier in the day. She couldn't believe that

she'd totally lost her mind. Now that she'd calmed
down, she was able to think about the situation clearly.
Conviction caused Serena to bury her face in her hands
and cry out to God in repentance. She was embarrassed
by her actions since she was highly esteemed among
her colaborers in the ministry. Serena could blame her
actions on her own personal issues and struggles with
the thoughts that took root in her heart and mind.

She'd hurt herself in the process of trying to put the
woman in the choke hold. Closing her eyes, the images of
what she'd done played vividly in her mind. She was sick
of the devil taking from her family, hurting them, and
trying to destroy them all. Angry at God for not stepping
in to keep Nathaniel's son from dying, Serena fumed
with tears building up behind her closed eyes. Like a dam
ready to break, she fought to keep the tears from bursting
out by straining to keep her eyelids sealed until she could
collect herself.

Nathaniel was dealing with his own pain and dis-
couragement from the loss of Shalimar. He felt sorry for
himself and for Melissa who had to be transferred to a
mental health facility. She'd gone into a depression and
somehow tried to commit suicide by using a plastic bag
that had been inadvertently left on her hospital tray in
the wee hours of the morning. She had been despondent
when he'd gone to see her each time after she found out
the baby had passed.

"Nathaniel!" Serena yelled.

The piercing sound of Serena's voice snatched Nathaniel from his daydreaming. He groaned inwardly as
it was time to face another song on the record that had
represented his broken life. "I'm calling now, baby." He
picked up the cordless phone and hit number three on
the phone which was the number programmed to speed
dial the doctor's office for emergencies.

Serena moaned and rolled over onto her side while Nathaniel got instructions on what to do. He was exhausted emotionally for trying not to display the full magnitude of his sadness of the passing of his son. He tried to be cognizant of Serena's feelings and didn't want her to think that he cared about Melissa and Shalimar more than he cared about the pending birth of their own child.

"Okay, we'll see you soon." Nathaniel nodded his head in approval as if he could be seen through the other end of the phone.

"Are we meeting Dr. Sinclair at the hospital?"

"Yes, and that means you need to shower and get dressed. I want you to wait right here for me to return to get you. I'm going to start the shower and adjust the water for you first. Then I'll check your maternity bag to make sure that everything on your list is in there." Nathaniel had mixed emotions about the birth of the baby. He was afraid that something would go terribly wrong with their child despite the results of Serena's last ultrasound. The doctors were positive that other than the expected low birth weight, their baby would be fine.

Sprinting through the house to the bathroom, Nathaniel caught a glimpse of himself in the mirror and paused. Standing there, he examined the dark circles resting under his eyes accompanied by puffiness from sleepless nights. His eyes were red, and he seemed to have lost his luster for life. Frustrated over the lack of control he felt he had in his life, he slammed his fists down on the counter. Every fiery dart thrown by the enemy pierced his heart, and he believed that if he looked down he would see a trail of blood from his wounded heart.

"Each day that passes brings me closer to the possibility of me losing my wife. God, how could you continue to take from me? What is it about me that would cause you to allow so much heartache and pain? When will it ever be enough?" Nathaniel's shoulders heaved up and down before he gave into the pain he'd kept pent up ever since the nurses took his son from the operating room. The baby didn't stand a chance at life.

The wall in the bathroom held Nathaniel up as he leaned on it holding his head in hands. He covered his mouth to muffle his cries, but he felt like his chest would explode from trying to be strong for everyone. "Who, God . . . Who's going to be strong for me?" He beat himself in the chest with all of his might.

Serena heard Nathaniel's desperate pleas in the bathroom. The pain in her heart outweighed the pain in her back and in her belly. She didn't really give Nathaniel the chance to mourn the loss of his son. She'd given him lip service when she assured him that they would get through the storm together. Serena had been selfish yet again, being consumed with her own issues. Although she hated that he'd lost his son to death, she was more concerned about her life and how Nathaniel would treat their own child.

She called out to him, but he didn't hear her. She called out yet again, not louder but softer as to not disturb him from becoming free from the bondage that held him captive. The more she stood behind her man in the physical, she acknowledged that she hadn't been standing behind him spiritually or emotionally. Although her body was wracked with pain, she withstood her own discomfort to really be there for Nathaniel by praying for him, and then herself.

Nathaniel had made a mental decision, and that was to be true to himself and to his feelings from here on out. He was tired of trying to be strong for Serena, but he needed to be able to express himself without the fears of what Serena would do or say. It wasn't fair for him to have to pretend that he was okay when he really wasn't for the sake of constantly trying to prove himself to her.

With her prayer complete, Serena waddled into the bathroom and hugged Nathaniel from behind. "I'm sorry," she whispered clinging to his backside as tight as she could without putting pressure on her stomach. He trembled in her arms, and she grasped the front of his shirt to hold onto him and assure him that she had his back.

Nathaniel felt in the core of his being that God was finally listening to his heart. He pulled Serena's hands from around his waist and pulled her in front of him. "Baby, that's all I've wanted . . . for you to really have my back. I know I've hurt you in ways unimaginable, but I regret it all. Serena, I'm paying for my mistakes in a grave way. While I try to wrap my mind around why God is punishing me to this degree, I can't fathom it," he vented.

"I feel like my soul has been ripped from my body and the only thing left is my shell. I haven't been happy since all of this mess began, and I'm disappointed in myself for allowing things to get so out of hand. I allowed my need to feel appreciated, and my wants outweighed my common sense and resolve. I've lost enough, and now I'm afraid of losing you, Serena Jackson. I love you more than life itself, and I won't make it without you. *We* won't make it without you." Nathaniel rubbed Serena's swollen belly.

Serena tensed at Nathaniel's touch. "I have some fault in the reason why we're here in this place. I didn't handle you the right way because I was blinded by my illness. I've been afraid that since Melissa was crazy about you and would be around long after I'm gone, I thought that you thought you'd married the wrong woman. I can't tell you how blessed I was when you stayed by my side as I fought cancer the first go-round." Serena's eyes glistened with tears.

"Baby, are you still in pain?" Nathaniel had forgotten about the shower he was supposed to be preparing for her.

"The aching in my back is getting sharper, but it's only radiating on the left side. I just want this done and over with. I've been asking God to grant me some time with our baby. Isn't it amazing that every time we've gone in to try to have its sex determined, the baby was either asleep or wouldn't open its legs. So we have no choice but to wait until the birth, and the way I feel, I believe we are closer now than ever before. Honey, I don't want us to be sad and constantly thinking about all of the things that we've fallen short at." Serena looked up at Nathaniel with a smile that outshined the tears she'd shed over and over again within the last eight months.

"I promise that I can be there for you again regardless of what comes our way. We are in this together," Nathaniel promised Serena. "Let's get you ready for the hospital. I'm ready to meet our little blessing, which is the greatest gift we can share." He kissed the tip of Serena's nose, her forehead, and then her lips before grabbing her hand and leading her over to the tub to begin her shower.

Chapter 32

Crystal and Tremaine were on their way to dinner. She'd been having a hard time with the drama from the church and folks overexaggerating about what happened that Sunday with Sherry. Tremaine was tired of seeing Crystal mope around as if the world had ended. He'd been trying unsuccessfully for the last week to get her out of the house, so he was pleasantly surprised that she'd finally agreed to go out to dinner this time.

The Thanksgiving holiday was marred by the passing of Baby Shalimar and so there was no big dinner at Crystal's. There was no family gathering where laughter and fun, along with fellowship, usually rang out during the holiday season. No one had heard from Jonathan, Amina never had that conversation with her birth mother, and Melissa had been transferred to Cherry Psychiatric Hospital in Goldsboro, North Carolina.

Tremaine had planned a nice dinner at Brasa's Brazilian Steakhouse because he was ready to make Crystal his wife. Nervous jitters traveled through him as he drove along to the restaurant. The ride was a quiet one since it was obvious that they were both preoccupied, satisfied to linger in their own separate worlds, allowing the jazz to fill the air and be the deterrent for any conversation. Happy for the silence, Tremaine rehearsed in his mind how he would propose to Crystal.

Crystal's cell phone rang in her pocketbook, and she reached into it to retrieve it. She didn't need to check to see who was calling since Amina had programmed her phone with specific ringtones for each of them. She answered, "Hey, Serena, how are you?" She lay back on the headrest to resume her conversation. They had talked briefly earlier that day. Serena had apologized for trying to beat Sherry down, and although Crystal wasn't pleased with the way things went down, she could definitely understand why they went the way they did.

"Mommy, I'm on my way to the hospital. I've been having back spasms or some kind of excruciating pain that radiates to the front of my belly. My left leg hurts too. I don't think I hit it on anything, but it's been happening on and off. Maybe it's nothing too serious. The doctor seems to think that the baby is coming tonight sometime," Serena informed her.

Crystal reached over to turn the radio down before responding. "Serena, did you say that you're having the baby?" She wanted to make sure she'd heard the right thing.

"Yes, Mommy, we're on our way to Duke and Dr. Sinclair will meet us there. Are you busy? I called you on the home phone, but you didn't answer."

"Has your water broken, or are you just having contractions?" Crystal was concerned. She needed to make a decision on whether to go on out to dinner or go to the hospital to be with Serena.

"Mommy, well, I can't be sure since I was in the shower. Either way, I'm going to get checked out." Serena rubbed her belly while Nathaniel sped through town to the hospital.

"Chile, it's normal. Every pregnancy is different for each woman. Some have contractions in their abdomen and others have back contractions. To be honest with you, the back contractions are the worst." Crystal closed her eyes at the visual that flashed before her.

"Mom, how do you know that the ones in the back are more painful?"

"I know because I had back labor with you. So I guess this is a little payback for the pain you caused me while I labored with you for over fifteen hours." Crystal chuckled trying to lighten the mood. She didn't like hearing fear in her daughter's voice, and she knew then that she'd have to cancel her dinner plans and head on over to be with Serena.

"I hope that you can come over and be with me. I'm afraid of something going wrong. There's so much going on inside of me, and the one thing I am grateful for is that I won't have to endure the full labor process since I'm having a Caesarian section." Serena sighed on her end of the phone.

"Well, baby, you know I will be there, but first I must keep my date with Tremaine. He's been trying to get me out of this funk since service ended, and I don't want to disappoint him. Do you think that the baby will wait for Gi-Gi to get there before making its grand entrance?"

"I don't know what's going to happen once I get up on the maternity floor. I'm hoping that I will be fine. It's not like Nathaniel won't be with me, but can you call Amina and let her know what's going on?" Serena grimaced as a pain shot through to her left side. "You know she won't allow me to live it down if she's not a part of the baby's birth." Serena hadn't had formal Lamaze classes, but she had seen a lot of Lifetime movies where women were giving birth. She felt a sharp pain shoot across her stomach and had to catch her breath.

"I'll see you soon, and if anything happens before I get there, have Nathaniel call me so that I can rush dinner and get to you as quickly as possible." Crystal peeped over at Tremaine to see if his demeanor changed with her last comment. The way he was all decked out, she knew that it wouldn't be a good thing to have to cut their time short.

"Okay, I need to concentrate on my breathing now so I've gotta go. Mommy, I love you, and please hurry," Serena said before clicking the END button on her cell phone.

"Is everything okay?" Tremaine asked as he maneuvered into the parking space nearest to the front door of the restaurant.

"Well, it looks like we are going to be having a baby tonight. I am truly hoping that we can get dinner in, and then get to the hospital before he or she comes." Crystal turned the volume on her cell phone up in order to make sure that she didn't miss any calls.

The ambiance inside of the restaurant was intoxicating. The warmth flowed from the fireplace and wrapped it's coziness around Crystal's shoulders as she was escorted to their table. She was impressed and smiled despite her desire to be with Serena. Tremaine pulled Crystal's chair out for her to sit down, and then he was seated.

The waiter came and took their drink orders, and they listened while he gave them the rundown on how their meals were prepared. There were colorful rocks on the table with one side being red and the other side being green. It was so dim in the room that Crystal couldn't make out the waiter's name, but it wasn't important because she allowed Tremaine to order for her.

Tremaine admired Crystal's beauty. She'd worn her hair pinned up with soft curls on the sides of her face. The tense look that had creased her otherwise flawless facial features was now gone, and he hoped that he was the reason that her frown had been replaced with a smile. His eyes gleamed with love each time he looked at her; he felt as if he couldn't breathe. Having gone through such a horrible divorce that he didn't think he'd ever recover from made Tremaine afraid to love again, and the thought of anyone loving him from a pure place intrigued him. He believed that Crystal was the woman for him.

Crystal looked across the table at Tremaine with love bursting in her heart for him. She was glad that he was able to convince her to go out. Inwardly, Crystal hoped that Tremaine was pleased with her efforts to get dolled up for him. He was quiet and reserved that evening, and it caused Crystal to get a little nervous, even though she tried playing it off by busying herself with her cloth napkin. She was thoroughly impressed with the Christmas décor in the establishment. The colors were bold and beautiful.

Tremaine held his hand out for Crystal's hand. When she obliged him, he studied the texture of her fingers and the softness of her skin. His heart skipped with joy as she relaxed at the smooth and calculated way he rubbed her inner palm. "Crystal, thanks so much for joining me for dinner tonight. I know that there's a lot going on in your world, but I'm blessed to be able to take part in it." He smiled.

Butterflies flitted around in Crystal's belly, and she giggled. The serene atmosphere helped her to just enjoy the moment and her man. She was tired of thinking and worrying about everything and everyone. Her kids were grown and would make their own decisions in life. But one thing Crystal had a hard time learning was that she could want the best for her family, yet it was up to them to make good decisions and to do the right thing. Jonathan was still missing in action, and she was almost positive that he'd gone back to drinking.

"What's on your mind? You look like you're a million miles away from here and from me." Tremaine tooted his lips into a pout. Lacing his long fingers into her slender ones, he pulled her hand up to his lips and placed a lingering kiss on the back of it.

Crystal shook her head as if to erase the heavy thoughts from her mind. "I was just thinking about how I've done all I can as a parent, and that I need to cut the umbilical cord with my children. After spending so much time trying to rewrite our history by going back and striving to prove to them that for once they would come first in my life, I realize that it's impossible to fix the things that have already happened."

Trepidation tried climbing its way into Tremaine's heart and although his knees were shaking he found the courage he needed and stood in front of Crystal. He never took his eyes off of the love of his life. "I never thought that I'd find happiness, never thought my heart could be healed or that my mind would change about women in general after my wife left me. The day I met you in the hospital before speaking to you, my heart was beating wildly in my chest at the sight of you." Tremaine laughed as he reminisced.

"Honey, what's going on?" Crystal got the feeling that Tremaine was about to propose, and she became anxious. She withdrew her sweaty hand from his and used her dinner napkin to wipe them both down.

"Pastor Crystal Sampson, you've given me a new lease on life. You're the reason I smile, the reason I'm able to love and be happy. I believe that God has ordained for you to become my wife." Tremaine looked intently into her eyes, hoping that she would take him seriously.

"But, honey, I . . ." Crystal tried to speak to no avail.

"Shhh, just listen to me. Now with as much that's great about you, one thing you are going to have to do is let me be the man and lead sometimes," he schooled Crystal. He was adamant that she wouldn't steal his joy and that he wasn't leaving the restaurant without an answer to his proposal.

He cleared his throat and readjusted his tie which felt like it was strangling him all of a sudden. "Now, if I can finish what I was saying, Madame . . . You've been the sunshine in my life for the last two years, and I'm tired of going home to my own place. I want to go home and make a life with you. Waking up next to you every morning has been my desire for a long time now, and you're cooking has kept me coming around too," he said laughing.

"Everything you've done has always been for someone else, and now I want to take care of you. We're not spring chickens anymore, you know. All I want for you to do is give me the chance to show you how good life can be. Please, let me show you."

Crystal watched Tremaine bend down on one knee, and her hands flew up to her face. Tears gleamed in her eyes as she bowed her head to meet his eyes which glistened with tears of joy and love. He didn't have to reach for her hand. She gave him hers in anticipation of the proposal.

The couple was oblivious to the crowd that had gathered around them as Tremaine recited the words that he'd practiced all day long since leaving the jewelry store. "Baby, will you do me the honor of making me the happiest man on the planet by accepting this proposal? Will you marry me?" Tremaine flashed his perfect smile while he wrangled out a black velvet jewelry box. Opening the small box, he flashed the ring in front of her face.

Crystal happened to look up at that moment and saw a sea of smiling faces. Embarrassed from the attention, she blushed. She looked lovingly at Tremaine and said, "Of course, I will marry you, my love. I thought you'd never ask." She wiggled her fingers waiting for him to place the ring on her finger.

The crowd clapped wildly and shared their well wishes to the couple and dispersed into other areas of the restaurant. Crystal hadn't paid any attention to the actual ring due to all of the onlookers standing around. She had to push her hand in the direction of a sliver of light that was barely enough for her to see the vintage Cushion Halo diamond engagement ring. Squealing with delight, she jumped up quicker than she should have and latched onto Tremaine's neck.

"Baby, I'm glad that you love it," Tremaine laughed. "That's why I've been working like a Hebrew slave the last few months. I wanted to get you the best thing out there because you deserve nothing less than all I have to give." Tremaine pecked Crystal on the lips.

Finally they were able to eat dinner in peace. Neither of them could stop smiling, and Crystal felt like her hard work had paid off. She believed that now it was her time to be happy and to allow the man in her life take the lead.

Chapter 33

Nathaniel sat holding his son, Meshach Jeremiah Jackson, as Serena rested. He was exhausted but wouldn't change the events of the day for anything in the world. As he rocked his baby boy, he marveled at how his little man wiggled in the cocoon of blankets. Nathaniel was ecstatic that Meshach was as perfect as he could be. He weighed in at five pounds and the doctors were confident that in a week or so, his weight would pick up. If it were possible for Nathaniel to hold onto that moment forever, he wouldn't ever let Meshach go. God gave life, and He took it away as He saw fit. *The promise.*

"Where's my grandbaby?" Crystal said as she and Tremaine walked into the room hand in hand, wearing huge smiles on their faces.

The noise startled the newborn because he let out a holler that sounded more like a squeak. Nathaniel watched as Crystal crossed the room to kiss Serena on the forehead, and then made a beeline over to him and the baby.

Nathaniel's arms automatically went upward as he introduced Meshach to Crystal, who cupped him in her arm raining kisses on his small cheek and nuzzled his nose. He handed the baby to his grandmother and vacated the rocking chair for Crystal to sit down, then strolled over to where Tremaine was.

"Hey, Daddy, how's it going?" Tremaine had heard about what had been going on with Nathaniel, and he would remain quiet about it for the time being. This was a day of celebration, and Tremaine didn't want to over-shadow the baby's birth with any conversation about Melissa.

"It's going." Nathaniel rubbed his head and marveled at the joy he felt in his heart.

"I tell you, God is blowing my mind still to this moment. I mean, He took my firstborn, and not even a month later, it's like God's replaced him with Meshach. My heart still hurts and sometimes I don't know if I'm coming or going because everything I knew to be solid and true has been wrecked by my own actions." Nathaniel shook his head wearing the feeling of despair.

"Man, you've got to hang in there. You know the old saying, live and learn. What would be the point of going through life not having to endure some hardships or disappointments? We all have sinned and fallen short of the glory of God. You've got to learn that when you won't forgive yourself, it's a sin." Tremaine patted Nathaniel on the back and smiled.

Crystal chimed in, "How did Serena do during the birth?" She glanced over at Serena who seemed to be sleeping deeply. "She's mighty tired, huh? When's the last time she was awake?" Crystal felt a twinge in her gut that said something's not right.

"She's been asleep ever since we returned from the operating room. Even when I tried to wake her to let her know that the nurse was bringing the baby in, she barely stirred. Hmm, it has been awhile. Maybe I should get the nurse in here to check on her."

Nathaniel's heart raced at the thought of something happening to Serena. He leaned over her bed rail and pushed the nurse's button, immediately having flash-backs of Melissa right before she was about to give birth to Shalimar. He fought back waves of nausea, but the sick feeling sank to the pit of his gut and anchored there.

The nurse came in, stopping at the door and pulling the foam soap from the fixture on the wall. "Hi, is everything all right?" She smiled at Nathaniel.

"Thanks for coming as quickly as you did. I was just wondering if you could check my wife's vitals. I'm worried that she's been sleeping for so long and before she had the C-section she was so anxious to see our son. I know she'd be happy to see that he's perfect, but I haven't been able to wake her." Nathaniel stood to the side fearing the worst.

"Okay, I'm just going to get something." She went back to the hallway and pulled a blood pressure machine into the room. Taking Serena's blood pressure, once, and then twice, the nurse hit the nurse's call button. She turned at look at the family. "Now, I don't want to alarm you; however, Mrs. Jackson's blood pressure is dangerously low, and I'm not sure why." She turned back to Serena and checked her dressings from the C-section.

Tremaine went to the nurse's station in order to have someone from the nursery come and get the baby to take him back until they could find out what was going on. When he turned to go back to the room, he saw the doctors flying into the room, which caused him to walk faster. He entered the room only to be ushered back out.

The door opened. Crystal could be heard hollering through her tears, and Tremaine fought again to go to her aid. He needed to get in there or get her out of there, so he strong-armed his way into the room. "I'm her husband, and Serena is her daughter," he said walking over to pull Crystal out of the way and to try to calm her down.

Nathaniel stood back feeling as if was having an out-of-body experience. He didn't understand how he could be so calm as he stood there and watched those doctors pump on Serena's chest and try to jump-start her heart. Standing there in shock, he couldn't cry, couldn't feel or think. Nathaniel couldn't understand what was happening right before his eyes. He had questions but couldn't find his voice in order to ask what had happened.

Crystal hadn't been able to stop crying when a doctor demanded that they vacate the room or he would have security called. Tremaine held onto her tightly and tried reassuring her that everything would be okay after awhile. Despondently, the trio left Serena's room and headed to the waiting room while the doctor worked on Serena. Praying wasn't an option at the moment, but she knew that when the doctor came out to the waiting room over an hour later with a somber look on her face that it would take lots of prayer in order for her family to get through the next moments, hours, days, weeks, and possibly even years.

"I'm so sorry, Pastor Sampson," Dr. Sinclair said. She looked like she'd been crying.

"What was it? What happened to her, Doctor?" Nathaniel demanded to know.

"After you all left, we had Serena transported to have an MRI done to look at all of her vital organs," Dr. Sinclair explained. She turned so that everyone could see her face while she talked. "When we transported her from the bed to the imaging machine, the lab technician noticed that there was some minor swelling in Serena's left leg, probably due to her pregnancy. Unfortunately, it seems as if she had a blood clot that traveled up through her bloodstream until it reached her lungs. Serena didn't complain about anything except for the normal pregnancy blues. You know, minor aches, pains, and fatigue. I'm sure that most of the fatigue was due to the severity of the cancer in the bone more than from the baby. Research does show that cancer patients have an increased percentage of deep vein thrombosis." Dr. Sinclair seemed to be in deep thought as the quietness surrounded her.

Tremaine remained in place, rubbing Crystal's shoulders and telling her he loved her as he listened to the doctor's diagnosis. He'd seen so many patients expire right before his very eyes, and each time it took something out of him. Tears fell from his eyes as his heart ached for his fiancée and her family which he loved like his own.

"Someone needs to call Amina and have her try to reach her father," Tremaine said above Crystal's head with his eyes fixed on Nathaniel, who hadn't stopped pacing the waiting room floor.

"Ah, man, I was supposed to call Amina while we were en route to dinner." Crystal thought back to the last conversation she'd had with her daughter. "She needed me to be here with her, but I wasn't, and now look at what's happened," Crystal blurted out.

Her phone rang just as she was about to reach into her satchel to call Amina. "Hello, Pastor Sampson speaking."

"Gran-Gran, is that you?" Amina's tone was laced with concern.

"Yes, baby, it's me." Crystal was struggling to tell Amina what was going on.

"Gran, I had a horrible dream. It was about Auntie Serena. Is she okay?" Amina asked.

"Baby girl, I need you to pray like never before for your auntie, and then call your daddy. Tell him it's a family emergency, and he needs to come out of hiding and show his support and love for his sister."

"Gran, please, what is it? You're making me afraid, and this sharp pain in my gut tells me that my dream may have been a warning from God. Gran—"

"Just do what I tell you now and have James bring you down to Duke Hospital. I'm sure you will be pleased to know your cousin is doing well. He's a li'l boy, and his name is Meshach Jeremiah Jackson. So take care of your business and get down here. Amina, we're on the fifth floor in the children's hospital. I'll see you soon." Crystal wanted to leave some good news with Amina. She knew that their worlds would be rocked to the core once everyone got to the hospital.

Nathaniel left the waiting room. He needed to get some understanding on what happened to his wife. He couldn't silence the voices in his head as the events over the last month kept taunting him. Feeling like he was under some sort of demonic attack, he put his fists up and began to swing at the air. "No! I just can't believe it . . . God, you hate me, don't you? I know I haven't been the perfect person, but did you have to take everything from me that I love?" Nathaniel had become lost in his emotional breakdown and didn't hear Amina call out to him.

Amina and James rushed down the corridor to see Nathaniel self-destructing. James ran up to him and grabbed him since he didn't seem to hear Amina calling his name. She knew that whatever had happened was the reason she'd had the dream. Watching from a short distance away, Amina prayed and cried.

"Hey, man, I'm here." James had to reach out to grab one of Nathaniel's flailing arms in order to stop him from swinging and hollering in the hallway.

Nathaniel collapsed into James's arms and unleashed fresh tears and wails. James escorted him back to the waiting room to sit him down and let him mourn. Amina allowed the men to pass her by as she followed quietly behind them. She was glad that James was able to close down the recreation center so quickly when she'd called. He assured her that he wouldn't have wanted to be any other place than with the family. It was nothing for him to have the parents come and pick up their kids within the hour due to the medical emergency. Many of the parents sent well wishes with James to the hospital, but he decided that he'd let Nathaniel know about those at a later time.

Once Amina walked into the waiting room, Crystal looked weary yet strong. "Gran . . ." She moved quickly into her grandmother's arms. The contact alone seemed to release more tears and wails throughout the room. The sounds reverberated off the thin walls, leaving the room pregnant with spent emotion.

Dr. Sinclair stood aside and watched the family mourn in their own way. She remembered her interactions with Serena and became emotional all over again. Once everyone had calmed down, Dr. Sinclair said, "I just wanted to give everyone a chance to get here before I asked if you all wanted to go down to see Serena one more time." Dr. Sinclair looked cautiously around the room to gauge their faces. She was glad that the family had the room to themselves as grief overtook them.

"I need to go and see Auntie Serena. I can't imagine any of this being reality right now." Amina cried again. "Please take me to her . . . She was like a mother to me. She . . ." Amina whimpered as she waited for someone to tell her what room Serena was in.

James stepped up to take Amina's hand. "Baby, if you need me, I'll be happy to go with you to see Prophetess Serena." James lifted Serena's hand and kissed the back of it.

"Follow me this way." Dr. Sinclair prepared to lead the way.

Everyone stood to go, but Amina stopped them. "Please, let me spend a few moments with Auntie before you all come down. We've shared so much together, and I just need to go in and be with her," Amina said.

Nathaniel, Crystal, and Tremaine sat back down. Each of them wanted to give Amina the privacy that she needed.

Amina took calculated steps into the room after asking James to wait outside of the room, but not to go too far in case she needed him. When she looked at Serena, there was a small glow that encamped her face that resembled a halo. Amina marveled at how peaceful she looked. Her small frame was tucked away under the covers of the bed. She looked like she was sleeping and not dead. Brushing her hands over the covers, Amina cried silent tears. She'd paced the room a few times, and then pulled the lone that chair in the room over to Serena's bedside.

"Auntie, I can't believe that this has happened." Tears fell. "I still don't even know why you left me, but God showed me in a dream, Auntie." More tears. "I am so sorry that I wasn't here for you because you've always been here for me. I don't know where Daddy is, and I don't even know where Sherry is, Auntie. What are we going to do now that you're gone?" Amina dropped her head onto the bed railing and cried for her loss.

She wasn't sure how much time had passed before she felt a hand on her shoulder. Looking up, she saw the family standing behind her. "I'm sorry if I took too long. I just wasn't ready to leave her," Amina explained.

Crystal had moved into the room and said, "It's all right, baby. We understand. We came down here because we need to let the hospital get Serena moved . . ." Crystal heard the cries from Nathaniel and stopped talking.

"Nooo . . ." Nathaniel broke down by Serena's bedside with James and Tremaine standing behind him also in tears. They gathered him into a group hug. In the midst of her own sorrow, Crystal noticed that Jonathan never made it to the hospital. The scene was surreal. Crystal couldn't believe that what had started out as a night of promise had ended up with so much hurt and pain.

Serena had passed on to glory three hours ago, and the family wasn't ready to let her go just yet. They'd taken turns having their last moments with Serena. They grabbed hands to pray that the angels of God had come to escort their loved one to the gates of heaven where they believed that Jesus Himself had ushered her into His glory. There would be no more suffering and no more pain for Serena. She'd completed the assignment of love, forgiveness, and selflessness by trading her life for the life of her child. They weren't sure how they would get through the hardest time of their lives. Only God knew.

Reading Group
Discussion Questions

1. The story opens with drama concerning Serena's health. You read that Serena's cancer had returned, which means that she had been afflicted before. Why do you think that God would allow her to become ill again, after He'd healed her?

2. Do you know of anyone who has been afflicted with cancer or a disease? How do you think Serena should have reacted since she was a child of God? What, if anything, would you have done differently?

3. Should jealousy be added to one of the seven deadly sins? Melissa had some issues with the spirit of jealousy, or do you think she really had issues with Serena? Why is jealousy such a destructive spirit?

4. Can you blame Nathaniel for cheating on Serena with Melissa? Why or why not? Is this a forgivable transgression?

5. What should Serena have done when she first began to suspect that Nathaniel was being unfaithful?

6. Do you agree with Serena's decision to forego all medical treatments in order to bring a healthy baby into the world? Even at the cost of her life?

7. What do you think about Crystal and Tremaine's relationship? Will they make it together?

8. Jonathan goes through a restitution phase of some things he'd done wrong in the story. It was clear that

he had some issues. Do you believe that preacher's kids are the worst?

9. What are your thoughts on James's character?
10. Would you like to see this story continue?

Author Bio

Lachá M. Scott is living her dreams of becoming an author. She loves to read and is the president of Victorious Ladies Book Club in Durham, North Carolina. Lachá is the mother of three beautiful daughters and has one grandson. She is the senior pastor of No Greater Love Christian Church, No. 2, in North Carolina.

UC HIS GLORY BOOK CLUB!

www.uchisglorybookclub.net

UC His Glory Book Club is the spirit-inspired brain-child of Joylynn Ross, Author and Acquisitions Editor of Urban Christian, and Kendra Norman-Bellamy, Author for Urban Christian. This is an online book club that hosts authors of Urban Christian. We welcome as members all men and women who have a passion for reading Christian-based fiction.

UC His Glory Book Club pledges our commitment to provide support, positive feedback, encouragement, and a forum whereby members can openly discuss and review the literary works of Urban Christian authors.

There is no membership fee associated with UC His Glory Book Club; however, we do ask that you support the authors through purchasing, encouraging, providing book reviews, and of course, your prayers. We also ask that you respect our beliefs and follow the guidelines of the book club. We hope to receive your valuable input, opinions, and reviews that build up, rather than tear down our authors.

What We Believe:

—We believe that Jesus is the Christ, Son of the Living God.

—We believe the Bible is the true, living Word of God.

—We believe all Urban Christian authors should use their God-given writing abilities to honor God and share the message of the written word God has given to each of them uniquely.

—We believe in supporting Urban Christian authors in their literary endeavors by reading, purchasing, and sharing their titles with our online community.

—We believe that everything we do in our literary arena should be done in a manner that will lead to God being glorified and honored.

We look forward to the online fellowship with you.

Please visit us often at:

www.uchisglorybookclub.net.

Many Blessings to You!

Shelia E. Lipsey,
President, UC His Glory Book Club

ORDER FORM
URBAN BOOKS, LLC
97 N. 18th Street
Wyandanch, NY 11798

Name (please print):_____

Address: _____

City/State: _____

Zip: _____

QTY	TITLES	PRICE
	By the Grace of God	$14.95
	Confessions Of A preachers Wife	$14.95
	Dance Into Destiny	$14.95
	Deliver Me From My Enemies	$14.95
	Desperate Decisions	$14.95
	Divorcing the Devil	$14.95
	Faith	$14.95
	First Comes Love	$14.95
	Flaws and All	$14.95
	Forgiven	$14.95
	Former Rain	$14.95
	Forsaken	$14.95

Shipping and handling-add $3.50 for 1st book, then $1.75 for each additional book.
Please send a check payable to:
Urban Books, LLC
Please allow 4-6 weeks for delivery

ORDER FORM
URBAN BOOKS, LLC
97 N. 18th Street
Wyandanch, NY 11798

Name (please print):_____

Address: _____

City/State: _____

Zip: _____

QTY	TITLES	PRICE
	From Sinner To Saint	$14.95
	From The Extreme	$14.95
	God Is In Love With You	$14.95
	God Speaks To Me	$14.95
	Grace And Mercy	$14.95
	Guilty Of Love	$14.95
	Happily Ever Now	$14.95
	Heaven Bound	$14.95
	His Grace His Mercy	$14.95
	His Woman His Wife His Widow	$14.95
	Illusions	$14.95
	In Green Pastures	$14.95

Shipping and handling-add $3.50 for 1st book, then $1.75 for each additional book.

Please send a check payable to:
    Urban Books, LLC
Please allow 4-6 weeks for delivery

ORDER FORM
URBAN BOOKS, LLC
97 N. 18th Street
Wyandanch, NY 11798

Name (please print):_____

Address: _____

City/State: _____

Zip: _____

QTY	TITLES	PRICE
	Into Each Life	$14.95
	Keep Your enemies Closer	$14.95
	Keeping Misery Company	$14.95
	Latter Rain	$14.95
	Living Consequences	$14.95
	Living Right On Wrong Street	$14.95
	Losing It	$14.95
	Love Honor Stray	$14.95
	Marriage Mayhem	$14.95
	Me, Myself and Him	$14.95
	Murder Through The Grapevine	$14.95
	My Father's House	$14.95

Shipping and handling-add $3.50 for 1st book, then $1.75 for each additional book.
Please send a check payable to:
Urban Books, LLC
Please allow 4-6 weeks for delivery

ORDER FORM
URBAN BOOKS, LLC
97 N. 18th Street
Wyandanch, NY 11798

Name (please print):_____

Address: _____

City/State: _____

Zip: _____

QTY	TITLES	PRICE

Shipping and handling-add $3.50 for 1st book, then $1.75 for each additional book.
Please send a check payable to:
Urban Books, LLC
Please allow 4–6 weeks for delivery